6-24-64

1462-64

8 vol. set $15.20

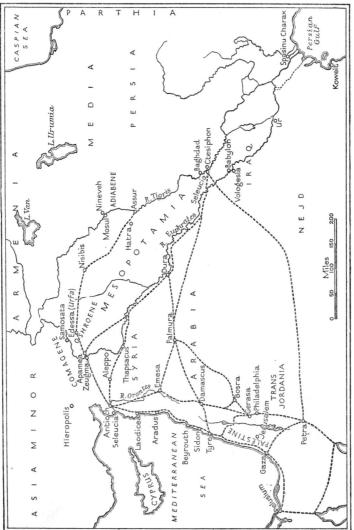

Map of the bilingual region of Arabia and Northern Syria in the time of Josephus, and of the neighbouring countries, to illustrate the place of origin and dissemination of S. Matthew's Gospel.

CHRIST THE LORD

From a Mosaic in the Apse of the Cathedral of Cefalu, Sicily, above the
High Altar. Twelfth century.

THE CLARENDON BIBLE

Under the general editorship of
BISHOP STRONG AND BISHOP WILD

THE GOSPEL

ACCORDING TO

SAINT MATTHEW

In the Revised Version

WITH INTRODUCTION AND COMMENTARY

BY

F. W. GREEN, B.D.

*Canon of Norwich Cathedral; Examining Chaplain to the
Bishop of Southwell; formerly Fellow and Tutor of
Merton College, Oxford*

OXFORD

AT THE CLARENDON PRESS

Oxford University Press, Amen House, London E.C.4

GLASGOW   NEW YORK   TORONTO   MELBOURNE   WELLINGTON
BOMBAY   CALCUTTA   MADRAS   KARACHI   KUALA LUMPUR
CAPE TOWN   IBADAN   NAIROBI   ACCRA

FIRST PUBLISHED 1936
REPRINTED (WITH CORRECTIONS) 1945, 1947, 1949, 1953, 1960

PRINTED IN GREAT BRITAIN

PREFACE

THE problem of the teaching of Holy Scripture at the present time presents many difficulties. There is a large and growing class of persons who feel bound to recognize that the progress of archaeological and critical studies has made it impossible for them to read, and still more to teach, it precisely in the old way. However strongly they may believe in inspiration, they cannot any longer set before their pupils, or take as the basis of their interpretation, the doctrine of the verbal inspiration of the Holy Scripture. It is with the object of meeting the requirements not only of the elder pupils in public schools, their teachers, students in training colleges, and others engaged in education, but also of the clergy, and the growing class of the general public which we believe takes an interest in Biblical studies, that the present series is projected.

The writers will be responsible each for his own contribution only, and their interpretation is based upon the belief that the books of the Bible require to be placed in their historical context, so that, as far as possible, we may recover the sense which they bore when written. Any application of them must rest upon this ground. It is not the writers' intention to set out the latest notions of radical scholars—English or foreign—nor even to describe the exact position at which the discussion of the various problems has arrived. The aim of the series is rather to put forward a constructive view of the books and their teaching, taking into consideration and welcoming results as to which there is a large measure of agreement among scholars.

In regard to form, subjects requiring comprehensive treatment are dealt with in Essays, whether forming part of the introduction or interspersed among the notes. The notes themselves are mainly concerned with the subject-matter of the books and the points of interest (historical, doctrinal, &c.) therein presented; they deal with the elucidation of words, allusions, and the like only so far as seems necessary to a proper comprehension of the author's meaning.

THOMAS STRONG } *General*
HERBERT WILD. } *Editors.*

TABLE OF CONTENTS

LIST OF ILLUSTRATIONS

List of Illustrations

INTRODUCTION

§ 1. *The place of S. Matthew in the Gospel Tradition*

THE Gospel according to S. Matthew, though by no means the first to be written, had from a very early date an undisputed position in the New Testament. Of all the known lists of the Gospels there are only two in which S. Matthew has any other place than the first, nor is any other book of the New Testament quoted with anything like the same frequency in early Christian writings. There are instances in which we find it quoted not as 'the Gospel according to S. Matthew' but simply as 'the Gospel'. It is not too much to say that few events in the history of the primitive Church can rival in interest and importance its sudden rise and rapid advance from comparative obscurity to the position of unchallenged supremacy which it still holds in the estimation of the Christian world.[1]

We may begin by asking what is the reason for this unanimous verdict? Among the chief reasons, of course, must be placed the challenge of its teaching. The Sermon on the Mount is often regarded as the essence of the Gospel of Christ, and it is only one of five great collections in which the writer has gathered all that he knew of the teaching of Jesus. Christianity has at all times loved to think of Christ as the great Teacher sitting in the midst of His disciples (Mt. 5¹); and although in reading S. Matthew[2] we cannot fail to recognize much of the harmonious arrangement of the teaching as the work of the Evangelist, it is Jesus that we hear speaking. It is otherwise in the Fourth Gospel, where the teaching of Christ appears to be given to the Church in the form of a summary, as it had been found to be true in the experience of Christians. In S. Matthew as in S. Luke, in spite of much editorial work, we are obviously much closer to the original form.

[1] The evidence for the widespread popularity of S. Matthew has been tabulated by Moffatt in the *Introduction to the Literature of the New Testament*, p. 14. It is perhaps not too much to say that, in the primitive Church writings, Mt. is always the Gospel employed unless the quotation wanted is not to be found in it.

[2] Usually in this book the Gospels will be denoted by the abbreviations Mt., Mk., Lk., Jn., except where it is the author rather than the Gospel itself that is referred to.

It is, however, much more than the literary remains of a great Teacher that we are given in S. Matthew. What we find there is the promulgation of the religion of Christ to the whole world by a *Church* teaching and ruling in His Name. It is this aspect of Matthew that has earned for it the name of the *ecclesiastical* or *liturgical* gospel. We shall have to examine its character and structure more closely from this point of view. But there can be no doubt that Matthew represents the movement towards *Catholicism* in the early Church—that is to say, it represents a reaction from the 'freedom of the Spirit' which breathes in S. Paul's Epistles and in St. Luke's Gospel, in the direction of something far more clearly defined in Church doctrine and order. It was in this respect that its readers found something new, which along with other features of the Gospel seemed to meet new and pressing needs of their time. As we shall see, the Catholic element in this Gospel has an important bearing on the question of its date. It marks it at once as belonging to a time when Christianity was beginning to find it necessary to strengthen its defences and define its creed. The long struggle between Christianity and Gnosticism[1] had already begun; and it was in view of the rivalry of the Gnostic sects that the Gospel of Catholic authority was early adopted as *the* Gospel by S. Ignatius, Bishop of Antioch (A.D. 115), and others who were the pioneers of the movement for the consolidation of the Church at the beginning of the second century A.D. At the same time it may be noted that Mt. was not the final stage in the development of the Gospel tradition. The last stage came once more from the Hellenistic side and is represented by the Fourth Gospel, published at Ephesus not long after Mt. It undertakes the difficult task of reconciling the Jewish and the Hellenistic aspects of Christianity. But it was a long time before that Gospel secured recognition in the greatest centres of Christianity, and it never succeeded in supplanting Mt. from its position of supremacy in the Canon of the New Testament.

[1] Gnosticism was a kind of theosophy deeply rooted and widespread in many forms in the oriental world. It was esoteric in character, and would have substituted a kind of freemasonry for Christianity. It was part of the movement which Harnack described as the 'acute Hellenization of Christianity'.

By Catholicism is meant not only the religion of authority and order, but also, and indeed primarily, a religion which is universal, transcending the divisions of nationality and sect. In this direction S. Matthew's Gospel goes beyond many books in the New Testament, even the Acts of the Apostles. Though predominantly Jewish in colouring, Matthew takes for granted the position for which S. Paul fought and suffered,[1] that 'the Gentiles are fellow heirs and of the same body and partakers of God's promise in Christ by the Gospel' (Eph. 3[6]). It is in Matthew that the Gentiles come to the light of the Messiah (Mt. 2[1]) and are given explicitly a right to the Baptism and teaching of the Christian Church.

Besides its intrinsic adaptation to the moral and spiritual conditions of the Church of its day, Mt. is designed to meet its rapidly developing liturgical needs. When Mt. was written, the ground plan of Christian worship was already in existence, with its recital of Scriptures, old and new, culminating in the solemn representation of the Lord's death, 'till He come', in the Breaking of Bread and the Prayers (1 Cor. 11[26], Acts 2[42]). Mt.'s stately periods and diction were clearly intended to be used in Christian meetings for worship under the presidency of the Bishop and his Presbyters. Mt. has never ceased to be the favourite choice for Lessons, Gospels, and public Reading in Church.

Features such as these, together with its strong appeal to apocalyptic feeling and its bold claim to apostolic authorship, go far to account for the immediate popularity of Mt. They also explain its rapid spread from the Eastern border of Greek-speaking Christianity, the region closest in touch with Judaism, with which the Gospel has obvious affinities, across the Pauline mission-field to Rome itself, where it quickly superseded the Marcan Gospel.

Its Purpose.

Thus the purpose of Mt. was not the writing of another Life of Jesus, that had already been done by Mark, with whose Gospel

[1] If, as seems likely, Mt. was the Gospel of a community which described itself by the designation of Nazarene (see note on 2[23]), it is interesting to note the existence of an Apocryphal Gospel called the Gospel of the Nazarenes, which combines in the same way an intense loyalty to the Jewish religion with a whole-hearted approval of the Gentile Mission of S. Paul and his followers (see Introd., p. 21.)

Mt. is clearly familiar.[1] Mt.'s purpose is at once dogmatic and liturgical. It is dogmatic in the sense that it seeks, in a time when the love of many was waxing cold (Mt. 24[12]), to contend earnestly 'for the faith once delivered unto the saints' (Jude 3). Its primary aim is 'to elaborate a great theme, which is none other than the universal claim of Jesus as the Son of God and the King of Israel' (McNeile). For Mt. consists not only of great teaching, but also of historical facts grouped together in such a way that we can draw certain conclusions; namely that Jesus, condemned by the Jews as a false Messiah and blasphemous usurper of the title of 'Son of God', has, nevertheless, been revealed to Israel as its Messiah, continuing thereby the Divine plan for mankind, in the line of the revelation to Israel, and accredited by works of divine power. It is this Christ as the King and the Lord in Glory that Mt. seeks to present to the faith and adoration of the people of God; not merely as an interesting character in history, but as a contemporary, regulating and ruling the Church through its hierarchy, yet Himself present there 'all the days' in the fullness of those redemptive acts which it is the purpose of liturgical worship to represent. In this respect Mt. is the liturgical counterpart of those great mosaic pictures which, like that given in the frontispiece, adorned the walls of the Christian basilicas and remain as a standing witness to the primitive belief about Jesus Christ.

§ 2. *Structure and Characteristics of Matthew*

(1) Not only has Mt. a unique position in the Gospel tradition, it has also a unique structure and pattern of its own.[2] It has an imposing unity of design no less remarkable than that of the Fourth Gospel. An analysis of the Gospel shows that it has been carefully

[1] According to Bacon, Rawlinson, and other authorities Mark is the Gospel of the Church of Rome and owed its prestige in the East to that fact. Similarly Streeter thinks that Lk. represents the Gospel of Caesarea and 'Q' that of Antioch, to which also he attributes Mt. But there is reason to believe that this is not so likely. See p. 20.

[2] Dr. Rendel Harris has discovered a very old fragment dating back to the second century, perhaps belonging to the Apologist Melito, Bishop of Sardis (A.D. 160); and apparently designed as a prologue to Matthew. It consists of six iambic lines the first two of which are as follows:

> Matthew curbs the rash error of the Jews
> Having muzzled it with the bridle of five discourses.

composed on a plan, consisting of a division into five Books containing the teaching of our Lord on five different subjects. Each one of the divisions is prefaced by a section of narrative which serves as an introduction to the discourse which follows. Every one is familiar with the first of these discourses—the Sermon on the Mount ; but it is not always understood that the Sermon is only the first, though the greatest, of five similar collections to which Sir John Hawkins has given the name of *perek*, the Hebrew word for 'chapter' ; because the plan appears to be based on the fivefold division of the Mosaic Law Code called the Pentateuch, for which the author of Mt. has so unbounded an admiration (Mt. 5^{17-20}). This interesting and distinctive structure, though not recognized by modern commentators until fifty years ago, was nevertheless familiar to antiquity. It was evidently these same five Books of Mt. that the ancient writer Papias (*c.* A.D. 140), whose statement about Mt. we shall have to examine carefully,[1] had before him when he composed his work called *The interpretation of the Lord's Oracles in five books.* It was, in fact, the first commentary on S. Matthew's Gospel. The ancient fragment already alluded to likewise bears witness to a feature of the Gospel well known in the second century. The five discourses have been given the following titles:

1. The new Ethics of Jesus and the Law (5–7).
2. Concerning Apostleship (9^{36}–11^{1}).
3. The Hiding and Revelation of the Mystery (13^{1-53}).
4. The Problem of Church Unity (18–19^{1}).
5. The Messianic Judgement (24–25).

Each one of these 'chapters' concludes with the almost identical formula: 'It came to pass that when Jesus had made an end of all these sayings,' &c. The purpose of this imposing structure is clear. The Evangelist means to surround the promulgation of the New Law and Covenant of God in Christ with the same majesty as accompanied the giving of the Law on Sinai, and to associate with it the same signs and wonders which were wrought by Jehovah when He delivered His people from the Land of Egypt and out of the house of bondage. In Streeter's words, 'an analysis of every one of these five discourses yields evidence that it was an

---

[1] See Introd., p. 16.

agglomeration put together by the writer of the Gospel.' Together they form what Moffatt describes as a 'massive unity'.

(2) *The Jewish background.* (*a*) Mt. prizes above all things the continuity between Christianity and Judaism, the old and the new. Next to its remarkable structure the most prominent characteristic of Mt. is the number of quotations from the Old Testament, which are evidently regarded as the credentials of the New Faith. There are more than 100 quotations and uses of the Old Testament, many of which have been taken over from Mk. But the most remarkable fact about these citations is that they are with few exceptions taken from the Greek and not from the Hebrew Bible. Those taken from Mk. are carefully brought into closer conformity with the LXX version. Even when Mt. follows some other version, the influence of the LXX is usually a marked feature in the quotation. This is one of the reasons which make it hard to believe that Mt. was originally written, as some think, in Hebrew. (*b*) Though Greek-speaking and habitually preferring the Septuagint to the Hebrew Bible, Matthew is deeply imbued with the spirit and the modes of expression of the Jewish Rabbis. His Greek has been described as 'Synagogue Greek'. The author has furnished an unconscious portrait of himself in the words placed in the mouth of Jesus in Mt. 13[52], 'every scribe who hath been made a disciple to the kingdom of heaven is like unto a man that is an householder who bringeth forth out of his treasure things new and old'. In other words, the writer is a converted Rabbi who has become a Church catechist. Whole volumes have been compiled of rabbinic parallels to the early teachings of Jesus. There is, of course, no reason to suppose that our Lord did not Himself make use of the rabbinic style in His teaching, but the parallels are twice as numerous in Mt. as in Mk. and Lk. Moreover that part of Mt. which is peculiar to him and which (following Bacon) we shall call N, is full of additions to the Marcan narrative which show a close resemblance to the rabbinic *Targums*, i.e. the paraphrases (with embellishments) of the Hebrew Scriptures made for the use of Aramaic congregations. Especially characteristic of rabbinic literature are the groupings in which the Evangelist delights; series of three or seven or ten miracle stories or parables; his love of proverbial sayings; his

stereotyped phraseology and repetition of formulae, of which Sir John Hawkins has noted no less than fifteen examples.[1] Tricks of style such as these, as well as his obvious legalism and devotion to the ideal of 'righteousness' and 'good works', justify the judgement that Matthew 'transferred to Christian writing as a catechist the same methods as characterized the Rabbi'.[2] At the same time Dr. Burney has pointed out that Matthew more than any other evangelist has presented the sayings of Jesus as perhaps they were originally uttered, with all the rhythm and parallelism of Hebrew Poetry.[3]

(3) 'Hebraic to the core' as Mt. obviously is, it would be quite a mistake to regard it as a Jewish or 'Ebionite' Gospel. Mt. is bitterly opposed to the official Judaism of his day. According to Zahn, Mt.'s sharp attack upon Judaism as governed and misled by the Sadducaic High Priests and Pharisaic Rabbis is so prominent a feature of the book as to justify his summary of the Gospel as an 'Apology of the Nazarene and his Church over against Judaism'. To Mt. Israel is no longer the chosen nation, not even a remnant; but utterly rejected and its scriptures and prerogatives transferred to the Christian Church. It is in the constitution of this Church, as the residuary legatee of the 'promise made of God unto our Fathers', that Mt. displays a marked interest; especially in the regulation and discipline of the Church through its hierarchy, of which S. Peter as Vicar of Christ on earth is the divinely appointed Head: its sacramental system and authority in faith and morals.

(4) These predominating characteristics of Mt. are, throughout the book, combined with a heightened interest in *eschatology*.[4]

[1] See *Horae Synopticae*, pp. 168–73.

[2] Bacon, *Studies in Matthew*, p. 132. Von Dobschütz ('Matthäus als Rabbi und Katechet', Z.N.W., 1928) conjectures that Matthew the converted Rabbi may well have been a disciple of the famous Johanan ben Zacchai (A.D. 10–80), a disciple of Hillel and one of the original founders of the Rabbinic School of teachers called 'Tannaim' at Jamnia, who carried on the tradition of Palestinian Judaism after the destruction of Jerusalem.

[3] *Poetry of Jesus*, p. 132.

[4] By 'eschatology' is meant the teaching about judgement and the end of the world, the vivid description of which constitutes the main theme of the apocalyptic literature, the output of which was considerable in the period between the end of the Old Testament and the completion of the New. See Charles, *Religious Development between the Old and New Testaments*, Home University Library.

There appears to be in Mt. a deliberate attempt to rekindle this form of religious feeling, perhaps under the influence of the growing Hellenization of Christianity. The solemn theme of Judgement resounds like a knell through the gospel, culminating in the tremendous picture, unequalled in literature, of the final separation of good and evil and of the ground on which that separation is made (25^{31}). The Judge is at the door. The decay of good works and the growth of lawlessness, by which Mt. means the decay of distinctively Christian morality, is sufficient evidence in his view of a world ripe for judgement. Every one of the five great Discourses concludes with a pointed allusion to the rewards and penalties of the Day of Judgement. In this respect Mt. has justly been described as the most apocalyptic of the Gospels.

§ 3. Sources and date of Matthew.

1. In spite of the unity of its structure, Mt., in common with the other Gospels, has all the marks of a composite document. In no department of the New Testament study has such progress been made in recent years as in the investigation of the origin and sources of the Gospels. Research has proceeded along two separate lines: (1) the relation of the first three Gospels to one another, usually known as the Synoptic Problem; and (2) the study of the 'pre-synoptic' origins of the Gospel form, called 'form-history', a method which has produced some striking discoveries.[1] The Synoptic problem arises, in Canon Streeter's words, 'from the fact that whenever the first three gospels give an account of the same incident they commonly do so in language which is often almost word for word identical.' Every one of the Synoptic Gospels has been subjected by critics to minute examination, with the result, as is now generally agreed, that the whole of Mk. is found in one form or another in either Mt. or Lk. or both. This fact is known as the *priority* of Mk. and it is, comparatively

[1] There is no space at this point to go at length into the question of the 'pre-synoptic' history of the Gospel form. It is largely technical and there is little agreement at present among scholars. It is however probable that the methods of form-criticism can be more usefully applied to Matthew than to any other of the Gospels. Some attempt accordingly is made in the appendix to give an account of the method and its importance in the study of the Gospels.

speaking, a new discovery, because it was for many centuries supposed that Mk. was an abridgement of the other two. This, however, is unlikely because where Mk. differs from the other two his version is usually more detailed than theirs. It is they who abridge Mk. in order to find room for the new material which they wish to insert (cf. Mk. $1^{14\,ff.}$ with Mt. $4^{18\,ff.}$, and Lk. $4^{16\,ff.}$).

The grounds on which the priority of Mk. to both Mt. and Lk. is based, have been summed up by Streeter as follows:

(a) Mt. reproduces 90 per cent. of the subject-matter of Mk. in language very nearly identical with that of Mk. Lk. does the same for rather more than half of Mk.

(b) In every average section which occurs in the three gospels the majority of the actual words used by Mk. are reproduced by Mt. and Lk. either alternately or both together.

(c) The relative order of incidents and sections in Mk. is in general supported both by Mt. and Lk.: when either of them deserts Mk. the other is usually found supporting him.[1]

2. In addition to the Gospel of Mark, the study of the Synoptic Problem disclosed a second source to which was given the name of Q (= German *Quelle*, a source), by which is meant the non-Marcan material in Mt. and Lk. From the close resemblances in language or content it is supposed that Mt. and Lk. had before them a written document which they both incorporated in their gospels. We cannot say what was the precise form of this source. Harnack thought that it was a document consisting almost wholly of sayings, but Streeter and Bacon maintain that Q was already a rudimentary gospel. The two evangelists, however, differ so widely in the use they respectively make of this source, that it has been thought they had different versions of it before them. Mark also appears to have known Q, and sometimes makes use of the source as in Mk. $3^{22\,ff.}$.

This theory of the relation of the Gospels to each other is known as the two-document hypothesis. It must, however, be pointed out that in the hands of Streeter it has become a four-document hypothesis. For he maintains that before it was combined with Mk., either by Luke or Matthew, Q had already been combined with their own special material. There is reason, as we shall see, to doubt

[1] Streeter, *Four Gospels*, pp. 200 ff.

whether this is exactly what happened in the case of Mt. But Streeter together with his predecessors, Bacon and Bartlet, seems to have demonstrated at any rate the existence of a proto-Luke.

3. That our present Mt. used Mk. must then be taken as practically certain. It is true that some distinguished scholars such as Zahn and Schlatter in Germany, the English scholar Dom Chapman, and the French Dominican Lagrange still maintain that Mt. represents an older and in many respects more trustworthy tradition than Mk., and the view of such scholars cannot be absolutely dismissed. We shall have presently to go into the question whether there was an Aramaic original of Mt. Lagrange thinks that Q, when combined with the N source of Mt., is quite sufficient of itself to have formed such an original Aramaic document. But even Zahn does not attempt any longer to deny that our *present Greek* Mt. has made use of Mk. It is, of course, obvious that all the Gospels are based on a Palestinian tradition which must originally have existed in Aramaic, but none of our present Gospels shows signs of having been translated; though Dr. Burney has produced interesting evidence that S. John was written by one who habitually thought in Aramaic.[1]

4. Assuming the priority of Mk. the following details may be specially noted in Mt.'s treatment of Mk.

(*a*) In the first 13 chapters Mt. has largely *rearranged* Mk. 1–6, but after 13^{54} the Marcan order is closely followed, especially in the story of the Passion. Mt.'s method in his rearrangement is obvious if, as Papias implies, the purpose of his gospel was to make a more 'orderly compilation of the oracles of the Lord' than Mk.'s unsystematic record of what he remembered of the teaching of Peter.[2]

(*b*) Mt. *abridges* Mk.; e.g. in the story of the Storm on the Lake Mt. has omitted almost all the picturesque details in Mk.'s account (Mt. 8^{23-7} and Mk. 4^{35-41}).[3]

---

[1] *Aramaic Origin of the Fourth Gospel.*

[2] Of Mk. Papias, comparing his Gospel unfavourably with Mt.'s, remarks: 'Mark, who had been Peter's interpreter, wrote down carefully, though not in order, the sayings and doings of Christ as far as he remembered them.'

[3] The omissions of Marcan material by Mt. consist of the sections Mk. 1^{23-8}; 3^{5-9}; 4^{26-9}; 7^{32-7}; 8^{22-6}; 9^{38-40}; 12^{41-4}. But the majority of these will be found to be omissions in appearance only.

(c) At the same time when Mt. omits anything in Mk. he *compensates* for it; e.g. Mt. omits the exorcism of Mk. 1²¹⁻⁸, but makes up for it by duplication in the story of the Gadarene Swine (Mt. 8²⁸⁻³⁴, compared with Mk. 5¹⁻²⁰). Another example of the same method may be seen in Mt. 20²⁹⁻³⁴, where there are two blind men instead of one (Mk. 10⁴⁶) in order to compensate for the omission of the healing in Mk. 8²²⁻⁶.

(d) Mt. *corrects* Mk. not only *stylistically* so as to bring his crude language, its redundancies and latinisms, into accordance with his more literary Greek, but also *dogmatically* or theologically; e.g. Mt. shrinks from putting into the mouth of Jesus the question 'Why callest thou me good?' in the story of the Rich Young Ruler (Mt. 19¹⁶⁻²⁴, Mk. 10¹⁷ff·). In the same way both Mt. and Lk. shrink from attributing passions such as anger to our Lord, where Mk. does not hesitate to do so (Mt. 12¹⁰, Mk. 3⁵), though it is only fair to say that some of these corrections may have only been for the sake of abbreviation.

(e) Not only does Mt. correct Mk., he undertakes at times to *rewrite* him; e.g. in the story of the Rich Young Ruler, to which we have just alluded, we have a good illustration of the way in which Mt. not only alters the theology of Mk. but also by a subtle change succeeds in completely altering the point of the story, which is now used to illustrate the ethical principle of the *counsels and precepts* of which Mk. knows nothing, (see note B, p. 152). As Bacon remarks, 'in more than one case by slight but skilfully applied touches of the pen, the writer of Mt. has succeeded in modifying to no slight extent the gospel that lay before him when it appeared to conflict with his own established tradition'.[1]

(f) Mt. appears to have dealt with Q in much the same way as with Mk. It is generally agreed that Mt. has preserved the contents of Q more faithfully than Lk., but not its order any more than that of Mk. All the five discourses of which Mt. is composed are, as we have seen, collections of Q material, most of which appears elsewhere in various positions in Lk. Mt. however, regarded it as his right to alter or enlarge what lay before him. A good example of Mt.'s enlargement of Q occurs in the parable of the Marriage of the King's Son where we find that he has made an addition of his

[1] *Op. cit.*, p. 87.

own, the parable of the Wedding Garment or The Uninvited Guest (22[11]).[1]

5. Finally it must be noted as a special characteristic of Mt.'s use of his sources, that he *conflates* or groups together material derived from various sources or different parts of the same source, e.g. Mt. 10, the charge to the Apostles is made up by conflating Mk. 3[13-19], 6[7-13], 13[9-13], with material from Q. and other non-Marcan sources.

6. *The N Source.*

There remains that large part of Mt. which is not accounted for either by Mk. or Q or by the practice of *midrashic* embellishment which we must expect to find in Jewish writers like the author of Mt. This part of the Gospel may be summarized as follows:

1. The Birth and Resurrection narratives.
2. The three Petrine supplements, i.e. the walking on the sea (14[28-31]); the promise to Peter (16[17-19]); the temple tax (17[24-7]), to which may be added the corresponding passage on discipline in the Church (18[15-20]).
3. Passage on celibacy (19[10-12]).
4. The suicide of Judas (27[3-10]).
5. Matthean features of the trial—Pilate's wife's dream (27[19]); the hand-washing (27[24]); the guard at the tomb (27[62-6], 28[11-15]); portents at Jesus' death (27[52]).
6. The eleven Scripture quotations scattered up and down the whole Gospel, which have not been derived from Mk. or Q but belong to a source peculiar to Mt., agreeing neither with the LXX nor the Hebrew Bible but quoted apparently from a special Aramaic version or from memory (1[23]; 2[6, 15, 18, 23]; 4[15-16]; 8[17]; 12[18-21]; 13[35]; 21[5]; 27[9]).

There can be little doubt that it is this source that represents the really Hebraic element in Mt., and which has led to the belief that Mt. was originally based on an Aramaic source. Much of this material is legendary in form, and its relation to the Marcan

---

[1] The Synagogue allowed a larger liberty of interpretation and addition to the Haggada or narrative portion of the 'Torah', in which parables were included, than was permitted to the Halacha, or ethical teaching and rule of conduct which required a maximum of precision and authority.

tradition has been aptly described by Streeter as like that of the mistletoe to the oak.[1] But while the contents of N display features unmistakably 'Haggadic', the soil from which they sprang is not that of Palestine, but, as McNeile remarks, they suggest an environment not in close touch with Jerusalem and outside the range of control which the Apostles may have been expected to exercise. The only episode which seems to be in any way connected with the local tradition of Jerusalem is that of the suicide of Judas; but even there the writer finds it necessary to translate the Aramaic word 'Akeldama' (Acts 1[19]). Otherwise, Jerusalem is almost ignored by this source, which knows nothing of the tradition which placed James the Lord's brother in authority there. The Lord's final commandments, like His first, were sent forth, according to N, not from Jerusalem but from Galilee.

To this source Bacon has given the name of N, standing for *Nazarene*. Burkitt, Rendel Harris, and others maintain that much of this material, and especially the Old Testament quotations embedded in it, formed part of a collection of testimonia or proof texts such as we know to have been in circulation in the second and third centuries A.D. Canon Streeter prefers to postulate as another source of our present Mt. a proto-Mt., in the same way as he has argued for a proto-Lk., as already combined with Q, to which a final redactor has added Mk. Allen thinks the N stories represent no more than a cycle of floating traditions not existing primarily in documentary form. Bacon, on the other hand, comes to the more probable because simpler conclusion that Mk., which had for a long time circulated with authority in Syria, received the addition of 'targums', some of which were Aramaic in origin, *before* the composition of Matthew, the result being that the Gospel of Mk. inevitably fell into disuse in that region.

7. *The Date of Mt.*

What inferences can we draw from the sources and other evidence as to the time when Mt. was written? The structure of the Gospel points at any rate to a later date than Mk., which most authorities are agreed was written at a date not far removed from the martyrdom of S. Peter and S. Paul at Rome (A.D. 64)

---

[1] *Four Gospels*, pp. 502 ff.

in the reign of Nero. The question is how much later? Moreover, if the date of a book is the date of the latest thing inserted in it by its author, then we must assume a date not earlier than the fall of Jerusalem in A.D. 70, for Matthew has allegorized a well-known parable of Jesus in a manner which presupposes that event (Mt. 22[1-14], cf. Lk. 14[16]). The question therefore becomes how much later than the fall of Jerusalem? It cannot, of course, be later than the Epistles of Ignatius (A.D. 115). But Mt. does not appear to be much more than two decades earlier. If we compare Mt. with other writings of the New Testament and outside it whose approximate date is known, we shall at once see that the first Gospel is a true product of that age. It suggests a period of which the distinguishing features correspond closely to those which we find in his Gospel. Exactly the same characteristics as we have already noticed in Mt. are reflected in many of the books of the New Testament, which are certainly to be placed in the last decade of the first century A.D. The Epistles of James and John lament that a religion of feelings or words is beginning to take the place of a religion of good works without which faith is dead (Jas. 2[14ff.]; 1 Jn. 3[17]); Jude makes the same appeal as Matthew to the certainty of judgement and consigns to the same outer darkness the workers of 'lawlessness' (4-13). Matthew, moreover, applies the same remedies as are found in the Pastoral Epistles, which are now usually dated from A.D. 90 to 95. Legalism and Church discipline are becoming universal weapons against the acute 'hellenization of Christianity' (1 Tim. 3, 4; 2 Tim. 2, 3; Tit. 2, 3). How far our Mt. contributed to, or was itself impelled along this movement it is impossible to say, but, as Bacon remarks, 'its dominant note coincides with that of the consolidating Church Catholic of the post-Pauline age'.

But we can perhaps get nearer still to an exact date. Persecution, though mentioned, is nowhere much emphasized in Mt. It is not like Mk. the Gospel of a martyr church. But it is exactly in this respect that Mt. displays close affinity, not only with the Pastoral and General Epistles, but with the Letters to the Seven Churches of Asia (Rev. 1-3), which are commonly regarded as being a later addition to the Apocalypse itself, which belongs almost certainly to the first part of the reign of Domitian (A.D. 90-5).

These Letters appear to look back upon a persecution which in the rest of the book is at its height. In the same way the Epistle of Clement, Bishop of Rome (A.D. 95), looks back on a persecution of which only a vivid memory remains. His concern also is with the question of insubordination and discipline in the Church. In fact these writings are far more concerned with the 'beguiling serpent' of false doctrine, heresy, and schism than with the 'roaring lion' of State persecution. Now Eusebius draws a clear line of demarcation between two periods of the reign of Domitian, one of severe persecution and social ostracism of Christians depicted so graphically in the Apocalypse, and a later period of comparative toleration. The Roman writer Hegesippus tells a story, of which there is no reason to doubt the substantial truth, that Domitian sent for James and Zacharias, the grandsons of James, from Jerusalem, and after examining them, dismissed them lightly as harmless peasants. It is to this period of the latter half of the reign of Domitian that Mt. is most probably to be assigned.[1]

§ 4. The Problem of Authorship and Origin

The first Gospel is an anonymous work. When first quoted in the letters of S. Ignatius of Antioch and others, it is cited as *The Gospel*. In no case is the title of a book in the New Testament part of the original document; nor does the title 'according to' necessarily imply belief as to authorship. It may only mean that the subject had been treated by others. There is reason to think that at the beginning of the second century A.D. Apostolic authorship was becoming a fixed qualification for inclusion in the slowly forming Canon of Scripture.[2] This added to the fact that more than one Gospel was, as we shall see, ascribed to the Apostle Matthew makes us wary of accepting at its face-value the only real evidence there is for the Matthean authorship of the first Gospel[3]—namely the famous fragment of Papias, Bishop of Hierapolis in Syria (c. A.D. 140).

---

[1] Eus. *H.E.* III. xx. 1–8, xxxii. 6–8; IV. vii. Bacon, op. cit., pp. 75 ff.
[2] The Second Epistle (so-called) of Peter is a work of unknown authorship and origin, an example of the use of a great name to secure inclusion in the Canon. See Streeter, *Primitive Church*, p. 191.
[3] Little confidence can be placed in the statement of Irenaeus (A.D. 180), that Mt. was composed when Peter and Paul were suffering martyrdom in

The Statement of Papias.

All that we know about this writer is derived from the historian Eusebius (A.D. 325) who quotes extracts from a work written by him on the Gospels. From these fragments we learn that Papias set greater store by what he could learn by word of mouth from trusted witnesses than by written narrative. The statement which he makes about S. Matthew's Gospel is as follows:

'*Matthew made an orderly compilation of the oracles of the Lord in the Hebrew language and each one translated them as he was able.*'[1]

This looks at first like a plain statement of fact which ought to be accepted as it stands. But in the first place it must be noted that Papias does not make it on the authority of an Elder, as he does the statement about Mk. He does not say from whom he heard it nor how he knew it. In the second place it is so difficult to believe that a late compilation from a fixed authoritative tradition, like Mt., could have been composed by an Apostle, who was presumably an eyewitness of the events, that it has been thought that by the 'oracles', was meant in this case the teaching of Jesus as distinguished from narrative of events. In other words, Papias meant that Matthew was the author of *Q*. Others again, such as Professor Burkitt and Dr. Rendel Harris, have thought that what Papias was referring to was the 'testimonia' or lists of proof texts from the Old Testament, which are so prominent a feature of the Gospel. There is no reason why either of these suggestions should not be true, but unfortunately it is not what Papias, who is after all our only evidence, actually says. For the expression 'Logia' is never used either in the LXX, Philo, or the post-apostolic writings merely to denote 'sayings', but

---

Rome. Irenaeus stands on the far side of a great gulf which separates the Church of the second century from that of the first. To the writers of the latter part of the second century, problems such as the authorship of the Fourth Gospel were as real as they are to-day. Irenaeus's statement, like the similar ones of Justin and Eusebius, is clearly based on that of Papias only.

[1] Papias, ap. Eusebius, *H.E.* III. xxxix Ματθαῖος μὲν οὖν Ἑβραΐδι διαλέκτῳ τὰ λόγια συνετάξατο, ἡρμήνευσε δ' αὐτὰ ὡς ἦν δυνατὸς ἕκαστος. Of Mk. Papias remarks, '*The Elder said*: Mark having been the interpreter of Peter, wrote accurately as much as he remembered, *not however in order*, the things done or said by Christ.' Eusebius remarks of Papias himself that he appeared to be a man of very limited intelligence. It should be noted that there is a variant reading συνεγράψατο.

in every case in the sense of *oracles* or *sacred scriptures*. We must therefore assume that Papias was referring to Mt.'s Gospel as we have it now, just as in the other statement he was referring to Mk.'s Gospel in its present form.[1] The statement can only mean that Matthew composed the sacred Gospel in the only form in which Papias accepted it: Mk. being regarded as an altogether inferior and second-hand production. No early writer who refers to the fragment appears to have the slightest doubt that he was referring to our present Matthew. The statement therefore must be taken or left for what it says. But in estimating its value it must be borne in mind that in the same fragment Papias assumes what is equally improbable, that the Apostle John composed the Apocalypse.

Was there a Hebrew Original?

Still more difficult to understand is Papias's further statement that the Gospel was written in Hebrew and then translated, presumably into Greek. For Matthew is a Greek writer dependent on Greek sources, and shows no sign of having been translated. Ever since Papias made the statement men have been searching for the Hebrew or Aramaic original of Matthew. As early as the second century A.D. we find the teacher Pantaenus, the learned head of the School of Christian philosophy at Alexandria, recording a journey which he has made to 'the nations of the east', about the year A.D. 180, in the course of which he penetrated as far as India. Among the Churches of that region he discovered a Gospel in Hebrew characters which they ascribed to the Apostle Matthew, alleging that it had been left with them by the Apostle Bartholomew. Eusebius,[2] to whom we owe this story, hesitates to admit that this was the original Hebrew of Matthew. But two later writers, Apollinaris of Laodicea and his more famous pupil S. Jerome, the great Latin father of the fourth century, had no such doubts. Apollinaris left behind large extracts from this Gospel which modern scholars call the Gospel of the Nazarenes, asserting it to be the original Mt.; while Jerome himself in his journey to the East claimed to have seen the original document. It is true

---

[1] Lightfoot's position on this vexed question remains unshaken. For other views see Sir J. Hawkins, *Oxford Studies in the Synoptic Problem,* pp. 106-7.   [2] *H.E.* V. x.

that there is considerable doubt whether Jerome is speaking the strict truth when he makes this claim. At any rate he was roundly denounced by his contemporaries for having discovered a Fifth Gospel. But it is suspicious that he has succeeded in seriously confusing it with another Apocryphal Gospel usually known as the Gospel according to the Hebrews. It is a pardonable mistake which is still often made at the present day.[1]

Now Bacon has advanced an ingenious theory that Papias was the victim of a similar confusion. The Gospel of the *Nazarenes*, the mutilated and 'targumed' version of Mt. which circulated in Syria, *was* written in Aramaic and translated into Greek, and resembled our Mt. closely enough to have been regarded as the original 'Hebrew' of the Gospel. Its claim to be the real Mt. misled Papias or those who were his informers.[2]

Why according to Matthew?

It is, of course, quite impossible to prove a theory of this kind. It remains an hypothesis, the best perhaps hitherto advanced in

[1] From the first there seems to have been a good deal of confusion between two apocryphal writings, both of which managed to get mixed up with our Mt., with very strange results, but they belong in fact to quite different regions. The *Greek* Gospel of the Hebrews (Ev. Heb.) circulated in the region known as Decapolis, on the far side of Jordan, where the spoken language had for centuries been Greek. This district was far more closely connected with Egypt than with the East, and that is why we find it constantly quoted by the Alexandrian Fathers, Clement and Origen. This gospel, which shows signs of dependence both on Mt. and Lk., was wholly Judaic in character and looked to James the Lord's brother as the head of the Christian Church. It repudiated Paul and probably also Peter as the leaders of the Gentile Mission, to which it is bitterly opposed. It is this Gospel which is designated the 'Gospel of the Twelve' by Origen and '*according to Matthew*' by Irenaeus, probably on account of its opening sentences, which single out Matthew, the one educated man among the Twelve, as the 'recorder of the testimony to Israel'. It is a title which fits it well, whereas it does not in the least fit our first Gospel. It was from this Gospel that in Bacon's theory the heading was transferred to our Mt. On the other hand, the Gospel of the Nazarenes (Ev. Naz.) is an *Aramaic* document and was translated into Greek. Its affinities are quite different from those of Ev. Heb. It circulated in the bilingual regions of northern Syria (Map at front) which looked to Antioch as their ecclesiastical centre and to Peter as the chief authority in the Christian Church. Eusebius himself confuses the two, but the quotation which he makes from Hegesippus (*H.E.* IV. xxii. 8) leaves no doubt of the difference between them.

[2] Bacon, *op. cit.*, pp. 41 ff. For the Apocryphal gospels the best English edition is that of Dr. Montague James, Clarendon Press, 1924.

explanation of Papias's cryptic statement. But it has the additional merit of throwing some light, however dim, on the traditional ascription of the Gospel to Matthew, for which Papias cannot be said to be alone responsible. Following a hint of McNeile, Bacon advances another interesting theory. We have seen that our Mt. was not the only Gospel to be ascribed to the Apostle. At some date unknown, but early enough for it to have become an established fact by the time of Papias, the heading 'according to Matthew' was by authority taken from the Apocryphal Gospel according to the Hebrews which was early attributed to Matthew, and transferred to the genuine product. He conjectures that they were 'at one time rival candidates for a place in the canon of scripture then in process of slow formation, and that the choice fell on the older and more original Gospel, which then formally received the apostolic name'. Both Streeter and Bacon are agreed that Councils were at an early date held at Rome concerning the books to be regarded as Scripture. Streeter is prepared to maintain that we have a genuine allusion to a council held at Rome in A.D. 130, at which the Roman Church accepted the First Gospel as apostolic, on the testimony, as he thinks, of the representatives of the Church of Antioch. Bacon goes a step farther and suggests that the very name of Matthew was on some such occasion either in Rome or Antioch authoritatively transferred from the Apocryphal Gospel to the Greek Mt. as being of the two the more deserving of the name.[1]

While, therefore, it is not impossible that the Apostle Matthew should have taken in hand, as Papias said, to make an 'orderly compilation' of the Gospel material such as it was, for the benefit of a particular Christian community (though the preface to Luke's Gospel makes this extremely unlikely), the probability is against the apostolic authorship of the First Gospel. The ascription to Matthew which, as we have seen, rests on no evidence save that of Papias, raises far more problems than it solves. Moreover, as will be seen in the note on Mt. 10^3, considerable doubt, as early as the time of Origen, was thrown on the very identity of Matthew the Apostle, and his identification with Levi the tax-collector is, in spite of Mt. 9^9, very far from certain.

[1] *Ibid.*, pp. 48–58. Streeter, *Four Gospels*, pp. 500 ff.

Birthplace of Mt.

It now remains only to ask what was the birthplace of this anonymous gospel, which, though so late and an obvious compilation, found its way to the very heart of the Christian world and was so soon to supersede all other gospels even in Rome. If, as we seem compelled to conclude, Mt. was not a Hebrew document composed by an apostle in Palestine, where did it come from?

While refusing to be impressed with the weight of patristic evidence in favour of the Matthean authorship, Streeter remarks that nevertheless the evidence of Papias and of Irenaeus has a certain *negative* value. It proves that Mt. was not produced either in Rome or Asia Minor, but was believed to have come originally from the East. The writer, as we have seen, is a stranger to Palestine, and his special source N is very far removed from the tradition of the Jerusalem circle. Much in the Gospel suggests Antioch, and Streeter maintains that it originated there. The connexion with Peter and of Peter with Antioch is undeniable; but Bacon contends that it is much more probable that Antioch represents the *second* stage in the canonization of Matthew, the stage which would require at that time the ascription to an apostle and the backing of an apostolic church. Antioch is the second stage as Rome is the third. We must look farther afield for the actual birthplace; and we must look for it, as McNeile says, at 'some place in Syria where the Christians were not in close touch with Jerusalem (as they would have been in Antioch), and where the tradition that reached him had grown up outside the range of control which apostles or other eyewitnesses would have exercised'.[1] These conditions, which are fundamental for Mt., point to a region more remote from the parent Church than Antioch ever was, and yet sufficiently in touch with it to recognize its claim to the primacy of Peter. Accordingly, Bacon asks, what more likely place to look for the origin of Mt. than among the Greek-speaking communities of northern and north-eastern Syria,[2] in which, as we have reason to believe, men took their type of teaching from Antioch and looked to Peter as sole arbiter of faith and practice, but retained echoes of oral 'targums' of the gospels?

[1] Bacon, *op. cit.*, pp. 15 ff.; Streeter, *op. cit.*, p. 500.
[2] See Map of the bilingual region of North Syria (front endpaper).

The country which stretched roughly from Aleppo in the north-west to the modern Mosul in Iraq on the Parthian border, is like all countries which have come under Moslem rule, 'a land of submerged civilizations'. It was, however, in the first century an important region with a vast Jewish population which probably represented the largest and wealthiest if not also the most influential branch of post-exilic Judaism. It was for this Eastern branch of Judaism that the historian Josephus composed the Aramaic version of his 'Jewish War'. The Babylonian Talmud remains as its most permanent memorial, and it is with the Talmud that the 'Synagogue Greek' of Matthew stands in closest affinity. In the great cities of this region, Antioch, Aleppo, Nisibis, Samosata—and above all Edessa, the modern Urfa, capital of Adiabene, a collection of Seleucid cities, Greek was still the dominant tongue and was habitually employed in the Jewish Synagogues. Hebrew was still cultivated by the Rabbis, and the submerged speech of the Ghettos, like the Yiddish of our great cities in England and America to-day, was the Aramaic of the whole Semitic world, destined later to emerge as the 'Syriac' of the oriental versions of the New Testament. There is evidence to show that this region was christianized from the earliest times. The new religion took root especially in the great cities, Damascus being the starting-point (Acts 9^{1-22}; Gal. 1^{17}). S. Paul himself speaks of missionary work in Syria before the first journey from Antioch into Asia. From Antioch Christianity spread rapidly along the great trade routes which from Trajan's time united the Parthian Empire with the Roman province of Syria. There is reason to think that the author of Acts was following a correct sequence of fact when he mentions as foremost among the witnesses of the Pentecostal outpouring of the Spirit 'Parthians and Medes and Elamites and the dwellers in Mesopotamia' before other later recipients of the Gospel. Our greatest authority on Syriac literature, Professor Burkitt, remarks that it is difficult to explain certain features in the rise of Christianity in Edessa except on the supposition that the original congregations were largely composed of converted Jews. A few miles north of Edessa lay Samosata, capital of Commagene, famous in the history of the Church for its connexion with Antioch and for the Jewish flavour of its Christianity. Between Edessa in the westernmost bend of the Euphrates and Nisibis in the far east stretched the broad and fertile plain of Adiabene, ruled since A.D. 40 by a royal house converted to Judaism.[1] It is in such a place as this that we may reasonably look for the conditions which could give rise to a writing in 'Synagogue Greek' like that of Matthew. Little enough remains of the noble and liberal Christianity of this region. It would be strange indeed if a region of such religious and cultural importance which produced the Babylonian Talmud should not have produced a first-rate Gospel of its own just as much as Jerusalem, Antioch, Ephesus, and Rome. And if this is so, what more likely than a Gospel designed for a bilingual district where Greek was habitually used in the synagogues, where the traces of Aramaic translations survived into the fourth century, and whose converts gloried in the typically oriental designation of Nazarene?

Coming from a region so rich in intellectual and spiritual resources, it is not so surprising, as at first seemed the case, that Mt., though 'relatively late and Jewish-Christian in character, but with its bold claims to Apostolic authority, marched triumphantly across the western mission-field of S. Paul from Antioch to Rome'. Spreading, so Bacon concludes, 'southward (in Aramaic) down the Euphrates towards India and (in the original Greek) westward toward Antioch, where Ignatius accepts it, most likely along with a claim that it was (perhaps in some broad sense) "according to Matthew", the third stage of the Gospel's advance towards canonization is a consequence of S. Ignatius's journey and of the immense effect of his martyrdom at Rome about A.D. 115. Rome, not Antioch, nor Ephesus, after due deliberation and consultation put the final stamp of its unparalleled authority upon the book, as authentic and Apostolic. Under this aegis its further triumph was assured.'[2]

---

[1] The story recounted by Eusebius, *H.E.* **I.** xiii, about King Abgar of Edessa, who was said to have written a letter to Jesus and was afterwards converted to Christianity by Addai, one of the seventy disciples, may have no foundation in fact, but is evidence of the belief in the very early evangelization of that district.   [2] Bacon, *op. cit.*, p. 58.

BIBLIOGRAPHY

THE following books, among many others, have been found useful in the studies necessary for the preparation of this commentary, only those being mentioned which are accessible to the majority of English readers.

1. INTRODUCTIONS.

   B. W. Bacon. *Studies in Matthew*. The posthumous work of one of the most profound and original students of the Gospels in modern times.

   J. Vernon Bartlet. Article 'Matthew' in Hastings's *Dictionary of the Bible*. Though written thirty years ago, it is still the best introduction to Matthew in any language.

2. COMMENTARIES.

   A. H. McNeile. The classical commentary in English by a first-class Greek and Hebrew scholar.

   W. C. Allen. *International Critical Commentary*. Very valuable as a work of reference for its profound Rabbinic knowledge.

   A. Plummer. A commentary written to supplement Allen on the exegetical side, very full but somewhat out of date.

   P. A. Micklem. *Westminster Commentaries*. The best for the general reader.

   Lagrange. *Évangile selon Saint-Matthieu*. By far the most comprehensive of all modern commentaries, by a French Dominican for many years a resident in the Holy Land.

   W. F. Slater and G. H. Box. *Century Bible*, new edition, 1926. The best small commentary, brought thoroughly up to date by the late Professor G. H. Box.

   B. T. D. Smith. *The Cambridge Bible*, both in the Greek and in the English text.

3. GENERAL.

   A. E. J. Rawlinson. *Gospel according to Mark* (*Westminster Commentaries*). Indispensable for the modern study of the Gospels.

   B. H. Streeter. *The Four Gospels*. The most important book on the Synoptic problem.

   F. C. Burkitt. *The Gospel History and its Transmission*.

   F. C. Burkitt. *Christian Beginnings*, 1921 (a small but indispensable book by a great authority on the Gospel tradition).

   F. C. Burkitt. *Earliest Sources for the Life of Jesus*.

   B. K. Rattey. *Growth and Structures of the Gospels*, Oxford, 1935.

   A. G. Hebert. *Liturgy and Society*, 1935. A valuable essay on the importance of the liturgical element in Christian tradition.

Bibliography

Vincent Taylor. *The Formation of the Gospel Tradition.*

B. S. Easton. *The Gospel in the Gospels.* A popular study of the same subject by a leading American scholar.

Abrahams. *Studies in Pharisaism and the Gospels,* series i and ii. A very valuable contribution to the study of the Gospels from the standpoint of a learned Jew.

Moore. *Judaism.* The most valuable recent book on the Jewish background at a date later than the Gospels.

The Commentaries by Bishop Blunt and H. Balmforth on Mk. and Lk. respectively, in this series.

Oesterley and Box. *Religion and Worship of the Synagogue.* A useful work on the doctrines and liturgical aspects of Judaism for the New Testament period.

The Editor desires to record his thanks to the Literary Executor of the late Prof. B. W. Bacon and to Dr. K. E. Kirk for permission to make quotations from their works cited in this Commentary. To Prof. Bacon's book especially is owed the division and general arrangement here adopted, as well as many of the chapter headings, &c. His thanks are specially due to the Rev. E. A. Parr, Sacrist of Norwich Cathedral, for much generous labour in the correcting of the proofs.

THE GOSPEL ACCORDING TO
ST. MATTHEW

PREAMBLE

Genealogy of Jesus.

1 [1]THE book of the [2]generation of Jesus Christ, the son of David, the son of Abraham.

2 Abraham begat Isaac; and Isaac begat Jacob; and Jacob
3 begat Judah and his brethren; and Judah begat Perez and Zerah of Tamar; and Perez begat Hezron; and Hezron begat
4 [3]Ram; and [3]Ram begat Amminadab; and Amminadab begat
5 Nahshon; and Nahshon begat Salmon; and Salmon begat Boaz of Rahab; and Boaz begat Obed of Ruth; and Obed begat
6 Jesse; and Jesse begat David the king.

7 And David begat Solomon of her *that had been the wife* of Uriah; and Solomon begat Rehoboam; and Rehoboam begat
8 Abijah; and Abijah begat [4]Asa; and [4]Asa begat Jehoshaphat;
9 and Jehoshaphat begat Joram; and Joram begat Uzziah; and Uzziah begat Jotham; and Jotham begat Ahaz; and Ahaz
10 begat Hezekiah; and Hezekiah begat Manasseh; and Manasseh
11 begat [5]Amon; and [5]Amon begat Josiah; and Josiah begat Jechoniah and his brethren, at the time of the [6]carrying away to Babylon.

12 And after the [6]carrying away to Babylon, Jechoniah begat
13 [7]Shealtiel; and [7]Shealtiel begat Zerubbabel; and Zerubbabel begat Abiud; and Abiud begat Eliakim; and Eliakim begat
14 Azor; and Azor begat Sadoc; and Sadoc begat Achim; and
15 Achim begat Eliud; and Eliud begat Eleazar; and Eleazar
16 begat Matthan; and Matthan begat Jacob; and Jacob begat Joseph the husband of Mary, of whom was born Jesus, who is called Christ.

17 So all the generations from Abraham unto David are fourteen generations; and from David unto the [8]carrying away to Babylon fourteen generations; and from the [8]carrying away to Babylon unto the Christ fourteen generations.

---

[1] Or, *The genealogy of Jesus Christ* [2] Or, *birth*: as in ver. 18.
[3] Gr. *Aram.* [4] Gr. *Asaph.* [5] Gr. *Amos.* [6] Or, *removal to Babylon*
[7] Gr. *Salathiel.* [8] Or, *removal to Babylon*

His miraculous birth. The Annunciation to Joseph.

18 Now the ¹birth ²of Jesus Christ was on this wise: When his mother Mary had been betrothed to Joseph, before they came
19 together she was found with child of the ³Holy Ghost. And Joseph her husband, being a righteous man, and not willing to make her a public example, was minded to put her away privily.
20 But when he thought on these things, behold, an angel of the Lord appeared unto him in a dream, saying, Joseph, thou son of David, fear not to take unto thee Mary thy wife: for that
21 which is ⁴conceived in her is of the Holy Ghost. And she shall bring forth a son; and thou shalt call his name JESUS; for it is
22 he that shall save his people from their sins. Now all this is come to pass, that it might be fulfilled which was spoken by the Lord through the prophet, saying,
23 Behold, the virgin shall be with child, and shall bring forth a son,
And they shall call his name ⁵Immanuel;
24 which is, being interpreted, God with us. And Joseph arose from his sleep, and did as the angel of the Lord commanded
25 him, and took unto him his wife; and knew her not till she had brought forth a son: and he called his name JESUS.

Astrologers do homage to Him.

2 Now when Jesus was born in Bethlehem of Judæa in the days of Herod the king, behold, ⁶wise men from the east
2 came to Jerusalem, saying, ⁷Where is he that is born King of the Jews? for we saw his star in the east, and are come to wor-
3 ship him. And when Herod the king heard it, he was troubled,
4 and all Jerusalem with him. And gathering together all the chief priests and scribes of the people, he inquired of them where
5 the Christ should be born. And they said unto him, In Bethlehem of Judæa: for thus it is written ⁸by the prophet,
6 And thou Bethlehem, land of Judah,
Art in no wise least among the princes of Judah:
For out of thee shall come forth a governor,
Which shall be shepherd of my people Israel.
7 Then Herod privily called the ⁶wise men, and learned of them

---

¹ Or, *generation*: as in ver. 1.   ² Some ancient authorities read *of the Christ*.   ³ Or, *Holy Spirit*: and so throughout this book.   ⁴ Gr. *begotten*.   ⁵ Gr. *Emmanuel*.   ⁶ Gr. *Magi*. Compare Esther i. 13; Dan. ii. 12.   ⁷ Or, *Where is the King of the Jews that is born?*   ⁸ Or, *through*

8 carefully ¹what time the star appeared. And he sent them to
Bethlehem, and said, Go and search out carefully concerning the
young child ; and when ye have found *him*, bring me word, that

THE GROTTO OF THE NATIVITY

9 I also may come and worship him. And they, having heard the
  king, went their way ; and lo, the star, which they saw in the
  east, went before them, till it came and stood over where the
10 young child was. And when they saw the star, they rejoiced
11 with exceeding great joy. And they came into the house and
  saw the young child with Mary his mother ; and they fell down

¹ Or, *the time of the star that appeared*

and worshipped him; and opening their treasures they offered
12 unto him gifts, gold and frankincense and myrrh. And being
warned *of God* in a dream that they should not return to Herod,
they departed into their own country another way.

CHRISTMAS DAY AT BETHLEHEM

*Herod tries to kill Him. Flight into Egypt and Martyrdom of the
Innocents.*

13   Now when they were departed, behold, an angel of the Lord
appeareth to Joseph in a dream, saying, Arise and take the
young child and his mother, and flee into Egypt, and be thou
there until I tell thee: for Herod will seek the young child to
14 destroy him. And he arose and took the young child and his
15 mother by night, and departed into Egypt; and was there until
the death of Herod: that it might be fulfilled which was spoken
by the Lord through the prophet, saying, Out of Egypt did I
16 call my son. Then Herod, when he saw that he was mocked of
the ¹wise men, was exceeding wroth, and sent forth, and slew
all the male children that were in Bethlehem, and in all the
borders thereof, from two years old and under, according to the
17 time which he had carefully learned of the ¹wise men. Then

¹ Gr. *Magi.*

THE CHURCH OF THE NATIVITY AT BETHLEHEM

BETHLEHEM TO-DAY

was fulfilled that which was spoken [1]by Jeremiah the prophet,
saying,

18   A voice was heard in Ramah,
      Weeping and great mourning,
      Rachel weeping for her children;
      And she would not be comforted, because they are not.

His settlement in Nazareth in accordance with prophecy.

19   But when Herod was dead, behold, an angel of the Lord
20 appeareth in a dream to Joseph in Egypt, saying, Arise and
take the young child and his mother, and go into the land of
21 Israel: for they are dead that sought the young child's life. And
he arose and took the young child and his mother, and came
22 into the land of Israel. But when he heard that Archelaus was
reigning over Judæa in the room of his father Herod, he was
afraid to go thither; and being warned *of God* in a dream, he
23 withdrew into the parts of Galilee, and came and dwelt in a city
called Nazareth: that it might be fulfilled which was spoken [1]by
the prophets, that he should be called a Nazarene.

John baptizes the people.

3 And in those days cometh John the Baptist, preaching in
2 the wilderness of Judæa, saying, Repent ye; for the kingdom
3 of heaven is at hand. For this is he that was spoken of [1]by
Isaiah the prophet, saying,

      The voice of one crying in the wilderness,
      Make ye ready the way of the Lord,
      Make his paths straight.

4 Now John himself had his raiment of camel's hair, and a leathern
girdle about his loins; and his food was locusts and wild honey.
5 Then went out unto him Jerusalem, and all Judæa, and all the
6 region round about Jordan; and they were baptized of him in
7 the river Jordan, confessing their sins. But when he saw many
of the Pharisees and Sadducees coming to his baptism, he said
unto them, Ye offspring of vipers, who warned you to flee from
8 the wrath to come? Bring forth therefore fruit worthy of
9 [2]repentance: and think not to say within yourselves, We have
Abraham to our father: for I say unto you, that God is able of
10 these stones to raise up children unto Abraham. And even now
is the axe laid unto the root of the trees: every tree therefore
that bringeth not forth good fruit is hewn down, and cast into

        [1] Or, *through*   [2] Or, *your repentance*

11 the fire. I indeed baptize you ¹with water unto repentance: but he that cometh after me is mightier than I, whose shoes I am not ²worthy to bear: he shall baptize you ¹with the Holy Ghost

THE MOUNT OF TEMPTATION

12 and *with* fire: whose fan is in his hand, and he will throughly cleanse his threshing-floor; and he will gather his wheat into the garner, but the chaff he will burn up with unquenchable fire.

Jesus being baptized is called by God.

13 Then cometh Jesus from Galilee to the Jordan unto John, to 14 be baptized of him. But John would have hindered him, saying,

¹ Or, *in* ² Gr. *sufficient*

I have need to be baptized of thee, and comest thou to me?
15 But Jesus answering said unto him, Suffer [1]*it* now: for thus it
becometh us to fulfil all righteousness. Then he suffereth him.
16 And Jesus, when he was baptized, went up straightway from
the water: and lo, the heavens were opened [2]unto him, and he
saw the Spirit of God descending as a dove, and coming upon
17 him; and lo, a voice out of the heavens, saying, [3]This is my
beloved Son, in whom I am well pleased.

He is put to the Test by Satan.

4 Then was Jesus led up of the Spirit into the wilderness to be
2 tempted of the devil. And when he had fasted forty days
3 and forty nights, he afterward hungered. And the tempter
came and said unto him, If thou art the Son of God, command
4 that these stones become [4]bread. But he answered and said, It
is written, Man shall not live by bread alone, but by every word
5 that proceedeth out of the mouth of God. Then the devil
taketh him into the holy city; and he set him on the [5]pinnacle
6 of the temple, and saith unto him, If thou art the Son of God,
cast thyself down: for it is written,

He shall give his angels charge concerning thee:
And on their hands they shall bear thee up,
Lest haply thou dash thy foot against a stone.

7 Jesus said unto him, Again it is written, Thou shalt not tempt
8 the Lord thy God. Again, the devil taketh him unto an exceeding high mountain, and sheweth him all the kingdoms of the
9 world, and the glory of them; and he said unto him, All these
things will I give thee, if thou wilt fall down and worship me.
10 Then saith Jesus unto him, Get thee hence, Satan: for it is
written, Thou shalt worship the Lord thy God, and him only
11 shalt thou serve. Then the devil leaveth him; and behold,
angels came and ministered unto him.

He chooses the darkest region for his Work.

12 Now when he heard that John was delivered up, he withdrew
13 into Galilee; and leaving Nazareth, he came and dwelt in
Capernaum, which is by the sea, in the borders of Zebulun and
14 Naphtali: that it might be fulfilled which was spoken [6]by Isaiah
the prophet, saying,

[1] Or, *me*   [2] Some ancient authorities omit *unto him.*   [3] Or, *This is
my Son; my beloved in whom I am well pleased.* See ch. xii. 18.   [4] Gr.
loaves.   [5] Gr. *wing.*   [6] Or, *through*

15   The land of Zebulun and the land of Naphtali,
        ¹Toward the sea, beyond Jordan,
        Galilee of the ²Gentiles,

VIEW FROM THE MOUNT OF TEMPTATION

16   The people which sat in darkness
        Saw a great light,
        And to them which sat in the region and shadow of death,
        To them did light spring up.
17   From that time began Jesus to preach, and to say, Repent
ye; for the kingdom of heaven is at hand.

¹ Gr. *The way of the sea.*   ² Gr. *nations*: and so elsewhere.

He calls four disciples.

18 And walking by the sea of Galilee, he saw two brethren,
Simon who is called Peter, and Andrew his brother, casting a net
19 into the sea; for they were fishers. And he saith unto them, Come
20 ye after me, and I will make you fishers of men. And they
21 straightway left the nets, and followed him. And going on from
thence he saw other two brethren, [1]James the *son* of Zebedee,
and John his brother, in the boat with Zebedee their father,
22 mending their nets; and he called them. And they straightway
left the boat and their father, and followed him.

He evangelizes.

23 And [2]Jesus went about in all Galilee, teaching in their
synagogues, and preaching the [3]gospel of the kingdom, and
healing all manner of disease and all manner of sickness among
24 the people. And the report of him went forth into all Syria: and
they brought unto him all that were sick, holden with divers
diseases and torments, [4]possessed with devils, and epileptic,
25 and palsied; and he healed them. And there followed him great
multitudes from Galilee and Decapolis and Jerusalem and
Judæa and *from* beyond Jordan.

FIRST BOOK OF MATTHEW. CONCERNING DISCIPLESHIP

THE SERMON ON THE MOUNT

The Beatitudes.

5 And seeing the multitudes, he went up into the mountain:
2 and when he had sat down, his disciples came unto him: and
he opened his mouth and taught them, saying,

3 Blessed are the poor in spirit: for theirs is the kingdom of
heaven.

4 [5]Blessed are they that mourn: for they shall be comforted.

5 Blessed are the meek: for they shall inherit the earth.

6 Blessed are they that hunger and thirst after righteousness:
for they shall be filled.

7 Blessed are the merciful: for they shall obtain mercy.

8 Blessed are the pure in heart: for they shall see God.

9 Blessed are the peacemakers: for they shall be called sons
of God.

[1] Or, *Jacob*: and so elsewhere.　　[2] Some ancient authorities read *he*.
[3] Or, *good tidings*: and so elsewhere.　　[4] Or, *demoniacs*　　[5] Some
ancient authorities transpose ver. 4 and 5.

10 Blessed are they that have been persecuted for righteousness'
11 sake: for theirs is the kingdom of heaven. Blessed are ye when
men shall reproach you, and persecute you, and say all manner

THE MOUNT OF BEATITUDES

12 of evil against you falsely, for my sake. Rejoice, and be exceeding glad: for great is your reward in heaven: for so persecuted
they the prophets which were before you.

The Responsibilities of Christians.

13 Ye are the salt of the earth: but if the salt have lost its savour,
wherewith shall it be salted? it is thenceforth good for nothing,
14 but to be cast out and trodden under foot of men. Ye are the

15 light of the world. A city set on a hill cannot be hid. Neither do
   men light a lamp, and put it under the bushel, but on the stand;
16 and it shineth unto all that are in the house. Even so let your
   light shine before men, that they may see your good works, and
   glorify your Father which is in heaven.

The New Commandments.

17   Think not that I came to destroy the law or the prophets:
18 I came not to destroy, but to fulfil. For verily I say unto you,
   Till heaven and earth pass away, one jot or one tittle shall in no
   wise pass away from the law, till all things be accomplished.
19 Whosoever therefore shall break one of these least commandments, and shall teach men so, shall be called least in the kingdom of heaven: but whosoever shall do and teach them, he
20 shall be called great in the kingdom of heaven. For I say unto
   you, that except your righteousness shall exceed *the righteousness* of the scribes and Pharisees, ye shall in no wise enter into
   the kingdom of heaven.

Christian Law of Self-Control.

21   Ye have heard that it was said to them of old time, Thou
   shalt not kill; and whosoever shall kill shall be in danger of the
22 judgement: but I say unto you, that every one who is angry
   with his brother [1]shall be in danger of the judgement; and whosoever shall say to his brother, [2]Raca, shall be in danger of the
   council; and whosoever shall say, [3]Thou fool, shall be in danger
23 [4]of the [5]hell of fire. If therefore thou art offering thy gift at the
   altar, and there rememberest that thy brother hath aught
24 against thee, leave there thy gift before the altar, and go thy
   way, first be reconciled to thy brother, and then come and offer
25 thy gift. Agree with thine adversary quickly, whiles thou art
   with him in the way; lest haply the adversary deliver thee to
   the judge, and the judge [6]deliver thee to the officer, and thou
26 be cast into prison. Verily I say unto thee Thou shalt by no
   means come out thence, till thou have paid the last farthing.

Christian Law of Purity.

27   Ye have heard that it was said, Thou shalt not commit
28 adultery: but I say unto you, that every one that looketh on a

---

[1] Many ancient authorities insert *without cause.*   [2] An expression of
contempt.   [3] Or, *Moreh*, a Hebrew expression of condemnation.
[4] Gr. *unto* or *into.*   [5] Gr. *Gehenna of fire.*   [6] Some ancient authorities
omit *deliver thee.*

woman to lust after her hath committed adultery with her
29 already in his heart. And if thy right eye causeth thee to
stumble, pluck it out, and cast it from thee: for it is profitable
for thee that one of thy members should perish, and not thy
30 whole body be cast into ¹hell. And if thy right hand causeth
thee to stumble, cut it off, and cast it from thee: for it is
profitable for thee that one of thy members should perish, and
not thy whole body go into ¹hell.

The name Jeshua, the Hebrew form of
Jesus, upon an Ossuary from Jerusalem.
Early Imperial Period. The letter on the
extreme right is *Yod*, the smallest letter
in the Hebrew alphabet. (Mt. v. 18.)

Christian Law of Marriage.

31   It was said also, Whosoever shall put away his wife, let him
32 give her a writing of divorcement: but I say unto you, that
every one that putteth away his wife, saving for the cause of
fornication, maketh her an adulteress: and whosoever shall
marry her when she is put away committeth adultery.

Christian Law of Truth.

33   Again, ye have heard that it was said to them of old time,
Thou shalt not forswear thyself, but shalt perform unto the
34 Lord thine oaths: but I say unto you, Swear not at all; neither
35 by the heaven, for it is the throne of God; nor by the earth, for
it is the footstool of his feet; nor ²by Jerusalem, for it is the city
36 of the great King. Neither shalt thou swear by thy head, for
37 thou canst not make one hair white or black. ³But let your
speech be, Yea, yea; Nay, nay: and whatsoever is more than
these is of ⁴the evil *one*.

¹ Gr. *Gehenna*.   ² Or, *toward*   ³ Some ancient authorities read *But
your speech shall be.*   ⁴ Or, *evil*: as in ver. 39; vi. 13.

Of Renunciation of Rights.

38 Ye have heard that it was said, An eye for an eye, and a tooth
39 for a tooth: but I say unto you, Resist not [1]him that is evil: but
whosoever smiteth thee on thy right cheek, turn to him the
40 other also. And if any man would go to law with thee, and take
41 away thy coat, let him have thy cloke also. And whosoever
42 shall [2]compel thee to go one mile, go with him twain. Give to
him that asketh thee, and from him that would borrow of thee
turn not thou away.

Of Love.

43 Ye have heard that it was said, Thou shalt love thy neighbour,
44 and hate thine enemy: but I say unto you, Love your enemies,
45 and pray for them that persecute you; that ye may be sons of
your Father which is in heaven: for he maketh his sun to rise
on the evil and the good, and sendeth rain on the just and the
46 unjust. For if ye love them that love you, what reward have
47 ye? do not even the [3]publicans the same? And if ye salute your
brethren only, what do ye more *than others?* do not even the
48 Gentiles the same? Ye therefore shall be perfect, as your
heavenly Father is perfect.

The Christian Lex orandi. Almsgiving.

6 Take heed that ye do not your righteousness before men, to
be seen of them: else ye have no reward with your Father
which is in heaven.
2 When therefore thou doest alms, sound not a trumpet before
thee, as the hypocrites do in the synagogues and in the streets,
that they may have glory of men. Verily I say unto you,
3 They have received their reward. But when thou doest alms
4 let not thy left hand know what thy right hand doeth: that
thine alms may be in secret: and thy Father which seeth in
secret shall recompense thee.

Praying.

5 And when ye pray, ye shall not be as the hypocrites: for they
love to stand and pray in the synagogues and in the corners
of the streets, that they may be seen of men. Verily I say unto
6 you, They have received their reward. But thou, when thou

---

[1] Or, *evil*   [2] Gr. *impress.*   [3] That is, *collectors or renters of*
Roman taxes: and so elsewhere.

prayest, enter into thine inner chamber, and having shut thy door, pray to thy Father which is in secret, and thy Father 7 which seeth in secret shall recompense thee. And in praying

A page of the *Codex Sinaiticus*, a Greek MS. of the fourth century, formerly in the Monastery of St. Catherine on Mount Sinai, removed by Tischendorf in 1859 to St. Peterburg, since 1933 in the British Museum. It contains the New Testament, much of the Old, and two early Christian books, the Epistle of Barnabas and the Shepherd of Hermas. The part shown runs from Mt. 6. 4 to 6. 32.

use not vain repetitions, as the Gentiles do: for they think that 8 they shall be heard for their much speaking. Be not therefore like unto them: for [1]your Father knoweth what things ye have need of, before ye ask him.

[1] Some ancient authorities read *God your Father*.

The Lord's Prayer.

9 After this manner therefore pray ye: Our Father which art in
10 heaven, Hallowed be thy name. Thy kingdom come. Thy will
11 be done, as in heaven, so on earth. Give us this day [1]our daily
12 bread. And forgive us our debts, as we also have forgiven our
13 debtors. And bring us not into temptation, but deliver us from
14 [2]the evil *one*.[3] For if ye forgive men their trespasses, your
15 heavenly Father will also forgive you. But if ye forgive not
men their trespasses, neither will your Father forgive your
trespasses.

Fasting.

16 Moreover when ye fast, be not, as the hypocrites, of a sad
countenance: for they disfigure their faces, that they may be
seen of men to fast. Verily I say unto you, They have received
17 their reward. But thou, when thou fastest, anoint thy head,
18 and wash thy face; that thou be not seen of men to fast, but of
thy Father which is in secret: and thy Father, which seeth in
secret, shall recompense thee.

Christian Law of Property.

19 Lay not up for yourselves treasures upon the earth, where
moth and rust doth consume, and where thieves [4]break through
20 and steal: but lay up for yourselves treasures in heaven, where
neither moth nor rust doth consume, and where thieves do not
21 [4]break through nor steal: for where thy treasure is, there will
22 thy heart be also. The lamp of the body is the eye: if therefore
23 thine eye be single, thy whole body shall be full of light. But
if thine eye be evil, thy whole body shall be full of darkness. If
therefore the light that is in thee be darkness, how great is the
24 darkness! No man can serve two masters: for either he will
hate the one, and love the other; or else he will hold to one, and
25 despise the other. Ye cannot serve God and mammon. Therefore I say unto you, Be not anxious for your life, what ye shall
eat, or what ye shall drink; nor yet for your body, what ye shall
put on. Is not the life more than the food, and the body than
26 the raiment? Behold the birds of the heaven, that they sow not,
neither do they reap, nor gather into barns; and your heavenly
Father feedeth them. Are not ye of much more value than they?

[1] Gr. *our bread for the coming day.*   [2] Or, *evil*   [3] Many authorities, some ancient, but with variations, add *For thine is the kingdom, and the
power, and the glory, for ever. Amen.*   [4] Gr. *dig through.*

27 And which of you by being anxious can add one cubit unto his
28 ¹stature? And why are ye anxious concerning raiment? Consider the lilies of the field, how they grow; they toil not, neither
29 do they spin: yet I say unto you, that even Solomon in all his
30 glory was not arrayed like one of these. But if God doth so clothe the grass of the field, which to-day is, and to-morrow is cast into the oven, *shall he* not much more *clothe* you, O ye of
31 little faith? Be not therefore anxious, saying, What shall we eat? or, What shall we drink? or, Wherewithal shall we be
32 clothed? For after all these things do the Gentiles seek; for your heavenly Father knoweth that ye have need of all these
33 things. But seek ye first his kingdom, and his righteousness;
34 and all these things shall be added unto you. Be not therefore anxious for the morrow: for the morrow will be anxious for itself. Sufficient unto the day is the evil thereof.

Christian Law of Prudence.

In relation to Brothers.

2 **7** Judge not, that ye be not judged. For with what judgement ye judge, ye shall be judged: and with what measure ye
3 mete, it shall be measured unto you. And why beholdest thou the mote that is in thy brother's eye, but considerest not the
4 beam that is in thine own eye? Or how wilt thou say to thy brother, Let me cast out the mote out of thine eye; and lo, the
5 beam is in thine own eye? Thou hypocrite, cast out first the beam out of thine own eye; and then shalt thou see clearly to cast out the mote out of thy brother's eye.

In relation to those without.

6   Give not that which is holy unto the dogs, neither cast your pearls before the swine, lest haply they trample them under their feet, and turn and rend you.

7   Ask, and it shall be given you; seek, and ye shall find; knock,
8 and it shall be opened unto you: for every one that asketh receiveth; and he that seeketh findeth; and to him that
9 knocketh it shall be opened. Or what man is there of you, who,
10 if his son shall ask him for a loaf, will give him a stone; or if he
11 shall ask for a fish, will give him a serpent? If ye then, being evil, know how to give good gifts unto your children, how much more shall your Father which is in heaven give good things to them that ask him?

¹ Or, *age*

The Golden Rule.

12　All things therefore whatsoever ye would that men should do unto you, even so do ye also unto them: for this is the law and the prophets.

In relation to our own Salvation. The Two Ways.

13　Enter ye in by the narrow gate: for wide [1]is the gate, and broad is the way, that leadeth to destruction, and many be they that
14　enter in thereby. [2]For narrow is the gate, and straitened the way, that leadeth unto life, and few be they that find it.

In relation to Spiritual Persons.

(i) *Prophets and Teachers.*

15　Beware of false prophets, which come to you in sheep's
16　clothing, but inwardly are ravening wolves. By their fruits ye shall know them. Do *men* gather grapes of thorns, or figs of
17　thistles? Even so every good tree bringeth forth good fruit; but
18　the corrupt tree bringeth forth evil fruit. A good tree cannot bring forth evil fruit, neither can a corrupt tree bring forth good
19　fruit. Every tree that bringeth not forth good fruit is hewn
20　down, and cast into the fire. Therefore by their fruits ye shall know them.

(ii) *Exorcists.*

21　Not every one that saith unto me, Lord, Lord, shall enter into the kingdom of heaven; but he that doeth the will of my
22　Father which is in heaven. Many will say to me in that day, Lord, Lord, did we not prophesy by thy name, and by thy name cast out [3]devils, and by thy name do many [4]mighty works?
23　And then will I profess unto them, I never knew you: depart from me, ye that work iniquity.

The Two Houses. Hearers and Doers.

24　Every one therefore which heareth these words of mine, and doeth them, shall be likened unto a wise man, which built his
25　house upon the rock: and the rain descended, and the floods came, and the winds blew, and beat upon that house; and it fell
26　not: for it was founded upon the rock. And every one that heareth these words of mine, and doeth them not, shall be likened unto a foolish man, which built his house upon the

---

[1] Some ancient authorities omit *is the gate.*　　[2] Many ancient authorities read *How narrow is the gate, &c.*　　[3] Gr. *demons.*　　[4] Gr. *powers.*

27 sand: and the rain descended, and the floods came, and the winds blew, and smote upon that house; and it fell: and great was the fall thereof.

28 And it came to pass, when Jesus ended these words, the mul-
29 titudes were astonished at his teaching: for he taught them as *one* having authority, and not as their scribes.

SECOND BOOK OF MATTHEW. CONCERNING APOSTLESHIP

A. INTRODUCTORY NARRATIVE

Three Faith-healings.

8 And when he was come down from the mountain, great
2 multitudes followed him. And behold, there came to him a leper and worshipped him, saying, Lord, if thou wilt, thou canst
3 make me clean. And he stretched forth his hand, and touched him, saying, I will; be thou made clean. And straightway his
4 leprosy was cleansed. And Jesus saith unto him, See thou tell no man; but go thy way, shew thyself to the priest, and offer the gift that Moses commanded, for a testimony unto them.

5 And when he was entered into Capernaum, there came unto
6 him a centurion, beseeching him, and saying, Lord, my [1]servant
7 lieth in the house sick of the palsy, grievously tormented. And
8 he saith unto him, I will come and heal him. And the centurion answered and said, Lord, I am not [2]worthy that thou shouldest come under my roof: but only say [3]the word, and my [1]servant
9 shall be healed. For I also am a man [4]under authority, having under myself soldiers: and I say to this one, Go, and he goeth; and to another, Come, and he cometh; and to my [5]servant, Do
10 this, and he doeth it. And when Jesus heard it, he marvelled, and said to them that followed, Verily I say unto you, [6]I have
11 not found so great faith, no, not in Israel. And I say unto you, that many shall come from the east and the west, and shall [7]sit down with Abraham, and Isaac, and Jacob, in the kingdom of
12 heaven: but the sons of the kingdom shall be cast forth into the outer darkness: there shall be the weeping and gnashing of
13 teeth. And Jesus said unto the centurion, Go thy way; as thou

[1] Or, *boy*   [2] Gr. *sufficient.*   [3] Gr. *with a word.*   [4] Some ancient authorities insert *set*: as in Luke vii. 8.   [5] Gr. *bond-servant.*
[6] Many ancient authorities read *With no man in Israel have I found so great faith.*   [7] Gr. *recline.*

hast believed, *so* be it done unto thee. And the [1]servant was healed in that hour.

14 And when Jesus was come into Peter's house, he saw his
15 wife's mother lying sick of a fever. And he touched her hand, and the fever left her; and she arose, and ministered unto him.
16 And when even was come, they brought unto him many [2]possessed with devils: and he cast out the spirits with a word,
17 and healed all that were sick: that it might be fulfilled which was spoken [3]by Isaiah the prophet, saying, Himself took our infirmities, and bare our diseases.

Vocations, Exorcisms, and Mighty Works.

18 Now when Jesus saw great multitudes about him, he gave
19 commandment to depart unto the other side. And there came [4]a scribe, and said unto him, [5]Master, I will follow thee whither-
20 soever thou goest. And Jesus saith unto him, The foxes have holes, and the birds of the heaven *have* [6]nests; but the Son of
21 man hath not where to lay his head. And another of the disciples said unto him, Lord, suffer me first to go and bury my
22 father. But Jesus saith unto him, Follow me; and leave the dead to bury their own dead.

23 And when he was entered into a boat, his disciples followed
24 him. And behold, there arose a great tempest in the sea, insomuch that the boat was covered with the waves: but he was
25 asleep. And they came to him, and awoke him, saying, Save,
26 Lord; we perish. And he saith unto them, Why are ye fearful, O ye of little faith? Then he arose, and rebuked the winds and
27 the sea; and there was a great calm. And the men marvelled, saying, What manner of man is this, that even the winds and the sea obey him?

28 And when he was come to the other side into the country of the Gardarenes, there met him two [2]possessed with devils, coming forth out of the tombs, exceeding fierce, so that no man
29 could pass by that way. And behold, they cried out, saying, What have we to do with thee, thou Son of God? art thou come
30 hither to torment us before the time? Now there was afar off
31 from them a herd of many swine feeding. And the [7]devils besought him, saying, If thou cast us out, send us away into the
32 herd of swine. And he said unto them, Go. And they came out, and went into the swine: and behold, the whole herd rushed

---

[1] Or, *boy*   [2] Or, *demoniacs*   [3] Or, *through*   [4] Gr. *one scribe*.
[5] Or, *Teacher*   [6] Gr. *lodging-places*.   [7] Gr. *demons*.

33 down the steep into the sea, and perished in the waters. And they that fed them fled, and went away into the city, and told everything, and what was befallen to them that were ¹possessed

VIEW OF THE SEA OF GALILEE FROM THE MOUNT OF BEATITUDES

34 with devils. And behold, all the city came out to meet Jesus: and when they saw him, they besought *him* that he would depart from their borders.

9 And he entered into a boat, and crossed over, and came into
2 his own city. And behold, they brought to him a man sick of the palsy, lying on a bed: and Jesus seeing their faith said unto

¹ Or, *demoniacs*

the sick of the palsy, [1]Son, be of good cheer; thy sins are for-
3 given. And behold, certain of the scribes said within themselves,
4 This man blasphemeth. And Jesus [2]knowing their thoughts
5 said, Wherefore think ye evil in your hearts? For whether is
easier, to say, Thy sins are forgiven; or to say, Arise, and walk?
6 But that ye may know that the Son of man hath [3]power on
earth to forgive sins (then saith he to the sick of the palsy),
7 Arise, and take up thy bed, and go unto thy house. And he arose,
8 and departed to his house. But when the multitudes saw it,
they were afraid, and glorified God, which had given such
[3]power unto men.

A Vocation to Apostleship given.

9 And as Jesus passed by from thence, he saw a man, called
Matthew, sitting at the place of toll: and he saith unto him,
Follow me. And he arose, and followed him.
10 And it came to pass, as he [4]sat at meat in the house, behold,
many publicans and sinners came and sat down with Jesus and
11 his disciples. And when the Pharisees saw it, they said unto his
disciples, Why eateth your [5]Master with the publicans and
12 sinners? But when he heard it, he said, They that are [6]whole
13 have no need of a physician, but they that are sick. But go ye
and learn what *this* meaneth, I desire mercy, and not sacrifice:
for I came not to call the righteous, but sinners.
14 Then come to him the disciples of John, saying, Why do we
15 and the Pharisees fast [7]oft, but thy disciples fast not? And
Jesus said unto them, Can the sons of the bride-chamber mourn,
as long as the bridegroom is with them? but the days will come,
when the bridegroom shall be taken away from them, and then
16 will they fast. And no man putteth a piece of undressed cloth
upon an old garment; for that which should fill it up taketh
17 from the garment, and a worse rent is made. Neither do *men*
put new wine into old [8]wine-skins: else the skins burst, and the
wine is spilled, and the skins perish: but they put new wine into
fresh wine-skins, and both are preserved.

Three Wonders performed.

18 While he spake these things unto them, behold, there came
[9]a ruler, and worshipped him, saying, My daughter is even now

[1] Gr. *Child*.   [2] Many ancient authorities read *seeing*.   [3] Or, *authority*
[4] Gr. *reclined*: and so always.   [5] Or, *Teacher*   [6] Gr. *strong*.   [7] Some
ancient authorities omit *oft*.   [8] That is, *skins used as bottles*.   [9] Gr.
one ruler.

dead: but come and lay thy hand upon her, and she shall live.
19 And Jesus arose, and followed him, and *so did* his disciples.
20 And behold, a woman, who had an issue of blood twelve years,
21 came behind him, and touched the border of his garment: for
she said within herself, If I do but touch his garment, I shall be
22 [1]made whole. But Jesus turning and seeing her said, Daughter,
be of good cheer; thy faith hath [2]made thee whole. And the
23 woman was [1]made whole from that hour. And when Jesus came
into the ruler's house, and saw the flute-players, and the crowd
24 making a tumult, he said, Give place: for the damsel is not dead,
25 but sleepeth. And they laughed him to scorn. But when the
crowd was put forth, he entered in, and took her by the hand;
26 and the damsel arose. And [3]the fame hereof went forth into all
that land.

27 And as Jesus passed by from thence, two blind men followed
him, crying out, and saying, Have mercy on us, thou son of
28 David. And when he was come into the house, the blind men
came to him: and Jesus saith unto them, Believe ye that I am
29 able to do this? They say unto him, Yea, Lord. Then touched
he their eyes, saying, According to your faith be it done unto
30 you. And their eyes were opened. And Jesus [4]strictly charged
31 them, saying, See that no man know it. But they went forth,
and spread abroad his fame in all that land.

32 And as they went forth, behold, there was brought to him a
33 dumb man possessed with a [5]devil. And when the [5]devil was
cast out, the dumb man spake: and the multitudes marvelled,
34 saying, It was never so seen in Israel. But the Pharisees said,
[6]By the prince of the [7]devils casteth he out [7]devils.

B. Discourse on Apostleship.

Delegation of Power to the Apostles.

35 And Jesus went about all the cities and the villages, teaching
in their synagogues, and preaching the gospel of the kingdom,
and healing all manner of disease and all manner of sickness.
36 But when he saw the multitudes, he was moved with compassion for them, because they were distressed and scattered, as
37 sheep not having a shepherd. Then saith he unto his disciples,
38 The harvest truly is plenteous, but the labourers are few. Pray

[1] Or, *saved*   [2] Or, *saved thee*   [3] Gr. *this fame.*   [4] Or, *sternly*
[5] Gr. *demon.*   [6] Or, *In*   [7] Gr. *demons.*

ye therefore the Lord of the harvest, that he send forth labourers into his harvest.

10 And he called unto him his twelve disciples, and gave them authority over unclean spirits, to cast them out, and to heal all manner of disease and all manner of sickness. 2 Now the names of the twelve apostles are these: The first, Simon, who is called Peter, and Andrew his brother; James the 3 *son* of Zebedee, and John his brother; Philip, and Bartholomew; Thomas, and Matthew the publican; James the *son* of Alphæus, 4 and Thaddæus; Simon the [1]Cananæan, and Judas Iscariot, who also [2]betrayed him.

The Charge to the Apostles.

5 These twelve Jesus sent forth, and charged them, saying,

Go not into *any* way of the Gentiles, and enter not into any 6 city of the Samaritans: but go rather to the lost sheep of the 7 house of Israel. And as ye go, preach, saying, The kingdom of 8 heaven is at hand. Heal the sick, raise the dead, cleanse the 9 lepers, cast out [3]devils: freely ye received, freely give. Get you 10 no gold, nor silver, nor brass in your [4]purses; no wallet for *your* journey, neither two coats, nor shoes, nor staff: for the labourer 11 is worthy of his food. And into whatsoever city or village ye shall enter, search out who in it is worthy; and there abide till 12 ye go forth. And as ye enter into the house, salute it. And if 13 the house be worthy, let your peace come upon it: but if it be not worthy, let your peace return to you. And whosoever shall 14 not receive you, nor hear your words, as ye go forth out of that 15 house or that city, shake off the dust of your feet. Verily I say unto you, It shall be more tolerable for the land of Sodom and Gomorrah in the day of judgement, than for that city.

Encouragement to meet Persecutions.

16 Behold, I send you forth as sheep in the midst of wolves: be 17 ye therefore wise as serpents, and [5]harmless as doves. But beware of men: for they will deliver you up to councils, and in 18 their synagogues they will scourge you; yea and before governors and kings shall ye be brought for my sake, for a testimony 19 to them and to the Gentiles. But when they deliver you up, be not anxious how or what ye shall speak: for it shall be given 20 you in that hour what ye shall speak. For it is not ye that

[1] Or, *Zealot.* See Luke vi. 15; Acts i. 13. [2] Or, *delivered him up*: and so always. [3] Gr. *demons.* [4] Gr. *girdles.* [5] Or, *simple*

21 speak, but the Spirit of your Father that speaketh in you. And brother shall deliver up brother to death, and the father his child: and children shall rise up against parents, and [1]cause
22 them to be put to death. And ye shall be hated of all men for my name's sake: but he that endureth to the end, the same shall
23 be saved. But when they persecute you in this city, flee into the next: for verily I say unto you, Ye shall not have gone through the cities of Israel, till the Son of man be come.

24 A disciple is not above his [2]master, nor a [3]servant above his
25 lord. It is enough for the disciple that he be as his [2]master, and the [3]servant as his lord. If they have called the master of the house [4]Beelzebub, how much more *shall they call* them of his
26 household! Fear them not therefore: for there is nothing covered, that shall not be revealed; and hid, that shall not be
27 known. What I tell you in the darkness, speak ye in the light:
28 and what ye hear in the ear, proclaim upon the housetops. And be not afraid of them which kill the body, but are not able to kill the soul: but rather fear him which is able to destroy both
29 soul and body in [5]hell. Are not two sparrows sold for a farthing?
30 and not one of them shall fall on the ground without your
31 Father: but the very hairs of your head are all numbered. Fear
32 not therefore; ye are of more value than many sparrows. Every one therefore who shall confess [6]me before men, [7]him will I also
33 confess before my Father which is in heaven. But whosoever shall deny me before men, him will I also deny before my Father which is in heaven.

34 Think not that I came to [8]send peace on the earth: I came
35 not to [8]send peace, but a sword. For I came to set a man at variance against his father, and the daughter against her
36 mother, and the daughter in law against her mother in law:
37 and a man's foes *shall be* they of his own household. He that loveth father or mother more than me is not worthy of me; and he that loveth son or daughter more than me is not worthy of
38 me. And he that doth not take his cross and follow after me,
39 is not worthy of me. He that [9]findeth his [10]life shall lose it; and he that [11]loseth his [10]life for my sake shall find it.

Reward for Kindly Reception.

40 He that receiveth you receiveth me, and he that receiveth me

---

[1] Or, *put them to death* [2] Or, *teacher* [3] Gr. *bondservant.*
[4] Gr. *Beelzebul*: and so elsewhere. [5] Gr. *Gehenna* [6] Gr. *in me.*
[7] Gr. *in him.* [8] Gr. *cast.* [9] Or, *found* [10] Or, *soul* [11] Or, *lost*

41 receiveth him that sent me. He that receiveth a prophet in the name of a prophet shall receive a prophet's reward; and he that receiveth a righteous man in the name of a righteous man shall
42 receive a righteous man's reward. And whosoever shall give to drink unto one of these little ones a cup of cold water only, in the name of a disciple, verily I say unto you, he shall in no wise lose his reward.

11 And it came to pass, when Jesus had made an end of commanding his twelve disciples, he departed thence to teach and preach in their cities.

THIRD BOOK OF MATTHEW. CONCERNING THE HIDING OF THE MYSTERY OF THE KINGDOM OF GOD FROM ISRAEL AND ITS REVELATION TO THE FOLLOWERS OF JESUS.

A. Israel is Offended at the Gospel

John the Baptist and Jesus.

2 Now when John heard in the prison the works of the Christ,
3 he sent by his disciples, and said unto him, Art thou he that
4 cometh, or look we for another? And Jesus answered and said unto them, Go your way and tell John the things which ye do
5 hear and see: the blind receive their sight, and the lame walk, the lepers are cleansed, and the deaf hear, and the dead are raised up, and the poor have ¹good tidings preached to them.
6 And blessed is he, whosoever shall find none occasion of stum-
7 bling in me. And as these went their way, Jesus began to say unto the multitudes concerning John, What went ye out into
8 the wilderness to behold? a reed shaken with the wind? But what went ye out for to see? a man clothed in soft *raiment*?
9 Behold, they that wear soft *raiment* are in kings' houses. ²But wherefore went ye out? to see a prophet? Yea, I say unto you,
10 and much more than a prophet. This is he, of whom it is written,

Behold, I send my messenger before thy face,
Who shall prepare thy way before thee.

11 Verily I say unto you, Among them that are born of women

---

¹ Or, *the gospel*   ² Many ancient authorities read *But what went ye out to see? a prophet?*

there hath not arisen a greater than John the Baptist: yet he that is ¹but little in the kingdom of heaven is greater than he.
12 And from the days of John the Baptist until now the kingdom of heaven suffereth violence, and men of violence take it by
13 force. For all the prophets and the law prophesied until John.
14 And if ye are willing to receive ²*it*, this is Elijah, which is to
15 come. He that hath ears ³to hear, let him hear. But whereunto
16 shall I liken this generation? It is like unto children sitting in
17 the marketplaces, which call unto their fellows, and say, We piped unto you, and ye did not dance; we wailed, and ye did
18 not ⁴mourn. For John came neither eating nor drinking, and
19 they say, He hath a ⁵devil. The Son of man came eating and drinking, and they say, Behold, a gluttonous man, and a wine-bibber, a friend of publicans and sinners! And wisdom ⁶is justified by her ⁷works.

Judgement on the Unrepentant Cities.

20   Then began he to upbraid the cities wherein most of his
21 ⁸mighty works were done, because they repented not. Woe unto thee, Chorazin! woe unto thee, Bethsaida! for if the ⁸mighty works had been done in Tyre and Sidon which were done in you, they would have repented long ago in sackcloth
22 and ashes. Howbeit I say unto you, it shall be more tolerable
23 for Tyre and Sidon in the day of judgement, than for you. And thou, Capernaum, shalt thou be exalted unto heaven? thou shalt ⁹go down unto Hades: for if the ⁸mighty works had been done in Sodom which were done in thee, it would have remained
24 until this day. Howbeit I say unto you, that it shall be more tolerable for the land of Sodom in the day of judgement, than for thee.

Fullness of the Revelation to Jesus and His Followers.

25   At that season Jesus answered and said, I ¹⁰thank thee, O Father, Lord of heaven and earth, that thou didst hide these things from the wise and understanding, and didst reveal them
26 unto babes: yea, Father, ¹¹for so it was well-pleasing in thy sight.
27 All things have been delivered unto me of my Father: and no one knoweth the Son, save the Father; neither doth any

---

¹ Gr. *lesser.*   ² Or, him   ³ Some ancient authorities omit *to hear.*
⁴ Gr. *beat the breast.*   ⁵ Gr. *demon.*   ⁶ Or, *was*   ⁷ Many ancient
authorities read *children*: as in Luke vii. 35.   ⁸ Gr. *powers.*   ⁹ Many
ancient authorities read *be brought down.*   ¹⁰ Or, *praise*   ¹¹ Or, *that*

know the Father, save the Son, and he to whomsoever the Son
28 willeth to reveal *him*. Come unto me, all ye that labour and
29 are heavy laden, and I will give you rest. Take my yoke upon
you, and learn of me; for I am meek and lowly in heart: and ye
30 shall find rest unto your souls. For my yoke is easy, and my
burden is light.

Pharisaic Opposition.

12 At that season Jesus went on the sabbath day through the
cornfields; and his disciples were an hungred, and began to
2 pluck ears of corn, and to eat. But the Pharisees, when they
saw it, said unto him, Behold, thy disciples do that which it is not
3 lawful to do upon the sabbath. But he said unto them, Have
ye not read what David did, when he was an hungred, and they
4 that were with him; how he entered into the house of God, and
[1]did eat the shewbread, which it was not lawful for him to eat,
neither for them that were with him, but only for the priests?
5 Or have ye not read in the law, how that on the sabbath day the
priests in the temple profane the sabbath, and are guiltless?
6 But I say unto you, that [2]one greater than the temple is here.
7 But if ye had known what this meaneth, I desire mercy, and
8 not sacrifice, ye would not have condemned the guiltless. For
the Son of man is lord of the sabbath.

9 And he departed thence, and went into their synagogue: and
10 behold, a man having a withered hand. And they asked him,
saying, Is it lawful to heal on the sabbath day? that they might
11 accuse him. And he said unto them, What man shall there be
of you, that shall have one sheep, and if this fall into a pit on
the sabbath day, will he not lay hold on it, and lift it out?
12 How much then is a man of more value than a sheep! Where-
13 fore it is lawful to do good on the sabbath day. Then saith he
to the man, Stretch forth thy hand. And he stretched it forth;
14 and it was restored whole, as the other. But the Pharisees went
out, and took counsel against him, how they might destroy him.
15 And Jesus perceiving *it* withdrew from thence: and many fol-
16 lowed him; and he healed them all, and charged them that they
17 should not make him known: that it might be fulfilled which
was spoken by [3]Isaiah the prophet, saying,

18   Behold, my servant whom I have chosen;
My beloved in whom my soul is well pleased:

---

[1] Some ancient authorities read *they did eat*.   [2] Gr. *a greater thing.*
Or, *through*

I will put my Spirit upon him,
And he shall declare judgement to the Gentiles.

19 He shall not strive, nor cry aloud;
Neither shall any one hear his voice in the streets.

20 A bruised reed shall he not break,
And smoking flax shall he not quench,
Till he send forth judgement unto victory.

21 And in his name shall the Gentiles hope.

Open Challenge of the Pharisees.

22 Then was brought unto him [1]one possessed with a devil,
blind and dumb: and he healed him, insomuch that the dumb
23 man spake and saw. And all the multitudes were amazed, and
24 said, Is this the son of David? But when the Pharisees heard
it, they said, This man doth not cast out [2]devils, but [3]by Beelze-
25 bub the prince of the [2]devils. And knowing their thoughts he
said unto them, Every kingdom divided against itself is brought
to desolation; and every city or house divided against itself
26 shall not stand: and if Satan casteth out Satan, he is divided
27 against himself; how then shall his kingdom stand? And if I
[3]by Beelzebub cast out [2]devils, [3]by whom do your sons cast
28 them out? therefore shall they be your judges. But if I [3]by the
Spirit of God cast out [2]devils, then is the kingdom of God come
29 upon you. Or how can one enter into the house of the strong
man, and spoil his goods, except he first bind the strong *man*?
30 and then he will spoil his house. He that is not with me is
against me; and he that gathereth not with me scattereth.
31 Therefore I say unto you, Every sin and blasphemy shall be
forgiven [4]unto men; but the blasphemy against the Spirit shall
32 not be forgiven. And whosoever shall speak a word against the
Son of man, it shall be forgiven him; but whosoever shall speak
against the Holy Spirit, it shall not be forgiven him, neither in
33 this [5]world, nor in that which is to come. Either make the tree
good, and its fruit good; or make the tree corrupt, and its fruit
34 corrupt: for the tree is known by its fruit. Ye offspring of
vipers, how can ye, being evil, speak good things? for out of
35 the abundance of the heart the mouth speaketh. The good man
out of his good treasure bringeth forth good things: and the evil
36 man out of his evil treasure bringeth forth evil things. And I

[1] Or, *a demoniac*   [2] Gr. *demons.*   [3] Or, *in*   [4] Some ancient
authorities read *unto you men.*   [5] Or, *age*

say unto you, that every idle word that men shall speak, they
37 shall give account thereof in the day of judgement. For by thy
words thou shalt be justified, and by thy words thou shalt be
condemned.

Final Demand for a Proof of Jesus' Claim to Power.

38 Then certain of the scribes and Pharisees answered him,
39 saying, [1]Master, we would see a sign from thee. But he answered
and said unto them, An evil and adulterous generation seeketh
after a sign; and there shall no sign be given to it but the sign
40 of Jonah the prophet: for as Jonah was three days and three
nights in the belly of the [2]whale; so shall the Son of man be
41 three days and three nights in the heart of the earth. The men
of Nineveh shall stand up in the judgement with this generation,
and shall condemn it: for they repented at the preaching of
42 Jonah; and behold, [3]a greater than Jonah is here. The queen
of the south shall rise up in the judgement with this generation,
and shall condemn it: for she came from the ends of the earth
to hear the wisdom of Solomon; and behold, [3]a greater than
43 Solomon is here. But the unclean spirit, when [4]he is gone out of
the man, passeth through waterless places, seeking rest, and
44 findeth it not. Then [4]he saith, I will return into my house
whence I came out; and when [4]he is come, [4]he findeth it empty,
45 swept, and garnished. Then goeth [4]he, and taketh with [5]him-
self seven other spirits more evil than [5]himself, and they enter
in and dwell there: and the last state of that man becometh
worse than the first. Even so shall it be also unto this evil
generation.

Spiritual Family of Jesus.

46 While he was yet speaking to the multitudes, behold, his
mother and his brethren stood without, seeking to speak to
47 him. [6]And one said unto him, Behold, thy mother and thy
48 brethren stand without, seeking to speak to thee. But he
answered and said unto him that told him, Who is my mother?
49 and who are my brethren? And he stretched forth his hand
towards his disciples, and said, Behold, my mother and my
50 brethren! For whosoever shall do the will of my Father which
is in heaven, he is my brother, and sister, and mother.

---

[1] Or, *Teacher*   [2] Gr. *sea-monster*.   [3] Gr. *more than*.   [4] Or, *it*
[5] Or, *itself*   [6] Some ancient authorities omit ver. 47.

B. The Teaching in Parables

13 On that day went Jesus out of the house, and sat by the sea
² side. And there were gathered unto him great multitudes,
so that he entered into a boat, and sat; and all the multitude
stood on the beach.

Parable of the Sower, or the Receptive and Unreceptive Soils.

3 And he spake to them many things in parables, saying,
4 Behold, the sower went forth to sow; and as he sowed, some
seeds fell by the way side, and the birds came and devoured
5 them: and others fell upon the rocky places, where they had not
much earth: and straightway they sprang up, because they had
6 no deepness of earth: and when the sun was risen, they were
scorched; and because they had no root, they withered away.
7 And others fell upon the thorns; and the thorns grew up, and
8 choked them: and others fell upon the good ground, and yielded
9 fruit, some a hundredfold, some sixty, some thirty. He that
hath ears[1], let him hear.

Why Jesus speaks in Parables

10 And the disciples came, and said unto him, Why speakest
11 thou unto them in parables? And he answered and said unto
them, Unto you it is given to know the mysteries of the kingdom
12 of heaven, but to them it is not given. For whosoever hath, to
him shall be given, and he shall have abundance: but whosoever
hath not, from him shall be taken away even that which he
13 hath. Therefore speak I to them in parables; because seeing
they see not, and hearing they hear not, neither do they under-
14 stand. And unto them is fulfilled the prophecy of Isaiah, which
saith,

By hearing ye shall hear, and shall in no wise understand;
And seeing ye shall see, and shall in no wise perceive:
15 For this people's heart is waxed gross,
And their ears are dull of hearing,
And their eyes they have closed;
Lest haply they should perceive with their eyes,
And hear with their ears,
And understand with their heart,
And should turn again,
And I should heal them.

[1] Some ancient authorities add here, and in ver. 43, *to hear*: as in Mark
iv. 9; Luke viii. 8.

16 But blessed are your eyes, for they see; and your ears, for they hear.
17 For verily I say unto you, that many prophets and righteous men desired to see the things which ye see, and saw them not; and to hear the things which ye hear, and heard them not.

Meaning of the Parable of the Sower.

18 Hear then ye the parable of the sower. When any one heareth
19 the word of the kingdom, and understandeth it not, *then* cometh the evil *one*, and snatcheth away that which hath been sown in
20 his heart. This is he that was sown by the way side. And he that was sown upon the rocky places, this is he that heareth the
21 word, and straightway with joy receiveth it; yet hath he not root in himself, but endureth for a while; and when tribulation or persecution ariseth because of the word, straightway he
22 stumbleth. And he that was sown among the thorns, this is he that heareth the word; and the care of the [1]world, and the deceitfulness of riches, choke the word, and he becometh un-
23 fruitful. And he that was sown upon the good ground, this is he that heareth the word, and understandeth it; who verily beareth fruit, and bringeth forth, some a hundredfold, some sixty, some thirty.

The Wheat and the Tares.

24 Another parable set he before them, saying, The kingdom of heaven is likened unto a man that sowed good seed in his field:
25 but while men slept, his enemy came and sowed [2]tares also
26 among the wheat, and went away. But when the blade sprang
27 up, and brought forth fruit, then appeared the tares also. And the [3]servants of the householder came and said unto him, Sir, didst thou not sow good seed in thy field? whence then hath it
28 tares? And he said unto them, [4]An enemy hath done this. And the [3]servants say unto him, Wilt thou then that we go and
29 gather them up? But he saith, Nay; lest haply while ye gather
30 up the tares, ye root up the wheat with them. Let both grow together until the harvest: and in the time of the harvest I will say to the reapers, Gather up first the tares, and bind them in bundles to burn them: but gather the wheat into my barn.

The Mustard Seed and the Leaven.

31 Another parable set he before them, saying, The kingdom of heaven is like unto a grain of mustard seed, which a man took,

[1] Or, *age* [2] Or, *darnel* [3] Gr. *bondservants.* [4] Gr. *A man that is an enemy.*

32 and sowed in his field: which indeed is less than all seeds; but when it is grown, it is greater than the herbs, and becometh a tree, so that the birds of the heaven come and lodge in the branches thereof.

33   Another parable spake he unto them; The kingdom of heaven is like unto leaven, which a woman took, and hid in three ¹measures of meal, till it was all leavened.

34   All these things spake Jesus in parables unto the multitudes;
35 and without a parable spake he nothing unto them: that it might be fulfilled which was spoken ²by the prophet, saying,

I will open my mouth in parables;
I will utter things hidden from the foundation ³of the world.

Meaning of the Parable of the Tares.

36   Then he left the multitudes, and went into the house: and his disciples came unto him, saying, Explain unto us the parable of
37 the tares of the field. And he answered and said, He that soweth
38 the good seed is the Son of man; and the field is the world; and the good seed, these are the sons of the kingdom; and the tares
39 are the sons of the evil *one*; and the enemy that sowed them is the devil: and the harvest is ⁴the end of the world; and the
40 reapers are angels. As therefore the tares are gathered up and
41 burned with fire; so shall it be in ⁴the end of the world. The Son of man shall send forth his angels, and they shall gather out of his kingdom all things that cause stumbling, and them
42 that do iniquity, and shall cast them into the furnace of fire:
43 there shall be the weeping and gnashing of teeth. Then shall the righteous shine forth as the sun in the kingdom of their Father. He that hath ears, let him hear.

The Hidden Treasure, the Costly Pearl, the Drag-net.

44   The kingdom of heaven is like unto a treasure hidden in the field; which a man found, and hid; and ⁵in his joy he goeth and selleth all that he hath, and buyeth that field.

45   Again, the kingdom of heaven is like unto a man that is a
46 merchant seeking goodly pearls: and having found one pearl of great price, he went and sold all that he had, and bought it.

47   Again, the kingdom of heaven is like unto a ⁶net, that was

¹ The word in the Greek denotes the Hebrew seah, a measure containing nearly a peck and a half.   ² Or, *through*   ³ Many ancient authorities omit *of the world.*   ⁴ Or, *the consummation of the age*
⁵ Or, *for joy thereof*   ⁶ Gr. *drag-net.*

48 cast into the sea, and gathered of every kind: which, when it was filled, they drew up on the beach; and they sat down, and
49 gathered the good into vessels, but the bad they cast away. So shall it be in [1]the end of the world: the angels shall come forth,
50 and sever the wicked from among the righteous, and shall cast them into the furnace of fire: there shall be the weeping and gnashing of teeth.

The Evangelist's Signature.

51 Have ye understood all these things? They say unto him,
52 Yea. And he said unto them, Therefore every scribe who hath been made a disciple to the kingdom of heaven is like unto a man that is a householder, which bringeth forth out of his treasure things new and old.

FOURTH BOOK OF MATTHEW. CONCERNING THE UNITY OF THE CHURCH

A. Introductory Narrative

53 And it came to pass, when Jesus had finished these parables,
54 he departed thence. And coming into his own country he taught them in their synagogue, insomuch that they were astonished, and said, Whence hath this man this wisdom, and these [2]mighty
55 works? Is not this the carpenter's son? is not his mother called Mary? and his brethren, James, and Joseph, and Simon, and
56 Judas? And his sisters, are they not all with us? Whence then
57 hath this man all these things? And they were [3]offended in him. But Jesus said unto them, A prophet is not without honour,
58 save in his own country, and in his own house. And he did not many [2]mighty works there because of their unbelief.

The Passion of John the Baptist.

14 At that season Herod the tetrarch heard the report con-
2 cerning Jesus, and said unto his servants, This is John the Baptist; he is risen from the dead; and therefore do these
3 powers work in him. For Herod had laid hold on John, and bound him, and put him in prison for the sake of Herodias, his
4 brother Philip's wife. For John said unto him, It is not lawful
5 for thee to have her. And when he would have put him to death, he feared the multitude, because they counted him as a
6 prophet. But when Herod's birthday came, the daughter of

[1] Or, *the consummation of the age*   [2] Gr. *powers.*   [3] Gr. *caused to stumble.*

7 Herodias danced in the midst, and pleased Herod. Whereupon he promised with an oath to give her whatsoever she should ask.
8 And she, being put forward by her mother, saith, Give me here

The reputed site of the feeding of the five thousand on the eastern shore of the Sea of Galilee.

9 in a charger the head of John the Baptist. And the king was grieved; but for the sake of his oaths, and of them which sat at
10 meat with him, he commanded it to be given; and he sent, and
11 beheaded John in the prison. And his head was brought in a charger, and given to the damsel: and she brought it to her
12 mother. And his disciples came, and took up the corpse, and buried him; and they went and told Jesus.

The Agape in Galilee.

13 Now when Jesus heard *it*, he withdrew from thence in a boat, to a desert place apart: and when the multitudes heard *thereof*,
14 they followed him [1]on foot from the cities. And he came forth, and saw a great multitude, and he had compassion on them,
15 and healed their sick. And when even was come, the disciples came to him, saying, The place is desert, and the time is already past; send the multitudes away, that they may go into the
16 villages, and buy themselves food. But Jesus said unto them,
17 They have no need to go away; give ye them to eat. And they
18 say unto him, We have here but five loaves, and two fishes.
19 And he said, Bring them hither to me. And he commanded the multitudes to [2]sit down on the grass; and he took the five loaves, and the two fishes, and looking up to heaven, he blessed, and brake and gave the loaves to the disciples, and the disciples to
20 the multitudes. And they did all eat, and were filled: and they took up that which remained over of the broken pieces, twelve
21 baskets full. And they that did eat were about five thousand men, beside women and children.

The Story of Peter's Failure and Restoration.

22 And straightway he constrained the disciples to enter into the boat, and to go before him unto the other side, till he should
23 send the multitudes away. And after he had sent the multitudes away, he went up into the mountain apart to pray: and when
24 even was come, he was there alone. But the boat [3]was now in the midst of the sea, distressed by the waves; for the wind was
25 contrary. And in the fourth watch of the night he came unto
26 them, walking upon the sea. And when the disciples saw him walking on the sea, they were troubled, saying, It is an appari-
27 tion; and they cried out for fear. But straightway Jesus spake
28 unto them, saying, Be of good cheer; it is I; be not afraid. And Peter answered him and said, Lord, if it be thou, bid me come
29 unto thee upon the waters. And he said, Come. And Peter went down from the boat, and walked upon the waters, [4]to
30 come to Jesus. But when he saw the wind[5], he was afraid; and
31 beginning to sink, he cried out, saying, Lord, save me. And immediately Jesus stretched forth his hand, and took hold of

[1] Or, *by land*   [2] Gr. *recline.*   [3] Some ancient authorities read *was many furlongs distant from the land.*   [4] Some ancient authorities read *and came.*   [5] Many ancient authorities add *strong.*

him, and saith unto him, O thou of little faith, wherefore didst
32 thou doubt? And when they were gone up into the boat, the
33 wind ceased. And they that were in the boat worshipped him,
saying, Of a truth thou art the Son of God.

34 And when they had crossed over, they came to the land, unto
35 Gennesaret. And when the men of that place knew him, they
sent into all that region round about, and brought unto him all
36 that were sick; and they besought him that they might only
touch the border of his garment: and as many as touched were
made whole.

The Law of Clean and Unclean.

2 **15** Then there come to Jesus from Jerusalem Pharisees and
scribes, saying, Why do thy disciples transgress the tradition of the elders? for they wash not their hands when they eat
3 bread. And he answered and said unto them, Why do ye also
transgress the commandment of God because of your tradition?
4 For God said, Honour thy father and thy mother: and, He that
5 speaketh evil of father or mother, let him [1]die the death. But
ye say, Whosoever shall say to his father or his mother, That
wherewith thou mightest have been profited by me is given *to*
6 *God*; he shall not honour his father[2]. And ye have made void
7 the [3]word of God because of your tradition. Ye hypocrites, well
did Isaiah prophesy of you, saying,

8   This people honoureth me with their lips;
       But their heart is far from me.
9   But in vain do they worship me,
       Teaching *as their* doctrines the precepts of men.

10 And he called to him the multitude, and said unto them, Hear,
11 and understand: Not that which entereth into the mouth defileth the man; but that which proceedeth out of the mouth,
12 this defileth the man. Then came the disciples, and said unto
him, Knowest thou that the Pharisees were [4]offended, when they
13 heard this saying? But he answered and said, Every [5]plant
14 which my heavenly Father planted not, shall be rooted up. Let
them alone: they are blind guides. And if the blind guide the
15 blind, both shall fall into a pit. And Peter answered and said
16 unto him, Declare unto us the parable. And he said, Are ye also
17 even yet without understanding? Perceive ye not, that whatsoever goeth into the mouth passeth into the belly, and is cast

[1] Or, *surely die*   [2] Some ancient authorities add *or his mother*.   [3] Some
ancient authorities read *law*.   [4] Gr. *caused to stumble*.   [5] Gr. *planting*.

18 out into the draught? But the things which proceed out of the
19 mouth come forth out of the heart; and they defile the man. For
out of the heart come forth evil thoughts, murders, adulteries,
20 fornications, thefts, false witness, railings: these are the things
which defile the man: but to eat with unwashen hands defileth
not the man.

An Example of the New Law of Cleansing by Faith.

21 And Jesus went out thence, and withdrew into the parts of
22 Tyre and Sidon. And behold, a Canaanitish woman came out
from those borders, and cried, saying, Have mercy on me, O
Lord, thou son of David; my daughter is grievously vexed with
23 a [1]devil. But he answered her not a word. And his disciples
came and besought him, saying, Send her away; for she crieth
24 after us. But he answered and said, I was not sent but unto the
25 lost sheep of the house of Israel. But she came and worshipped
26 him, saying, Lord, help me. And he answered and said, It is not
27 meet to take the children's [2]bread and cast it to the dogs. But
she said, Yea, Lord: for even the dogs eat of the crumbs which
28 fall from their masters' table. Then Jesus answered and said
unto her, O woman, great is thy faith: be it done unto thee even
as thou wilt. And her daughter was healed from that hour.

The Agape in Peraea.

29 And Jesus departed thence, and came nigh unto the sea of
30 Galilee; and he went up into the mountain, and sat there. And
there came unto him great multitudes, having with them the
lame, blind, dumb, maimed, and many others, and they cast
31 them down at his feet; and he healed them: insomuch that the
multitude wondered, when they saw the dumb speaking, the
maimed whole, and the lame walking, and the blind seeing: and
they glorified the God of Israel.

32 And Jesus called unto him his disciples, and said, I have
compassion on the multitude, because they continue with me
now three days and have nothing to eat: and I would not send
33 them away fasting, lest haply they faint in the way. And the
disciples say unto him, Whence should we have so many loaves
34 in a desert place, as to fill so great a multitude? And Jesus
saith unto them, How many loaves have ye? And they said,
35 Seven, and a few small fishes. And he commanded the multitude
36 to sit down on the ground; and he took the seven loaves and the

---

[1] Gr. demon.   [2] Or, loaf

fishes; and he gave thanks and brake, and gave to the disciples,
37 and the disciples to the multitudes. And they did all eat, and
were filled: and they took up that which remained over of the
38 broken pieces, seven baskets full. And they that did eat were
39 four thousand men, beside women and children. And he sent

THE SNOWS OF MT. HERMON, seen from the Sea of Galilee.

away the multitudes, and entered into the boat, and came into
the borders of Magadan.

16 And the Pharisees and Sadducees came, and tempting
2 him asked him to shew them a sign from heaven. But he
answered and said unto them, ¹When it is evening, ye say, *It
3 will be* fair weather: for the heaven is red. And in the morning,
It will be foul weather to-day: for the heaven is red and lowring.
Ye know how to discern the face of the heaven; but ye cannot
4 *discern* the signs of the times. An evil and adulterous generation
seeketh after a sign; and there shall no sign be given unto it, but
the sign of Jonah. And he left them, and departed.

¹ The following words, to the end of ver. 3, are omitted by some of the
most ancient and other important authorities.

The Conversation about Leaven.

5 And the disciples came to the other side and forgot to take
6 [1]bread. And Jesus said unto them, Take heed and beware of
7 the leaven of the Pharisees and Sadducees. And they reasoned
8 among themselves, saying, [2]We took no [1]bread. And Jesus
perceiving it said, O ye of little faith, why reason ye among
9 yourselves, because ye have no [1]bread? Do ye not yet perceive,
neither remember the five loaves of the five thousand, and how
10 many [3]baskets ye took up? Neither the seven loaves of the four
11 thousand, and how many [3]baskets ye took up? How is it that
ye do not perceive that I spake not to you concerning [1]bread?
12 But beware of the leaven of the Pharisees and Sadducees. Then
understood they how that he bade them not beware of the
leaven of [1]bread, but of the teaching of the Pharisees and
Sadducees.

*Peter's Confession of the Christ and the Revelation to Peter as the
Foundation of the Unity of the Church.*

13 Now when Jesus came into the parts of Cæsarea Philippi, he
asked his disciples, saying, Who do men say [4]that the Son of
14 man is? And they said, Some *say* John the Baptist; some,
15 Elijah: and others, Jeremiah, or one of the prophets. He saith
16 unto them, But who say ye that I am? And Simon Peter
answered and said, Thou art the Christ, the Son of the living
17 God. And Jesus answered and said unto him, Blessed art thou,
Simon Bar-Jonah: for flesh and blood hath not revealed it unto
18 thee, but my Father which is in heaven. And I also say unto
thee, that thou art [5]Peter, and upon this [6]rock I will build my
church; and the gates of Hades shall not prevail against it.
19 I will give unto thee the keys of the kingdom of heaven: and
whatsoever thou shalt bind on earth shall be bound in heaven:
and whatsoever thou shalt loose on earth shall be loosed in
20 heaven. Then charged he the disciples that they should tell no
man that he was the Christ.
21 From that time began [7]Jesus to shew unto his disciples, how
that he must go unto Jerusalem, and suffer many things of the
elders and chief priests and scribes, and be killed, and the third
22 day be raised up. And Peter took him, and began to rebuke

---

[1] Gr. *loaves*.   [2] Or, It is *because we took no bread*.   [3] *Basket* in ver. 9
and 10 represents different Greek words.   [4] Many ancient authorities
read *that I the Son of man am*. See Mark viii. 27; Luke ix. 18.   [5] Gr.
Petros.   [6] Gr. *petra*.   [7] Some ancient authorities read *Jesus Christ*.

ST. PETER AS A BISHOP, WITH ST. PAUL AND ST. ANDREW
From a thirteenth century wall-painting in the Ante-reliquary
Chapel at Norwich Cathedral.

him, saying, ¹Be it far from thee, Lord: this shall never be unto
23 thee. But he turned, and said unto Peter, Get thee behind me,
Satan: thou art a stumblingblock unto me: for thou mindest

¹ Or, God *have mercy on thee*

24 not the things of God, but the things of men. Then said Jesus unto his disciples, If any man would come after me, let him
25 deny himself, and take up his cross, and follow me. For whosoever would save his [1]life shall lose it: and whosoever shall lose
26 his [1]life for my sake shall find it. For what shall a man be profited, if he shall gain the whole world, and forfeit his [1]life?
27 or what shall a man give in exchange for his [1]life? For the Son of man shall come in the glory of his Father with his angels; and then shall he render unto every man according to his [2]deeds.
28 Verily I say unto you, There be some of them that stand here, which shall in no wise taste of death, till they see the Son of man coming in his kingdom.

The Divine Nature of Jesus revealed in the Transfiguration.

17 And after six days Jesus taketh with him Peter, and James, and John his brother, and bringeth them up into
2 a high mountain apart: and he was transfigured before them: and his face did shine as the sun, and his garments became white
3 as the light. And behold, there appeared unto them Moses and
4 Elijah talking with him. And Peter answered, and said unto Jesus, Lord, it is good for us to be here: if thou wilt, I will make here three [3]tabernacles; one for thee, and one for Moses, and one
5 for Elijah. While he was yet speaking, behold, a bright cloud overshadowed them: and behold, a voice out of the cloud, saying, This is my beloved Son, in whom I am well pleased; hear
6 ye him. And when the disciples heard it, they fell on their face,
7 and were sore afraid. And Jesus came and touched them and
8 said, Arise, and be not afraid. And lifting up their eyes, they saw no one, save Jesus only.
9 And as they were coming down from the mountain, Jesus commanded them, saying, Tell the vision to no man, until the
10 Son of man be risen from the dead. And his disciples asked him, saying, Why then say the scribes that Elijah must first come?
11 And he answered and said, Elijah indeed cometh, and shall
12 restore all things: but I say unto you, that Elijah is come already, and they knew him not, but did unto him whatsoever they listed.
13 Even so shall the Son of man also suffer of them. Then understood the disciples that he spake unto them of John the Baptist.

Jesus heals an Epileptic Boy.

14 And when they were come to the multitude, there came to
15 him a man, kneeling to him, and saying, Lord, have mercy on

[1] Or, *soul*   [2] Gr. *doing.*   [3] Or, *booths*

my son: for he is epileptic, and suffereth grievously: for oft-
16 times he falleth into the fire, and oft-times into the water. And
I brought him to thy disciples, and they could not cure him.
17 And Jesus answered and said, O faithless and perverse generation, how long shall I be with you? how long shall I bear with
18 you? bring him hither to me. And Jesus rebuked him; and the
[1]devil went out from him: and the boy was cured from that hour.
19 Then came the disciples to Jesus apart, and said, Why could
20 not we cast it out? And he saith unto them, Because of your
little faith: for verily I say unto you, If ye have faith as a grain
of mustard seed, ye shall say unto this mountain, Remove hence
to yonder place; and it shall remove; and nothing shall be impossible unto you.[2]

B. Discourse on the Unity of the Church

Avoiding Occasions (i) *of giving Offence to the Civil Authorities.*

22   And while they [3]abode in Galilee, Jesus said unto them, The
23 Son of man shall be delivered up into the hands of men; and
they shall kill him, and the third day he shall be raised up. And
they were exceeding sorry.
24   And when they were come to Capernaum, they that received
the [4]half-shekel came to Peter, and said, Doth not your [5]master
25 pay the [4]half-shekel? He saith, Yea. And when he came into
the house, Jesus spake first to him, saying, What thinkest thou,
Simon? the kings of the earth, from whom do they receive toll
26 or tribute? from their sons, or from strangers? And when he
said, From strangers, Jesus said unto him, Therefore the sons
27 are free. But, lest we cause them to stumble, go thou to the sea,
and cast a hook, and take up the fish that first cometh up; and
when thou hast opened his mouth, thou shalt find a [6]shekel:
that take, and give unto them for me and thee.

(ii) *Of Schism in the Church.*

18 In that hour came the disciples unto Jesus, saying, Who
2 then is [7]greatest in the kingdom of heaven? And he
3 called to him a little child, and set him in the midst of them, and
said, Verily I say unto you, Except ye turn, and become as little

---

[1] Gr. *demon.*   [2] Many authorities, some ancient, insert ver. 21 *But
this kind goeth not out save by prayer and fasting.* See Mark ix. 29.
[3] Some ancient authorities read *were gathering themselves together.*   [4] Gr.
didrachma.   [5] Or, *teacher*   [6] Gr. *stater.*   [7] Gr. *greater.*

children, ye shall in no wise enter into the kingdom of heaven.
4 Whosoever therefore shall humble himself as this little child,
5 the same is the [1]greatest in the kingdom of heaven. And whoso
6 shall receive one such little child in my name receiveth me: but
whoso shall cause one of these little ones which believe on me to
stumble, it is profitable for him that [2]a great millstone should
be hanged about his neck, and *that* he should be sunk in the
7 depth of the sea. Woe unto the world because of occasions of
stumbling! for it must needs be that the occasions come; but
8 woe to that man through whom the occasion cometh! And if
thy hand or thy foot causeth thee to stumble, cut it off, and
cast it from thee: it is good for thee to enter into life maimed or
halt, rather than having two hands or two feet to be cast into
9 the eternal fire. And if thine eye causeth thee to stumble, pluck
it out, and cast it from thee: it is good for thee to enter into life
with one eye, rather than having two eyes to be cast into the
10 [3]hell of fire. See that ye despise not one of these little ones; for
I say unto you, that in heaven their angels do always behold the
12 face of my Father which is in heaven.[4] How think ye? if any
man have a hundred sheep, and one of them be gone astray,
doth he not leave the ninety and nine, and go unto the moun-
13 tains, and seek that which goeth astray? And if so be that he
find it, verily I say unto you, he rejoiceth over it more than over
14 the ninety and nine which have not gone astray. Even so it is
not [5]the will of [6]your Father which is in heaven, that one of
these little ones should perish.

The Problem of Discipline in the Church.

15 And if thy brother sin [7]against thee, go, shew him his fault
between thee and him alone: if he hear thee, thou hast gained
16 thy brother. But if he hear *thee* not, take with thee one or two
more, that at the mouth of two witnesses or three every word
17 may be established. And if he refuse to hear them, tell it unto
the [8]church: and if he refuse to hear the [8]church also, let him be
18 unto thee as the Gentile and the publican. Verily I say unto
you, What things soever ye shall bind on earth shall be bound
in heaven: and what things soever ye shall loose on earth shall

---

[1] Gr. *greater*   [2] Gr. *a millstone turned by an ass.*   [3] Gr. *Gehenna of fire.*
[4] Many authorities, some ancient, insert ver. 11 *For the Son of man came to save that which was lost.* See Luke xix. 10.   [5] Gr. *a thing willed before your Father.*   [6] Some ancient authorities read *my.*   [7] Some ancient authorities omit *against thee.*   [8] Or, *congregation*

19 be loosed in heaven. Again I say unto you, that if two of you shall agree on earth as touching anything that they shall ask,
20 it shall be done for them of my Father which is in heaven. For where two or three are gathered together in my name, there am I in the midst of them.

THE RIVER JORDAN

Illustrated by the Parable of the Unmerciful Servant.

21   Then came Peter, and said to him, Lord, how oft shall my brother sin against me, and I forgive him? until seven times?
22 Jesus saith unto him, I say not unto thee, Until seven times;
23 but, Until ¹seventy times seven. Therefore is the kingdom of heaven likened unto a certain king, which would make a
24 reckoning with his ²servants. And when he had begun to reckon, one was brought unto him, which owed him ten thousand
25 ³talents. But forasmuch as he had not *wherewith* to pay, his lord commanded him to be sold, and his wife, and children, and
26 all that he had, and payment to be made. The ⁴servant there-

---

¹ Or, *seventy times and seven*   ² Gr. *bondservants.*   ³ This talent was probably worth about £240.   ⁴ Gr. *bondservant.*

fore fell down and worshipped him, saying, Lord, have patience
27 with me, and I will pay thee all. And the lord of that [1]servant,
being moved with compassion, released him, and forgave him
28 the [2]debt. But that [1]servant went out, and found one of his
fellow-servants, which owed him a hundred [3]pence: and he laid
hold on him, and took *him* by the throat, saying, Pay what thou
29 owest. So his fellow-servant fell down and besought him, say-
30 ing, Have patience with me, and I will pay thee. And he would
not: but went and cast him into prison, till he should pay that
31 which was due. So when his fellow-servants saw what was done,
they were exceeding sorry, and came and told unto their lord all
32 that was done. Then his lord called him unto him, and saith to
him, Thou wicked [1]servant, I forgave thee all that debt, because
33 thou besoughtest me: shouldest not thou also have had mercy
34 on thy fellow-servant, even as I had mercy on thee? And his
lord was wroth, and delivered him to the tormentors, till he
35 should pay all that was due. So shall also my heavenly Father do
unto you, if ye forgive not every one his brother from your hearts.

19 And it came to pass when Jesus had finished these words,
he departed from Galilee, and came into the borders of
2 Judæa beyond Jordan; and great multitudes followed him; and
he healed them there.

FIFTH BOOK OF MATTHEW. CONCERNING THE JUDGEMENT

A. Preliminary Events

Teachings on the Way to the Cross.

Marriage and Divorce.

3   And there came unto him [4]Pharisees, tempting him, and saying, Is it lawful *for a man* to put away his wife for every cause?
4 And he answered and said, Have ye not read, that he which
[5]made *them* from the beginning made them male and female,
5 and said, For this cause shall a man leave his father and mother,
and shall cleave to his wife; and the twain shall become one
6 flesh? So that they are no more twain, but one flesh. What
therefore God hath joined together, let not man put asunder.
7 They say unto him, Why then did Moses command to give a bill

---

[1] Gr. *bondservant.*   [2] Gr. *loan.*   [3] The word in the Greek denotes
a coin worth about eight pence halfpenny.   [4] Many authorities, some
ancient, insert *the.*   [5] Some ancient authorities read *created.*

8 of divorcement, and to put *her* away? He saith unto them, Moses for your hardness of heart suffered you to put away your
9 wives: but from the beginning it hath not been so. And I say unto you, Whosoever shall put away his wife, [1]except for fornication, and shall marry another, committeth adultery: [2]and he that marrieth her when she is put away committeth adultery.
10 The disciples say unto him, If the case of the man is so with his
11 wife, it is not expedient to marry. But he said unto them, All men cannot receive this saying, but they to whom it is given.
12 For there are eunuchs, which were so born from their mother's womb: and there are eunuchs, which were made eunuchs by men: and there are eunuchs, which made themselves eunuchs for the kingdom of heaven's sake. He that is able to receive it, let him receive it.

Christ's love for Children.

13   Then were there brought unto him little children, that he should lay his hands on them, and pray: and the disciples re-
14 buked them. But Jesus said, Suffer the little children, and forbid them not, to come unto me: for of such is the kingdom of
15 heaven. And he laid his hands on them, and departed thence.

Precepts and Counsels.

16   And behold, one came to him and said, [3] [4]Master, what good
17 thing shall I do, that I may have eternal life? And he said unto him, [5]Why askest thou me concerning that which is good? One there is who is good: but if thou wouldest enter into life, keep
18 the commandments. He saith unto him, Which? And Jesus said, Thou shalt not kill, Thou shalt not commit adultery, Thou
19 shalt not steal, Thou shalt not bear false witness, Honour thy father and thy mother: and, Thou shalt love thy neighbour as
20 thyself. The young man saith unto him, All these things have I
21 observed: what lack I yet? Jesus said unto him, If thou wouldest be perfect, go, sell that thou hast, and give to the poor, and thou shalt have treasure in heaven: and come, follow me.
22 But when the young man heard the saying, he went away sorrowful: for he was one that had great possessions.

[1] Some ancient authorities read *saving for the cause of fornication, maketh her an adulteress*: as in ch. v. 32.   [2] The following words, to the end of the verse, are omitted by some ancient authorities.   [3] Or, *Teacher* [4] Some ancient authorities read *Good Master*. See Mark x. 17; Luke xviii. 18.   [5] Some ancient authorities read *Why callest thou me good? None is good save one*, even *God*. See Mark x. 18; Luke xviii. 19.

23 And Jesus said unto his disciples, Verily I say unto you, It is
24 hard for a rich man to enter into the kingdom of heaven. And
again I say unto you, It is easier for a camel to go through a
needle's eye, than for a rich man to enter into the kingdom of
25 God. And when the disciples heard it, they were astonished
26 exceedingly, saying, Who then can be saved? And Jesus looking upon *them* said to them, With men this is impossible; but
with God all things are possible.

Rewards and Punishments.

27 Then answered Peter and said unto him, Lo, we have left all,
28 and followed thee; what then shall we have? And Jesus said
unto them, Verily I say unto you, that ye which have followed
me, in the regeneration when the Son of man shall sit on the
throne of his glory, ye also shall sit upon twelve thrones,
29 judging the twelve tribes of Israel. And every one that hath
left houses, or brethren, or sisters, or father, or mother,[1] or
children, or lands, for my name's sake, shall receive [2]a hundred-
30 fold, and shall inherit eternal life. But many shall be last *that
are* first; and first *that are* last.

*Illustrated by the first Parable of the Vineyard or the Dissatisfied
Wage-earners.*

20 For the kingdom of heaven is like unto a man that is a
householder, which went out early in the morning to hire
2 labourers into his vineyard. And when he had agreed with the
labourers for a [3]penny a day, he sent them into his vineyard.
3 And he went out about the third hour, and saw others standing
4 in the marketplace idle; and to them he said, Go ye also into
the vineyard, and whatsoever is right I will give you. And they
5 went their way. Again he went out about the sixth and the
6 ninth hour, and did likewise. And about the eleventh *hour* he
went out, and found others standing; and he saith unto them,
7 Why stand ye here all the day idle? They say unto him, Because no man hath hired us. He saith unto them, Go ye also
8 into the vineyard. And when even was come, the lord of the
vineyard saith unto his steward, Call the labourers, and pay
9 them their hire, beginning from the last unto the first. And
when they came that *were hired* about the eleventh hour, they
10 received every man a [3]penny. And when the first came, they

[1] Many ancient authorities add *or wife*: as in Luke xviii. 29.   [2] Some
ancient authorities read *manifold.*   [3] See marginal note on ch. xviii. 28.

supposed that they would receive more; and they likewise
11 received every man a [1]penny. And when they received it, they
12 murmured against the householder, saying, These last have
spent *but* one hour, and thou hast made them equal unto us,
which have borne the burden of the day and the [2]scorching heat.
13 But he answered and said to one of them, Friend, I do thee no
14 wrong: didst not thou agree with me for a [1]penny? Take up
that which is thine, and go thy way; it is my will to give unto
15 this last, even as unto thee. Is it not lawful for me to do what
I will with mine own? or is thine eye evil, because I am good?
16 So the last shall be first, and the first last.

Jesus again foretells His Sufferings and Death.

17   And as Jesus was going up to Jerusalem, he took the twelve
18 disciples apart, and in the way he said unto them, Behold, we
go up to Jerusalem; and the Son of man shall be delivered unto
the chief priests and scribes; and they shall condemn him to
19 death, and shall deliver him unto the Gentiles to mock, and to
scourge, and to crucify: and the third day he shall be raised up.

Request of the Sons of Zebedee. Service true Greatness.

20   Then came to him the mother of the sons of Zebedee with her
21 sons, worshipping *him*, and asking a certain thing of him. And
he said unto her, What wouldest thou? She saith unto him,
Command that these my two sons may sit, one on thy right
22 hand, and one on thy left hand, in thy kingdom. But Jesus
answered and said, Ye know not what ye ask. Are ye able to
23 drink the cup that I am about to drink? They say unto him,
We are able. He saith unto them, My cup indeed ye shall drink:
but to sit on my right hand, and on *my* left hand, is not mine
to give, but *it is for them* for whom it hath been prepared of my
24 Father. And when the ten heard it, they were moved with
25 indignation concerning the two brethren. But Jesus called
them unto him, and said, Ye know that the rulers of the Gentiles
lord it over them, and their great ones exercise authority over
26 them. Not so shall it be among you: but whosoever would be-
27 come great among you shall be your [3]minister; and whosoever
28 would be first among you shall be your [4]servant: even as the
Son of man came not to be ministered unto, but to minister, and
to give his life a ransom for many.

---

[1] See marginal note on ch. xviii. 28.   [2] Or, *hot wind*   [3] Or, *servant*
[4] Gr. *bondservant.*

29 And as they went out from Jericho, a great multitude followed
30 him. And behold, two blind men sitting by the way side, when
they heard that Jesus was passing by, cried out, saying, Lord,
31 have mercy on us, thou son of David. And the multitude rebuked them, that they should hold their peace: but they cried
out the more, saying, Lord, have mercy on us, thou son of
32 David. And Jesus stood still, and called them, and said, What
33 will ye that I should do unto you? They say unto him, Lord,
34 that our eyes may be opened. And Jesus, being moved with
compassion, touched their eyes: and straightway they received
their sight, and followed him.

At Jericho. The Last Days in and near Jerusalem. The Tri-
umphal Entry, Sunday, Nisan 10.

21 And when they drew nigh unto Jerusalem, and came unto
Bethphage, unto the mount of Olives, then Jesus sent
2 two disciples, saying unto them, Go into the village that is over
against you, and straightway ye shall find an ass tied, and a colt
3 with her: loose *them*, and bring *them* unto me. And if any one say
aught unto you, ye shall say, The Lord hath need of them; and
4 straightway he will send them. Now this is come to pass, that
it might be fulfilled which was spoken [1]by the prophet, saying,

5   Tell ye the daughter of Zion,
          Behold, thy King cometh unto thee,
          Meek, and riding upon an ass,
          And upon a colt the foal of an ass.

6 And the disciples went, and did even as Jesus appointed them,
7 and brought the ass, and the colt, and put on them their gar-
8 ments; and he sat thereon. And the most part of the multitude
spread their garments in the way; and others cut branches from
9 the trees, and spread them in the way. And the multitudes that
went before him, and that followed, cried, saying, Hosanna to the
son of David: Blessed *is* he that cometh in the name of the Lord;
10 Hosanna in the highest. And when he was come into Jerusalem,
11 all the city was stirred, saying, Who is this? And the multitudes
said, This is the prophet, Jesus, from Nazareth of Galilee.

The Challenge to the Temple Authorities.

12 And Jesus entered into the temple [2]of God, and cast out all
them that sold and bought in the temple, and overthrew the

---

[1] Or, *through*   [2] Many ancient authorities omit *of God*.

tables of the money-changers, and the seats of them that sold
13 the doves; and he saith unto them, It is written, My house shall
be called a house of prayer: but ye make it a den of robbers.
14 And the blind and the lame came to him in the temple: and he
15 healed them. But when the chief priests and the scribes saw
the wonderful things that he did, and the children that were
crying in the temple and saying, Hosanna to the son of David;
16 they were moved with indignation, and said unto him, Hearest
thou what these are saying? And Jesus saith unto them, Yea:
did ye never read, Out of the mouth of babes and sucklings thou
17 hast perfected praise? And he left them, and went forth out
of the city to Bethany, and lodged there.

The Parable of the Unfruitful Fig Tree.

18   Now in the morning as he returned to the city, he hungered.
19 And seeing [1]a fig tree by the way side, he came to it, and found
nothing thereon, but leaves only; and he saith unto it, Let there
be no fruit from thee henceforward for ever. And immediately
the fig tree withered away.

Debates in the Temple Precincts, Tuesday, Nisan 12.

20   And when the disciples saw it, they marvelled, saying, How
21 did the fig tree immediately wither away? And Jesus answered
and said unto them, Verily I say unto you, If ye have faith, and
doubt not, ye shall not only do what is done to the fig tree, but
even if ye shall say unto this mountain, Be thou taken up and
22 cast into the sea, it shall be done. And all things, whatsoever ye
shall ask in prayer, believing, ye shall receive.
23   And when he was come into the temple, the chief priests and
the elders of the people came unto him as he was teaching, and
said, By what authority doest thou these things? and who gave
24 thee this authority? And Jesus answered and said unto them,
I also will ask you one [2]question, which if ye tell me, I likewise
25 will tell you by what authority I do these things. The baptism
of John, whence was it? from heaven or from men? And they
reasoned with themselves, saying, If we shall say, From heaven;
26 he will say unto us, Why then did ye not believe him? But if
we shall say, From men; we fear the multitude; for all hold
27 John as a prophet. And they answered Jesus, and said, We
know not. He also said unto them, Neither tell I you by what
authority I do these things.

        [1] Or, *a single*   [2] Gr. *word.*

Parables of the two Sons and of the Usurping Husbandmen.

28 But what think ye? A man had two sons; and he came to
29 the first, and said, ¹Son, go work to-day in the vineyard. And
he answered and said, I will not: but afterward he repented
30 himself, and went. And he came to the second, and said likewise. And he answered and said, I *go,* sir: and went not.
31 Whether of the twain did the will of his father? They say, The
first. Jesus saith unto them, Verily I say unto you, that the
publicans and the harlots go into the kingdom of God before
32 you. For John came unto you in the way of righteousness, and
ye believed him not: but the publicans and the harlots believed
him: and ye, when ye saw it, did not even repent yourselves
afterward, that ye might believe him.

33 Hear another parable: There was a man that was a householder, which planted a vineyard, and set a hedge about it, and
digged a winepress in it, and built a tower, and let it out to
34 husbandmen, and went into another country. And when the
season of the fruits drew near, he sent his ²servants to the hus-
35 bandmen, to receive ³his fruits. And the husbandmen took his
²servants, and beat one, and killed another, and stoned another.
36 Again, he sent other ²servants more than the first: and they did
37 unto them in like manner. But afterward he sent unto them his
38 son, saying, They will reverence my son. But the husbandmen,
when they saw the son, said among themselves, This is the heir;
39 come, let us kill him, and take his inheritance. And they took
him, and cast him forth out of the vineyard, and killed him.
40 When therefore the lord of the vineyard shall come, what will
41 he do unto those husbandmen? They say unto him, He will
miserably destroy those miserable men, and will let out the
vineyard unto other husbandmen, which shall render him the
42 fruits in their seasons. Jesus saith unto them, Did ye never read
in the scriptures,

> The stone which the builders rejected,
> The same was made the head of the corner:
> This was from the Lord,
> And it is marvellous in our eyes?

43 Therefore say I unto you, The kingdom of God shall be taken
away from you, and shall be given to a nation bringing forth
44 the fruits thereof. ⁴And he that falleth on this stone shall be

¹ Gr. *Child.*   ² Gr. *bondservants.*   ³ Or, *the fruits of it*   ⁴ Some
ancient authorities omit ver. 44.

broken to pieces: but on whomsoever it shall fall, it will scatter
45 him as dust. And when the chief priests and the Pharisees
46 heard his parables, they perceived that he spake of them. And
when they sought to lay hold on him, they feared the multitudes,
because they took him for a prophet.

Parable of the Wedding-feast and of the Uninvited Guest.

22 And Jesus answered and spake again in parables unto
2 them, saying, The kingdom of heaven is likened unto a
3 certain king, which made a marriage feast for his son, and sent
forth his [1]servants to call them that were bidden to the marriage
4 feast: and they would not come. Again he sent forth other
[1]servants, saying, Tell them that are bidden, Behold, I have
made ready my dinner: my oxen and my fatlings are killed, and
5 all things are ready: come to the marriage feast. But they made
light of it, and went their ways, one to his own farm, another to
6 his merchandise: and the rest laid hold on his [1]servants, and
7 entreated them shamefully, and killed them. But the king was
wroth; and he sent his armies, and destroyed those murderers,
8 and burned their city. Then saith he to his [1]servants, The
wedding is ready, but they that were bidden were not worthy.
9 Go ye therefore unto the partings of the highways, and as many
10 as ye shall find, bid to the marriage feast. And those [1]servants
went out into the highways, and gathered together all as many
as they found, both bad and good: and the wedding was filled
11 with guests. But when the king came in to behold the guests, he
12 saw there a man which had not on a wedding-garment: and he
saith unto him, Friend, how camest thou in hither not having
13 a wedding-garment? And he was speechless. Then the king
said to the [2]servants, Bind him hand and foot, and cast him out
into the outer darkness; there shall be the weeping and gnash-
14 ing of teeth. For many are called, but few chosen.

The Pharisees and Herodians.

15   Then went the Pharisees, and took counsel how they might
16 ensnare him in *his* talk. And they send to him their disciples,
with the Herodians, saying, [3]Master, we know that thou art
true, and teachest the way of God in truth, and carest not for
17 any one: for thou regardest not the person of men. Tell us
therefore, What thinkest thou? Is it lawful to give tribute
18 unto Cæsar, or not? But Jesus perceived their wickedness, and

---

[1] Gr. *bondservants.*   [2] Or, *ministers*   [3] Or, *Teacher*

19 said, Why tempt ye me, ye hypocrites? Shew me the tribute
20 money. And they brought unto him a [1]penny. And he saith
21 unto them, Whose is this image and superscription? They say
unto him, Cæsar's. Then saith he unto them, Render therefore unto Cæsar the things that are Cæsar's; and unto God the
22 things that are God's. And when they heard it, they marvelled,
and left him, and went their way.

The Sadducees.

23 On that day there came to him Sadducees, [2]which say that
24 there is no resurrection: and they asked him, saying, [3]Master,
Moses said, If a man die, having no children, his brother [4]shall
25 marry his wife, and raise up seed unto his brother. Now there
were with us seven brethren: and the first married and deceased,
26 and having no seed left his wife unto his brother; in like manner
27 the second also, and the third, unto the [5]seventh. And after
28 them all the woman died. In the resurrection therefore whose
29 wife shall she be of the seven? for they all had her. But Jesus
answered and said unto them, Ye do err, not knowing the scrip-
30 tures, nor the power of God. For in the resurrection they neither
marry, nor are given in marriage, but are as angels [6]in heaven.
31 But as touching the resurrection of the dead, have ye not read
32 that which was spoken unto you by God, saying, I am the God
of Abraham, and the God of Isaac, and the God of Jacob? God
33 is not *the God* of the dead, but of the living. And when the
multitudes heard it, they were astonished at his teaching.

A Scribe.

34 But the Pharisees, when they heard that he had put the
35 Sadducees to silence, gathered themselves together. And one of
36 them, a lawyer, asked him a question, tempting him, [3]Master,
37 which is the great commandment in the law? And he said unto
him, Thou shalt love the Lord thy God with all thy heart, and
38 with all thy soul, and with all thy mind. This is the great and
39 first commandment. [7]And a second like *unto it* is this, Thou
40 shalt love thy neighbour as thyself. On these two commandments hangeth the whole law, and the prophets.

---

[1] See marginal note on ch. xviii. 28.   [2] Gr. *saying*.   [3] Or, *Teacher*
[4] Gr. *shall perform the duty of a husband's brother to his wife.* Compare
Deut. xxv. 5.   [5] Gr. *seven*.   [6] Many ancient authorities add
of God.   [7] Or, *And a second is like unto it, Thou shalt love &c.*

Jesus makes a Rejoinder.

41 Now while the Pharisees were gathered together, Jesus asked
42 them a question, saying, What think ye of the Christ? whose
43 son is he? They say unto him, *The son* of David. He saith unto
them, How then doth David in the Spirit call him Lord, saying,

44 The Lord said unto my Lord,
Sit thou on my right hand,
Till I put thine enemies underneath thy feet?

45 If David then calleth him Lord, how is he his son? And no one
46 was able to answer him a word, neither durst any man from that
day forth ask him any more questions.

Condemnation of the Scribes and Pharisees.

23 Then spake Jesus to the multitudes and to his disciples,
2 saying, The scribes and the Pharisees sit on Moses' seat:
3 all things therefore whatsoever they bid you, *these* do and
observe: but do not ye after their works; for they say, and do
4 not. Yea, they bind heavy burdens [1]and grievous to be borne,
and lay them on men's shoulders; but they themselves will not
5 move them with their finger. But all their works they do for to
be seen of men: for they make broad their phylacteries, and
6 enlarge the borders *of their garments*, and love the chief place at
7 feasts, and the chief seats in the synagogues, and the salutations
8 in the marketplaces, and to be called of men, Rabbi. But be
not ye called Rabbi: for one is your teacher, and all ye are
9 brethren. And call no man your father on the earth: for one is
10 your Father, [2]which is in heaven. Neither be ye called masters:
11 for one is your master, *even* the Christ. But he that is [3]greatest
12 among you shall be your [4]servant. And whosoever shall exalt
himself shall be humbled; and whosoever shall humble himself
shall be exalted.

13 But woe unto you, scribes and Pharisees, hypocrites! because ye shut the kingdom of heaven [5]against men: for ye enter
not in yourselves, neither suffer ye them that are entering in to
enter.[6]

15 Woe unto you, scribes and Pharisees, hypocrites! for ye com-

[1] Many ancient authorities omit *and grievous to be borne.*   [2] Gr. *the heavenly.*   [3] Gr. *greater.*   [4] Or, *minister*   [5] Gr. *before.*   [6] Some authorities insert here, or after ver. 12, ver. 14 *Woe unto you, scribes and Pharisees, hypocrites! for ye devour widows' houses, even while for a pretence ye make long prayers: therefore ye shall receive greater condemnation.* See Mark xii. 40; Luke xx. 47.

pass sea and land to make one proselyte; and when he is become so, ye make him twofold more a son of [1]hell than yourselves.

16   Woe unto you, ye blind guides, which say, Whosoever shall
swear by the [2]temple, it is nothing; but whosoever shall swear
17 by the gold of the [2]temple, he is [3]a debtor. Ye fools and blind:
for whether is greater, the gold, or the [2]temple that hath
18 sanctified the gold? And, Whosoever shall swear by the altar,
it is nothing; but whosoever shall swear by the gift that is upon
19 it, he is [3]a debtor. Ye blind: for whether is greater, the gift, or
20 the altar that sanctifieth the gift? He therefore that sweareth
21 by the altar, sweareth by it, and by all things thereon. And he
that sweareth by the [2]temple, sweareth by it, and by him that
22 dwelleth therein. And he that sweareth by the heaven, sweareth
by the throne of God, and by him that sitteth thereon.

23   Woe unto you, scribes and Pharisees, hypocrites! for ye tithe
mint and [4]anise and cummin, and have left undone the weightier
matters of the law, judgement, and mercy, and faith: but these
ye ought to have done, and not to have left the other undone.
24 Ye blind guides, which strain out the gnat, and swallow the
camel.

25   Woe unto you, scribes and Pharisees, hypocrites! for ye
cleanse the outside of the cup and of the platter, but within
26 they are full from extortion and excess. Thou blind Pharisee,
cleanse first the inside of the cup and of the platter, that the
outside thereof may become clean also.

27   Woe unto you, scribes and Pharisees, hypocrites! for ye are
like unto whited sepulchres, which outwardly appear beautiful,
but inwardly are full of dead men's bones, and of all unclean-
28 ness. Even so ye also outwardly appear righteous unto men,
but inwardly ye are full of hypocrisy and iniquity.

29   Woe unto you, scribes and Pharisees, hypocrites! for ye build
the sepulchres of the prophets, and garnish the tombs of the
30 righteous, and say, If we had been in the days of our fathers, we
should not have been partakers with them in the blood of the
31 prophets. Wherefore ye witness to yourselves, that ye are sons
32 of them that slew the prophets. Fill ye up then the measure
33 of your fathers. Ye serpents, ye offspring of vipers, how shall
34 ye escape the judgement of [1]hell? Therefore, behold, I send
unto you prophets, and wise men, and scribes: some of them
shall ye kill and crucify; and some of them shall ye scourge in

---

[1] Gr. *Gehenna*.   [2] Or, *sanctuary*. as in ver. 35.   [3] Or, *bound by*
his oath   [4] Or, *dill*

35 your synagogues, and persecute from city to city: that upon
you may come all the righteous blood shed on the earth, from
the blood of Abel the righteous unto the blood of Zachariah son
of Barachiah, whom ye slew between the sanctuary and the
36 altar. Verily I say unto you, All these things shall come upon
this generation.

37   O Jerusalem, Jerusalem, which killeth the prophets, and
stoneth them that are sent unto her! how often would I have
gathered thy children together, even as a hen gathereth her
38 chickens under her wings, and ye would not! Behold, your
39 house is left unto you [1]desolate. For I say unto you, Ye shall
not see me henceforth, till ye shall say, Blessed *is* he that
cometh in the name of the Lord.

B. The Final Discourse. The Judgement to Come

The Doom of Jerusalem.

24 And Jesus went out from the temple, and was going on
his way; and his disciples came to him to shew him the
2 buildings of the temple. But he answered and said unto them,
See ye not all these things? verily I say unto you, There shall
not be left here one stone upon another, that shall not be thrown
down.

Signs of the End.

(a) The Great Deception and the Rise of Lawlessness.

3   And as he sat on the mount of Olives, the disciples came unto
him privately, saying, Tell us, when shall these things be? and
what *shall be* the sign of thy [2]coming, and of [3]the end of the
4 world? And Jesus answered and said unto them, Take heed
5 that no man lead you astray. For many shall come in my name,
6 saying, I am the Christ; and shall lead many astray. And ye
shall hear of wars and rumours of wars: see that ye be not
troubled: for *these things* must needs come to pass; but the end
7 is not yet. For nation shall rise against nation, and kingdom
against kingdom: and there shall be famines and earthquakes
8 in divers places. But all these things are the beginning of
9 travail. Then shall they deliver you up unto tribulation, and
shall kill you: and ye shall be hated of all the nations for my
10 name's sake. And then shall many stumble, and shall deliver
11 up one another, and shall hate one another. And many false

[1] Some ancient authorities omit *desolate.*   [2] Gr. *presence.*
[3] Or, *the consummation of the age*

12 prophets shall arise, and shall lead many astray. And because
iniquity shall be multiplied, the love of the many shall wax
13 cold. But he that endureth to the end, the same shall be saved.
14 And ¹this gospel of the kingdom shall be preached in the whole
²world for a testimony unto all the nations; and then shall the
end come.

(b) The Desecrating Horror and Great Distress.

15   When therefore ye see the abomination of desolation, which
was spoken of ³by Daniel the prophet, standing in ⁴the holy
16 place (let him that readeth understand), then let them that are
17 in Judæa flee unto the mountains: let him that is on the house-
18 top not go down to take out the things that are in his house: and
19 let him that is in the field not return back to take his cloke. But
woe unto them that are with child and to them that give suck
20 in those days! And pray ye that your flight be not in the
21 winter, neither on a sabbath: for then shall be great tribulation,
such as hath not been from the beginning of the world until
22 now, no, nor ever shall be. And except those days had been
shortened, no flesh would have been saved: but for the elect's
sake those days shall be shortened.

(c) False Messiahs.

23   Then if any man shall say unto you, Lo, here is the Christ, or,
24 Here; believe ⁵it not. For there shall arise false Christs, and
false prophets, and shall shew great signs and wonders; so as to
25 lead astray, if possible, even the elect. Behold, I have told you
26 beforehand. If therefore they shall say unto you, Behold, he is
in the wilderness; go not forth: Behold, he is in the inner
27 chambers; believe ⁶it not. For as the lightning cometh forth
from the east, and is seen even unto the west; so shall be the
28 ⁷coming of the Son of man. Wheresoever the carcase is, there
will the ⁸eagles be gathered together.

(d) The Sign of the Son of Man.

29   But immediately, after the tribulation of those days, the sun
shall be darkened, and the moon shall not give her light, and the
stars shall fall from heaven, and the powers of the heavens shall
30 be shaken: and then shall appear the sign of the Son of man in
heaven: and then shall all the tribes of the earth mourn, and

¹ Or, *these good tidings*   ² Gr. *inhabited earth.*   ³ Or, *through*
⁴ Or, *a holy place*   ⁵ Or, him   ⁶ Or, them   ⁷ Gr. *presence.*
⁸ Or, *vultures*

they shall see the Son of man coming on the clouds of heaven
31 with power and great glory. And he shall send forth his angels
[1]with [2]a great sound of a trumpet, and they shall gather together his elect from the four winds, from one end of heaven to
the other.

32 Now from the fig tree learn her parable: when her branch is
now become tender, and putteth forth its leaves, ye know that
33 the summer is nigh; even so ye also, when ye see all these things,
34 know ye that [3]he is nigh, *even* at the doors. Verily I say unto
you, This generation shall not pass away, till all these things be
35 accomplished. Heaven and earth shall pass away, but my words
shall not pass away.

(e) The Imminence and Suddenness of the Advent.

36 But of that day and hour knoweth no one, not even the angels
37 of heaven, [4]neither the Son, but the Father only. And as *were*
38 the days of Noah, so shall be the [5]coming of the Son of man. For
as in those days which were before the flood they were eating
and drinking, marrying and giving in marriage, until the day
39 that Noah entered into the ark, and they knew not until the
flood came, and took them all away; so shall be the [5]coming of
40 the Son of man. Then shall two men be in the field; one is taken,
41 and one is left: two women *shall be* grinding at the mill; one is
taken, and one is left.

Therefore be ready, like Good Stewards.

42 Watch therefore: for ye know not on what day your Lord
43 cometh. [6]But know this, that if the master of the house had
known in what watch the thief was coming, he would have
watched, and would not have suffered his house to be [7]broken
44 through. Therefore be ye also ready: for in an hour that ye
45 think not the Son of man cometh. Who then is the faithful and
wise [8]servant, whom his lord hath set over his household, to
46 give them their food in due season? Blessed is that [8]servant,
47 whom his lord when he cometh shall find so doing. Verily I say
48 unto you, that he will set him over all that he hath. But if that
49 evil [8]servant shall say in his heart, My lord tarrieth; and shall
begin to beat his fellow-servants, and shall eat and drink with
50 the drunken; the lord of that [8]servant shall come in a day

[1] Many ancient authorities read *with a great trumpet, and they shall gather
&c.*   [2] Or, *a trumpet of great sound*   [3] Or, *it*   [4] Many authorities,
some ancient, omit *neither the Son.*   [5] Gr. *presence.*   [6] Or, *But this
ye know*   [7] Gr. *digged through.*   [8] Gr. *bondservant.*

when he expecteth not, and in an hour when he knoweth not,
51 and shall ¹cut him asunder, and appoint his portion with the
hypocrites: there shall be the weeping and gnashing of teeth.

Or like the Provident Bridesmaids.

Parable of the Ten Virgins.

25 Then shall the kingdom of heaven be likened unto ten
virgins, which took their ²lamps, and went forth to meet
2 the bridegroom. And five of them were foolish, and five were
3 wise. For the foolish, when they took their ²lamps, took no oil
4 with them: but the wise took oil in their vessels with their
5 ²lamps. Now while the bridegroom tarried, they all slumbered
6 and slept. But at midnight there is a cry, Behold, the bride-
7 groom! Come ye forth to meet him. Then all those virgins
8 arose, and trimmed their ²lamps. And the foolish said unto the
9 wise, Give us of your oil; for our ²lamps are going out. But the
wise answered, saying, Peradventure there will not be enough
for us and you: go ye rather to them that sell, and buy for
10 yourselves. And while they went away to buy, the bridegroom
came; and they that were ready went in with him to the
11 marriage feast: and the door was shut. Afterward come also
12 the other virgins, saying, Lord, Lord, open to us. But he
answered and said, Verily I say unto you, I know you not.
13 Watch therefore, for ye know not the day nor the hour.

Or like the Good and Faithful Servants.

Parable of the Entrusted Funds, or the Talents.

14   For *it is* as *when* a man, going into another country, called his
15 own ³servants, and delivered unto them his goods. And unto
one he gave five talents, to another two, to another one; to each
according to his several ability; and he went on his journey.
16 Straightway he that received the five talents went and traded
17 with them, and made other five talents. In like manner he also
18 that *received* the two gained other two. But he that received the
one went away and digged in the earth, and hid his lord's money.
19 Now after a long time the lord of those ³servants cometh, and
20 maketh a reckoning with them. And he that received the five
talents came and brought other five talents, saying, Lord, thou
deliveredst unto me five talents: lo, I have gained other five

---

¹ Or, *severely scourge him*   ² Or, *torches*   ³ Gr. *bondservants.*

21 talents. His lord said unto him, Well done, good and faithful
[1]servant: thou hast been faithful over a few things, I will set
22 thee over many things: enter thou into the joy of thy lord. And
he also that *received* the two talents came and said, Lord, thou
deliveredst unto me two talents: lo, I have gained other two
23 talents. His lord said unto him, Well done, good and faithful
[1]servant; thou hast been faithful over a few things, I will set
24 thee over many things: enter thou into the joy of thy lord. And
he also that had received the one talent came and said, Lord, I
knew thee that thou art a hard man, reaping where thou didst
25 not sow, and gathering where thou didst not scatter: and I was
afraid, and went away and hid thy talent in the earth: lo, thou
26 hast thine own. But his lord answered and said unto him, Thou
wicked and slothful [1]servant, thou knewest that I reap where I
27 sowed not, and gather where I did not scatter; thou oughtest
therefore to have put my money to the bankers, and at my
coming I should have received back mine own with interest.
28 Take ye away therefore the talent from him, and give it unto
29 him that hath the ten talents. For unto every one that hath
shall be given, and he shall have abundance: but from him that
30 hath not, even that which he hath shall be taken away. And
cast ye out the unprofitable [1]servant into the outer darkness:
there shall be the weeping and gnashing of teeth.

The Great Judgement: the Sheep and the Goats.

31   But when the Son of man shall come in his glory, and all the
angels with him, then shall he sit on the throne of his glory:
32 and before him shall be gathered all the nations: and he shall
separate them one from another, as the shepherd separateth the
33 sheep from the [2]goats: and he shall set the sheep on his right
34 hand, but the [2]goats on the left. Then shall the King say unto
them on his right hand, Come, ye blessed of my Father, inherit
the kingdom prepared for you from the foundation of the world:
35 for I was an hungred, and ye gave me meat: I was thirsty, and
36 ye gave me drink: I was a stranger, and ye took me in; naked,
and ye clothed me: I was sick, and ye visited me: I was in
37 prison, and ye came unto me. Then shall the righteous answer
him, saying, Lord, when saw we thee an hungred, and fed thee?
38 or athirst, and gave thee drink? And when saw we thee a
39 stranger, and took thee in? or naked, and clothed thee? And
40 when saw we thee sick, or in prison, and came unto thee? And

[1] Gr. *bondservant.*   [2] Gr. *kids.*

the King shall answer and say unto them, Verily I say unto you,
Inasmuch as ye did it unto one of these my brethren, *even* these
41 least, ye did it unto me. Then shall he say also unto them on
the left hand, [1]Depart from me, ye cursed, into the eternal fire
42 which is prepared for the devil and his angels: for I was an
hungred, and ye gave me no meat: I was thirsty, and ye gave
43 me no drink: I was a stranger, and ye took me not in; naked,
and ye clothed me not; sick, and in prison, and ye visited me
44 not. Then shall they also answer, saying, Lord, when saw we
thee an hungred, or athirst, or a stranger, or naked, or sick, or in
45 prison, and did not minister unto thee? Then shall he answer
them, saying, Verily I say unto you, Inasmuch as ye did it not
46 unto one of these least, ye did it not unto me. And these shall go
away into eternal punishment: but the righteous into eternal
life.

EPILOGUE

THE DEATH AND RESURRECTION OF THE MESSIAH

26 And it came to pass, when Jesus had finished all these
words, he said unto his disciples,

The Plot to kill Jesus. Wednesday, Nisan 13.

2 Ye know that after two days the passover cometh, and the Son
3 of man is delivered up to be crucified. Then were gathered
together the chief priests, and the elders of the people, unto the
4 court of the high priest, who was called Caiaphas; and they took
counsel together that they might take Jesus by subtilty, and
5 kill him. But they said, Not during the feast, lest a tumult arise
among the people.

The Anointing at Simon's House.

6 Now when Jesus was in Bethany, in the house of Simon the
7 leper, there came unto him a woman having [2]an alabaster cruse
of exceeding precious ointment, and she poured it upon his head,
8 as he sat at meat. But when the disciples saw it, they had
9 indignation, saying, To what purpose is this waste? For this
ointment might have been sold for much, and given to the poor.
10 But Jesus perceiving it said unto them, Why trouble ye the
11 woman? for she hath wrought a good work upon me. For ye
have the poor always with you; but me ye have not always.
12 For in that she [3]poured this ointment upon my body, she did it

[1] Or, *Depart from me under a curse*   [2] Or, *a flask*   [3] Gr. *cast.*

13 to prepare me for burial. Verily I say unto you, Wheresoever [1]this gospel shall be preached in the whole world, that also which this woman hath done shall be spoken of for a memorial of her.

The Traitor Judas.

14 Then one of the twelve, who was called Judas Iscariot, went 15 unto the chief priests, and said, What are ye willing to give me, and I will deliver him unto you? And they weighed unto him 16 thirty pieces of silver. And from that time he sought opportunity to deliver him *unto them.*

The Passover is prepared. Thursday, Nisan 14.

17 Now on the first *day* of unleavened bread the disciples came to Jesus, saying, Where wilt thou that we make ready for thee 18 to eat the passover? And he said, Go into the city to such a man, and say unto him, The [2]Master saith, My time is at hand: 19 I keep the passover at thy house with my disciples. And the disciples did as Jesus appointed them; and they made ready the passover.

The Farewell Supper.

20 Now when even was come, he was sitting at meat with the 21 twelve [3]disciples; and as they were eating, he said, Verily I say 22 unto you, that one of you shall betray me. And they were exceeding sorrowful, and began to say unto him every one, Is it 23 I, Lord? And he answered and said, He that dipped his hand 24 with me in the dish, the same shall betray me. The Son of man goeth, even as it is written of him: but woe unto that man through whom the Son of man is betrayed! good were it [4]for 25 that man if he had not been born. And Judas, which betrayed him, answered and said, Is it I, Rabbi? He saith unto him, Thou hast said.

The Institution of the Eucharist.

26 And as they were eating, Jesus took [5]bread, and blessed, and brake it; and he gave to the disciples, and said, Take, eat; this 27 is my body. And he took [6]a cup, and gave thanks, and gave 28 to them, saying, Drink ye all of it; for this is my blood of [7]the [8]covenant, which is shed for many unto remission of sins.

---

[1] Or, *these good tidings*   [2] Or, *Teacher*   [3] Many authorities, some ancient, omit *disciples.*   [4] Gr. *for him if that man.*   [5] Or, *a loaf*
[6] Some ancient authorities read *the cup.*   [7] Or, *the testament*   [8] Many ancient authorities insert *new.*

29 But I say unto you, I will not drink henceforth of this fruit of the vine, until that day when I drink it new with you in my Father's kingdom.

30 And when they had sung a hymn, they went out unto the mount of Olives.

THE CHAMBER OF THE LAST SUPPER

The Warning to Peter.

31 Then saith Jesus unto them, All ye shall be [1]offended in me this night: for it is written, I will smite the shepherd, and the

32 sheep of the flock shall be scattered abroad. But after I am

33 raised up, I will go before you into Galilee. But Peter answered

---

[1] Gr. *caused to stumble.*

and said unto him, If all shall be [1]offended in thee, I will never
34 be [1]offended. Jesus said unto him, Verily I say unto thee, that
this night, before the cock crow, thou shalt deny me thrice.
35 Peter saith unto him, Even if I must die with thee, *yet* will I not
deny thee. Likewise also said all the disciples.

In the Garden of Gethsemane.

36   Then cometh Jesus with them unto [2]a place called Gethsemane, and saith unto his disciples, Sit ye here, while I go
37 yonder and pray. And he took with him Peter and the two sons
38 of Zebedee, and began to be sorrowful and sore troubled. Then
saith he unto them, My soul is exceeding sorrowful, even unto
39 death: abide ye here, and watch with me. And he went forward
a little, and fell on his face, and prayed, saying, O my Father, if
it be possible, let this cup pass away from me: nevertheless, not
40 as I will, but as thou wilt. And he cometh unto the disciples,
and findeth them sleeping, and saith unto Peter, What, could
41 ye not watch with me one hour? [3]Watch and pray, that ye
enter not into temptation: the spirit indeed is willing, but the
42 flesh is weak. Again a second time he went away, and prayed,
saying, O my Father, if this cannot pass away, except I drink it,
43 thy will be done. And he came again and found them sleeping,
44 for their eyes were heavy. And he left them again, and went
away, and prayed a third time, saying again the same words.
45 Then cometh he to the disciples, and saith unto them, Sleep on
now, and take your rest: behold, the hour is at hand, and the
46 Son of man is betrayed into the hands of sinners. Arise, let us
be going: behold, he is at hand that betrayeth me.

Jesus is betrayed, arrested, and taken to Caiaphas.

47   And while he yet spake, lo, Judas, one of the twelve, came,
and with him a great multitude with swords and staves, from
48 the chief priests and elders of the people. Now he that betrayed
him gave them a sign, saying, Whomsoever I shall kiss, that is
49 he: take him. And straightway he came to Jesus, and said,
50 Hail, Rabbi; and [4]kissed him. And Jesus said unto him, Friend,
do that for which thou art come. Then they came and laid hands
51 on Jesus, and took him. And behold, one of them that were
with Jesus stretched out his hand, and drew his sword, and
smote the [5]servant of the high priest, and struck off his ear.

---

[1] Gr. *caused to stumble.*   [2] Gr. *an enclosed piece of ground.*   [3] Or, *Watch
ye, and pray that ye enter not*   [4] Gr. *kissed him much.*   [5] Gr. *bondservant.*

52 Then saith Jesus unto him, Put up again thy sword into its
place: for all they that take the sword shall perish with the
53 sword. Or thinkest thou that I cannot beseech my Father, and
he shall even now send me more than twelve legions of angels?

COURT-YARD IN THE HOUSE OF CAIAPHAS

54 How then should the scriptures be fulfilled, that thus it must be?
55 In that hour said Jesus to the multitudes, Are ye come out as
against a robber with swords and staves to seize me? I sat
56 daily in the temple teaching, and ye took me not. But all this
is come to pass, that the scriptures of the prophets might be
fulfilled. Then all the disciples left him, and fled.
57 And they that had taken Jesus led him away to *the house of*
Caiaphas the high priest, where the scribes and the elders were

58 gathered together. But Peter followed him afar off, unto the court of the high priest, and entered in, and sat with the officers, to see the end.

The Trial of the Messiah before His People.

59 Now the chief priests and the whole council sought false wit-
60 ness against Jesus, that they might put him to death; and they found it not, though many false witnesses came. But after-
61 ward came two, and said, This man said, I am able to destroy
62 the [1]temple of God, and to build it in three days. And the high priest stood up, and said unto him, Answerest thou nothing?
63 what is it which these witness against thee? But Jesus held his peace. And the high priest said unto him, I adjure thee by the living God, that thou tell us whether thou be the Christ, the
64 Son of God. Jesus saith unto him, Thou hast said: nevertheless I say unto you, Henceforth ye shall see the Son of man sitting at the right hand of power, and coming on the clouds of heaven.
65 Then the high priest rent his garments, saying, He hath spoken blasphemy: what further need have we of witnesses? behold,
66 now ye have heard the blasphemy: what think ye? They
67 answered and said, He is [2]worthy of death. Then did they spit in his face and buffet him: and some smote him [3]with the palms
68 of their hands, saying, Prophesy unto us, thou Christ: who is he that struck thee?

Peter disowns his Master.

69   Now Peter was sitting without in the court: and a maid came
70 unto him, saying, Thou also wast with Jesus the Galilæan. But he denied before them all, saying, I know not what thou sayest.
71 And when he was gone out into the porch, another *maid* saw him, and saith unto them that were there, This man also was
72 with Jesus the Nazarene. And again he denied with an oath, I
73 know not the man. And after a little while they that stood by came and said to Peter, Of a truth thou also art *one* of them; for
74 thy speech bewrayeth thee. Then began he to curse and to swear, I know not the man. And straightway the cock crew.
75 And Peter remembered the word which Jesus had said, Before the cock crow, thou shalt deny me thrice. And he went out, and wept bitterly.

---

[1] Or, *sanctuary*: as in ch. xxiii. 35; xxvii. 5.   [2] Gr. *liable to*.
[3] Or, *with rods*

The Trial of the Messiah before the Gentiles.

27 Now when morning was come, all the chief priests and the elders of the people took counsel against Jesus to put him 2 to death: and they bound him, and led him away, and delivered him up to Pilate the governor.

The Despair and Suicide of Judas.

3 Then Judas, which betrayed him, when he saw that he was condemned, repented himself, and brought back the thirty 4 pieces of silver to the chief priests and elders, saying, I have sinned in that I betrayed ¹innocent blood. But they said, What 5 is that to us? see thou *to it.* And he cast down the pieces of silver into the sanctuary, and departed; and he went away and 6 hanged himself. And the chief priests took the pieces of silver, and said, It is not lawful to put them into the ²treasury, since it 7 is the price of blood. And they took counsel, and bought with 8 them the potter's field, to bury strangers in. Wherefore that 9 field was called, The field of blood, unto this day. Then was fulfilled that which was spoken ³by Jeremiah the prophet, saying, And ⁴they took the thirty pieces of silver, the price of him that was priced, ⁵whom *certain* of the children of Israel did 10 price; and ⁶they gave them for the potter's field, as the Lord appointed me.

The Messiah is condemned to Death.

11 Now Jesus stood before the governor: and the governor asked him, saying, Art thou the King of the Jews? And Jesus said 12 unto him, Thou sayest. And when he was accused by the chief 13 priests and elders, he answered nothing. Then saith Pilate unto him, Hearest thou not how many things they witness against 14 thee? And he gave him no answer, not even to one word: 15 insomuch that the governor marvelled greatly. Now at ⁷the feast the governor was wont to release unto the multitude one 16 prisoner, whom they would. And they had then a notable 17 prisoner, called Barabbas. When therefore they were gathered together, Pilate said unto them, Whom will ye that I release

---

¹ Many ancient authorities read *righteous*.   ² Gr. *corbanas*, that is, *sacred treasury*. Compare Mark vii. 11.   ³ Or, *through*   ⁴ Or, *I took* ⁵ Or, *whom they priced on the part of the sons of Israel*   ⁶ Some ancient authorities read *I gave*.   ⁷ Or, *a feast*

18 unto you? Barabbas, or Jesus which is called Christ? For he
19 knew that for envy they had delivered him up. And while he
was sitting on the judgement-seat, his wife sent unto him, saying, Have thou nothing to do with that righteous man: for I
have suffered many things this day in a dream because of him.
20 Now the chief priests and the elders persuaded the multitudes
21 that they should ask for Barabbas, and destroy Jesus. But the
governor answered and said unto them, Whether of the twain
will ye that I release unto you? And they said, Barabbas.
22 Pilate saith unto them, What then shall I do unto Jesus which
23 is called Christ? They all say, Let him be crucified. And he
said, Why, what evil hath he done? But they cried out ex-
24 ceedingly, saying, Let him be crucified. So when Pilate saw
that he prevailed nothing, but rather that a tumult was arising,
he took water, and washed his hands before the multitude,
saying, I am innocent ¹of the blood of this righteous man: see
25 ye *to it.* And all the people answered and said, His blood *be* on
26 us, and on our children. Then released he unto them Barabbas:
but Jesus he scourged and delivered to be crucified.

Jesus is mocked by the Roman Soldiers.

27 Then the soldiers of the governor took Jesus into the ²palace,
28 and gathered unto him the whole ³band. And they ⁴stripped
29 him, and put on him a scarlet robe. And they plaited a crown
of thorns and put it upon his head, and a reed in his right hand;
and they kneeled down before him, and mocked him, saying,
30 Hail, King of the Jews! And they spat upon him, and took the
31 reed and smote him on the head. And when they had mocked
him, they took off from him the robe, and put on him his garments, and led him away to crucify him.

The Via Dolorosa and the Crucifixion.

32 And as they came out, they found a man of Cyrene, Simon by
name: him they ⁵compelled to go *with them,* that he might bear
33 his cross. And when they were come unto a place called Gol-
34 gotha, that is to say, The place of a skull, they gave him wine
to drink mingled with gall: and when he had tasted it, he would
35 not drink. And when they had crucified him, they parted his

---

¹ Some ancient authorities read *of this blood: see ye &c.*   ² Gr. *Prætorium.*
See Mark xv. 16.   ³ Or, *cohort*   ⁴ Some ancient authorities read *clothed.*
⁵ Gr. *impressed.*

36 garments among them, casting lots: and they sat and watched
37 him there. And they set up over his head his accusation written,
38 THIS IS JESUS THE KING OF THE JEWS. Then are there crucified
with him two robbers, one on the right hand, and one on the left.
39 And they that passed by railed on him, wagging their heads,
40 and saying, Thou that destroyest the ¹temple, and buildest it in
three days, save thyself: if thou art the Son of God, come down
41 from the cross. In like manner also the chief priests mocking
42 *him*, with the scribes and elders, said, He saved others; ²himself
he cannot save. He is the King of Israel; let him now come
43 down from the cross, and we will believe on him. He trusteth
on God; let him deliver him now, if he desireth him: for he said,
44 I am the Son of God. And the robbers also that were crucified
with him cast upon him the same reproach.

Portents at the Death of the Messiah.

45 Now from the sixth hour there was darkness over all the
46 ³land until the ninth hour. And about the ninth hour Jesus
cried with a loud voice, saying, Eli, Eli, lama sabachthani? that
47 is, My God, my God, ⁴why hast thou forsaken me? And some
of them that stood there, when they heard it, said, This man
48 calleth Elijah. And straightway one of them ran, and took a
sponge, and filled it with vinegar, and put it on a reed, and gave
49 him to drink. And the rest said, Let be; let us see whether
50 Elijah cometh to save him.⁵ And Jesus cried again with a loud
51 voice, and yielded up his spirit. And behold, the veil of the
¹temple was rent in twain from the top to the bottom; and the
52 earth did quake; and the rocks were rent; and the tombs were
opened; and many bodies of the saints that had fallen asleep
53 were raised; and coming forth out of the tombs after his resurrection they entered into the holy city and appeared unto many.
54 Now the centurion, and they that were with him watching
Jesus, when they saw the earthquake, and the things that were
done, feared exceedingly, saying, Truly this was ⁶the Son of
55 God. And many women were there beholding from afar, which
56 had followed Jesus from Galilee, ministering unto him: among
whom was Mary Magdalene, and Mary the mother of James and
Joses, and the mother of the sons of Zebedee.

---

¹ Or, *sanctuary*   ² Or, *can he not save himself?*   ³ Or, *earth*   ⁴ Or, *why
didst thou forsake me?*   ⁵ Many ancient authorities add *And another took
a spear and pierced his side, and there came out water and blood.* See John
xix. 34.   ⁶ Or, *a son of God*

THE VIA DOLOROSA

The Descent from the Cross and the Entombment.

57 And when even was come, there came a rich man from
Arimathæa, named Joseph, who also himself was Jesus' disciple:

The Rock of Calvary in the Church of the Holy Sepulchre at
Jerusalem. Legend connected the cleft in this rock with the
events recorded in Mt. 27^{51}.

58 this man went to Pilate, and asked for the body of Jesus. Then
59 Pilate commanded it to be given up. And Joseph took the body,
60 and wrapped it in a clean linen cloth, and laid it in his own
new tomb, which he had hewn out in the rock: and he rolled a
61 great stone to the door of the tomb, and departed. And Mary

Magdalene was there, and the other Mary, sitting over against the sepulchre.

The Events of Easter Eve.

62   Now on the morrow, which is *the day* after the Preparation,

Site of the tomb of Our Lord in the Church of the Holy Sepulchre.

the chief priests and the Pharisees were gathered together unto
63 Pilate, saying, Sir, we remember that that deceiver said, while
64 he was yet alive, After three days I rise again. Command therefore that the sepulchre be made sure until the third day, lest
haply his disciples come and steal him away, and say unto the
people, He is risen from the dead: and the last error will be

65 worse than the first. Pilate said unto them, [1]Ye have a guard:
66 go your way, [2]make it *as* sure as ye can. So they went, and made
the sepulchre sure, sealing the stone, the guard being with them.

THE RESURRECTION OF CHRIST. Mosaic in St. Mark's,
Venice. Eleventh century.

*The First Easter Sunday. The Resurrection of the Messiah. The
Women find the Sepulchre empty.*

28 Now late on the sabbath day, as it began to dawn toward
the first *day* of the week, came Mary Magdalene and the
2 other Mary to see the sepulchre. And behold, there was a great
earthquake; for an angel of the Lord descended from heaven,
3 and came and rolled away the stone, and sat upon it. His

[1] Or, *Take a guard*   [2] Gr. *make it sure, as ye know.*

4 appearance was as lightning, and his raiment white as snow: and
for fear of him the watchers did quake, and became as dead men.

5 And the angel answered and said unto the women, Fear not ye:

CHURCH OF THE HOLY SEPULCHRE

6 for I know that ye seek Jesus, which hath been crucified. He is
not here; for he is risen, even as he said. Come, see the place
7 ¹where the Lord lay. And go quickly, and tell his disciples, He
is risen from the dead; and lo, he goeth before you into Galilee;
there shall ye see him: lo, I have told you.

¹ Many ancient authorities read *where he lay.*

Jesus meets them.

8 And they departed quickly from the tomb with fear and great
9 joy, and ran to bring his disciples word. And behold, Jesus met
them, saying, All hail. And they came and took hold of his feet,
10 and worshipped him. Then saith Jesus unto them, Fear not: go
tell my brethren that they depart into Galilee, and there shall
they see me.

The Controversy about the Empty Tomb.

11 Now while they were going, behold, some of the guard came
into the city, and told unto the chief priests all the things that
12 were come to pass. And when they were assembled with the
elders, and had taken counsel, they gave large money unto the
13 soldiers, saying, Say ye, His disciples came by night, and stole
14 him away while we slept. And if this [1]come to the governor's
15 ears, we will persuade him, and rid you of care. So they took the
money, and did as they were taught: and this saying was spread
abroad among the Jews, *and continueth* until this day.

The Appearance to the Eleven in Galilee.

16 But the eleven disciples went into Galilee, unto the mountain
17 where Jesus had appointed them. And when they saw him,
they worshipped *him*: but some doubted.

The Apostolic Commission.

18 And Jesus came to them and spake unto them, saying, All
19 authority hath been given unto me in heaven and on earth. Go
ye therefore, and make disciples of all the nations, baptizing
them into the name of the Father and of the Son and of the
20 Holy Ghost: teaching them to observe all things whatsoever I
commanded you: and lo, I am with you [2]alway, even unto [3]the
end of the world.

[1] Or, *come to a hearing before the governor*   [2] Gr. *all the days.*
[3] Or, *the consummation of the age*

COMMENTARY

CHAPTERS 1 and 2. PROLOGUE

1¹⁻¹⁷. *The Genealogy of Jesus.*

1¹. The majestic exordium of the Gospel stamps it with a character which it retains throughout. It is couched in the language of an official document, which is clearly meant to give it at once the authority of scripture. It is to be the official account of the exalted Object of the Church's worship, Jesus Christ the Son of David and the King of Israel.

1. The genealogy which follows is clearly not intended to be in the strict sense of the word a pedigree of Jesus. It traces the descent of Joseph, while at the same time making it quite clear that Jesus was not his son. If we look at it closely we observe that it is the genealogical tree of the royal family of Israel, which could trace its descent back to David and the early forefathers of the race, Abraham, Isaac, and Jacob. The first of the kings is of course David and the last Zerubbabel (v. 13), who was the first post-exilic ruler, and was deposed by Darius in 510 B.C., probably for attempting a coronation (Zech. 6¹¹). After that time the dynasty of David was forgotten for a long period, during part of which the dynasty of the Maccabees and their descendants ruled in Israel. Shortly before the birth of Jesus disgust with the rule of half-Jewish princes, such as Herod the Great, led many in Pharisaic circles to desire a restoration of the House of David, and called attention to the prophecies in the Old Testament of such a restoration. The so-called Psalms of Solomon, a Pharisaic document of *circ.* 63 B.C., embody this aspiration. Mt. traces the descent of Joseph Ben-David through the royal line of Judah (v. 3), according to the prophecy of Gen. 49¹⁰, but also through Solomon, the legitimate and divinely appointed succession. Luke, on the other hand, follows a different and obscure line from Joseph to Salathiel, and thence to David. Probably the purpose of the genealogy in Lk. is to trace the pedigree of actual descent and it is therefore carried back to Adam, while Matthew's object was to trace the succession of the throne, and to show how Jesus, as a divinely ordained Messiah, was adopted into the true royal family of Israel. It is possible that this was done in reply to Jewish calumniators who denied the legitimate character of Jesus' claim to be Messiah.

2. Whichever reading is adopted in v. 16 (see note), it is clearly the intention of the writer to combine the genealogy, which traces the legal descent of Jesus to David with the doctrine of His supernatural birth, which is closely connected with it. Matthew regards as indispensable both Jesus' connexion with Israel, which places Him in the true line of descent, and His birth from the creative act of God, Who gives to mankind with Christ that which history could not bring by any process of natural evolution. This conjunction of Nature and Miracle, of evolution and creative act, recurs throughout the story of Jesus and is inseparable from it: it belongs to the foundation on which Christianity was laid. It is necessary to enter into this point of view if we are to understand the purpose of the writer and the story which he is about to unfold. The genealogy, therefore, even if Jesus were Joseph's own son, could never by itself prove the Messianic title of Jesus; and equally little did the miracle dispense with requirements of Scripture that He should be the Son of David; rather it fulfilled them, as indeed a fuller insight into its prophecies showed. It is for this reason that Mt. relates that by the special command of God, Jesus was given to Joseph Ben-David. The natural link by birth could not have bound Him more closely to the House of David than the declared will of God had expressly done.

3. It is interesting to note the prominent position of women in the genealogy; even of women on whose name there was some shadow, e.g. Thamar, Rahab the temple-slave of Jericho who sheltered the spies (Josh. 2[1]), and Bathsheba wife of Uriah the Hittite whom David caused to be killed that he might take her to wife (2 Sam. 11). Ruth was a Moabitess, and according to Deut. 23[3] 'an Ammonite or a Moabite shall not enter into the congregation of the Lord even to the tenth generation.' A possible reason for the inclusion of these names is that aspersions had from the first been cast by Jews upon the Mother of Jesus (cf. Jn. 8[41]). If the Jews were true to their own national history, they had no ground for condemning the new religion because of a suspicion, which was in fact baseless. Lagrange holds that the real reason is that they were all strangers; the fact that even the Messiah Himself, though Son of David, was not of the pure blood of Israel, conveying a rebuke against Jewish exclusiveness. This explanation provides another link with the O.T. in the book of Ruth, which is a tract written to oppose the exclusiveness of post-exilic Judaism, and itself concludes with the royal pedigree of David.

4. Note the artificial character of the threefold division of the

genealogy, which is regarded by Professor G. H. Box[1] as concealing an acrostic on the name of David which is in Hebrew numerically equivalent to $4+6+4 = 14$. Only the first division, however, corresponds to the actual generations recorded in the O.T. In order to make the second division fit, three generations of kings are omitted (Ahaz, Joash, and Amaziah), while the third, which after Zerubbabel it is impossible to verify, contains in Lk. 19 names to Mt.'s 13. The division, however, into three is characteristic of this Gospel. Bartlet suggests that the three divisions represent respectively the rise of the Hebrew Monarchy in David, its decline in Zerubbabel, and its restoration in Jesus the Messiah.

1^{1-2}. *book of the generation.* Cf. Gen. 2^4 and 5^1. The words probably refer to the whole of what follows in the Gospel.

1^2. David and Abraham are mentioned at the beginning because the latter received God's promise that in him all the families of the earth shall be blessed (Gen. 12^3); which promise was afterwards renewed to Judah and to David (2 Sam. 7), and has been finally realized in Jesus the Messiah. *The son of David* was the current name for the Messiah, especially since the hatred of the Pharisees for the Hasmonaean and Herodian dynasties had revived the hopes based on Scripture in the House of David.

1^{16}. The text in this verse appears in three forms. (1) That of the great Uncial MSS. $\aleph^2$ and B,[3] which is followed in A.V. and R.V. (2) The edition of the Syriac version of the Gospel still in the monastery on Mt. Sinai, known as the Sinaitic Syriac, had the following reading: *Joseph to whom was betrothed Mary the Virgin begat Jesus called the Messiah.* (3) The Uncial MS. Θ, supported by the Farrar group of minuscules representing the text probably used by Origen, read, *Joseph, to whom being betrothed Mary a Virgin begat Jesus.* All three forms of the text emphasize the supernatural character of the birth, but they express it in different ways. It makes, therefore, little difference which text is adopted. The existence of these very old variants is thought by some to suggest that the genealogy originally ended with the words *Joseph begat Jesus.* This, it is said, points to a time when the doctrine of the virgin birth of Jesus was not held by Christians. Apart from the fact that the genealogy is clearly the composition of the Evangelist himself who held that doctrine very strongly, the variant readings, if based on an accurate text, prove no more than that there were Jewish Christians, as admittedly there were, who believed Jesus to be the son of Joseph; a belief expressly contradicted by our Evangelist. On the whole subject of the virgin birth see Professor G. H. Box, *Virgin Birth of Jesus*, esp. pp. 215 ff.; G. L. Prestige, *The Virgin Birth*; Professor J. M. Creed, *St. Luke*; and H. Balmforth, *St. Luke* (Clarendon Bible, Note A); also Vincent Taylor, *The Virgin Birth*.

[1] *Virgin Birth of Jesus*, p. 12.   [2] Codex Sinaiticus.   [3] Codex Vaticanus.

I[18-24]. *The Miraculous Birth of Jesus. The Annunciation to Joseph.*

Both the accounts given by Lk. and by Mt. are based on a yet earlier tradition from which it appeared that Joseph had already taken Mary to his home to be his wife and that Jesus was born in their family, but was the child of Mary only.

I[18]. *Betrothed.* The Jewish law of marriage, as of divorce, differed from the Roman Law of the time. In Jewish Law not only an actual betrothal but the fact that one or other of the parties believed themselves to be betrothed constituted an affinity which prevented the marriage of their relations within the prohibited degrees. A girl once engaged became a widow if her fiancé died. Hence an engagement could not merely be broken off by mutual consent; the man must give the woman a writ (Heb. *Geṭ*) and pay a fine.[1] This is the situation expressed here by the words in v. 18 *before they came together* = before she was legally married to him. It was therefore before the final introduction of the two to one another that Mary, still in the house of her parents, was discovered by them to be with child.

I[19]. *A righteous man.* As many modern commentators are agreed Joseph believed from the beginning in Mary's innocence. Legally, the husband had the right to divorce the girl who had been given to him by espousal with her consent. It might even be his duty to do so, but he was not bound to do so according to the Mosaic law of divorce in Deut. 24[1 ff]. It is not, therefore, true to say that Joseph was bound by law to divorce Mary, even if he believed her guilty. But it would be absurd to say that it was for the sake of 'justice' that he did not denounce her, for whatever 'a righteous man' means, it cannot mean 'indulgent' or 'complacent.' Righteousness or justice in Mt. always consists not in the legal righteousness of the Pharisees, but in doing the will of God (Mt. 6[33]). The refusal, therefore, is a testimony on Joseph's part to the purity of Mary. Joseph knowing her innocence and marvelling at what had taken place conceals by silence a fact, the mysterious cause of which he does not yet know. At the same time he was in a dilemma; for while he could not now marry one who by all the evidence belonged to God alone, neither could he set her free without calling attention to her condition. What was he to do? He proposed in the presence of two witnesses, who might be the parents, to give her a private undated letter of divorce, in which case, according to Jewish law, there would be no need for the public authority to intervene.

---

[1] G. H. Box, *op. cit.*, pp. 209 ff.

1[18]. *The Holy Ghost.* The words as used presuppose the story of the Annunciation in Lk. 1[30], and suggest that the clause in the Apostles' Creed in one of its forms already existed. The phrase implies that the Conception was an act of God, not of man; for the Spirit in the O.T. is always the instrument of irresistible divine action through which God enters man and works in him. The same Spirit that moved on the face of the waters and made them fruitful (Gen. 1[2]) was also on this occasion the moving power in a creation no less wonderful than the first. As to Abraham and Sarah against all hope a child was born *after the spirit* (Gal. 4[29]), even so Jesus was born 'after the spirit'.

1[20, 21]. It has been pointed out by Burney and G. H. Box that the contents of these verses have all the characteristic marks of Hebrew poetry, the metre corresponding in pentameter form to that of the Benedictus (Lk. 1[68-79]):

> Joseph thou son of David fear not
> To take unto thee Mary thy wife:
> For that which is conceived within her
> Is of the Holy Spirit.
> And she shall bring forth a son; and thou shalt call
> His name Jesus;
> For it is he that shall save his people
> From their sins.

1[21]. *Jesus* is a Greek transcript of the Hebrew *Jeshua* or *Joshua* or *Hosea,* meaning *Jehovah is Salvation.* Mt.'s interpretation of the word is coloured by the Hellenistic hopes of a *Saviour,* a title given at that time to the Emperor Augustus as the bringer of a universal peace to mankind. There is no doubt that the Jews used the name in a nationalistic sense on amulets and rings; and as a personal name Joshua became common in various forms among the Jews. Jason in Acts 17[5] is another form of the same name. There is no real evidence, as Deissmann has pointed out, of the use of the name of Jesus as a cult-name anywhere in the Graeco-Roman world before the Christian era.[1]

his people. Gk. λαός, as so often in Mt., is the liturgical name for the royal people of Israel.

1[22]. The first instance of the formula which is characteristic of the Gospel wherever quotations from the O.T. occur. The use of the O.T. by the Jewish Christian Church was adopted from that of the Pharisees who were strong fatalists and believed that nothing took place without 'the determinate counsel and fore-knowledge of God' (Acts 2[23]). Any important event, therefore, that happened, no matter how unexpected, e.g. the death of the

[1] See the Essay in *Mysterium Christi,* pp. 2 ff.

Messiah, *must have* been purposed by God and *therefore* it must be found in the Scriptures which are the revelation of His purpose. This is a very different point of view from the use of the Scriptures by the early Church Fathers, who on their part adopted the view that the fact that an event had been prophesied was a miraculous guarantee of its truth.

I²³. *Behold, the virgin shall conceive.* From Isa. 7¹⁴. The Hebrew word *'almah*, here translated 'virgin', means no more than a young woman. But it is clear that the LXX in using the Gk. word *parthenos* to translate it knew of a tradition among the Jews that Isaiah had spoken of a supernatural birth of a Redeemer from a virgin. The quotation, as is always the case in Mt.'s N source, is neither from the Hebrew nor from the LXX, but probably from an Aramaic translation, perhaps a collection of such texts.

I²⁴⁻²⁵. *The Nativity of the Messiah.*

I²⁵. Mt. is entirely concerned with the virgin character of Mary at the time of the birth of Jesus, and Joseph's evidence for it. These words cannot be taken to imply that it was not afterwards preserved. An Old Latin and the Sin. Syriac version leave out the words altogether. They may be a gloss.

I²⁵. *Called his name Jesus.* By naming the Child Joseph publicly acknowledged Him as a lawfully born member of his family.

2¹⁻¹². THE EPIPHANY

I. The connexion of this story with the first chapter is clear. Because Jesus was by divine providence born into the house of Joseph He was therefore the Son of David, and because He was born by the Spirit of God He was not only one of many such sons, but *the* Son of David, the 'Emmanuel' of whom the promise spoke. Therewith the question arose as to His right to be the governor of Jerusalem. But in what relationship stood the *de facto* king of Jerusalem to Him? With him there could be no peace. Herod the Great had made it his life-work without scruple and without mercy to attain to one ambition, the name of king. Once obtained, he had no other object in his latter years than to bequeath it intact to his sons. The purpose, therefore, of the following collection of stories is to paint in ever-deepening tones the inevitable conflict between the earthly and the heavenly kingdom, the world and the Church, which enters so deeply into the rest of this Gospel and early Christianity as a whole.

2. The Epiphany story is legendary in form and must be read with due regard to the historical background against which it is written. The fact that it and the other incidents in this chapter are apparently not known either to Mk. or Lk. is of course no argument against their historical character; for Mk. or Lk. give us only the Palestinian tradition, and Mt., as we have seen, does not claim to give us that tradition (see Introduction, p. 13). He was following a different source altogether, which we have called N and which has close affinities with the Syrian lands beyond the Jordan. This Eastern world was at the beginning of our era undoubtedly agitated by a widespread movement of expectation of a *Saviour* to deliver civilization from the curse of war and its attendant miseries. The famous fourth Eclogue of Virgil and the so-called Sibylline Books represent the arrival in the West of a movement which had its origin in the hero-worship of the East and found its natural outlet in the worship of the Roman emperor as such a Saviour. The Messianic hopes of the Jews of the Babylonian Dispersion must have exercised a wide influence in the same region, and there is nothing at all improbable that these hopes should have been shared by Babylonian astrologers in close touch, as they were, with the many Jewish synagogues of northern Syria and Mesopotamia. There are, of course, many pagan parallels to this as there are to other stories in the Bible. Astronomical portents are a commonplace of classical literature.[1] Had not a star guided Aeneas to the place where the Eternal City should be founded?

> de caelo lapsa per umbras
> Stella facem ducens multa cum luce cucurrit.
> Illam summa super labentem culmina tecti
> Cernimus Idaea claram se condere silva,
> Signantemque vias.
>
> (Virgil, *Aeneid* ii. 694.)

Stars were often thought to foretell the birth of heroes and kings, e.g. that of Augustus.[2] Cicero tells a story of how in the night when the temple of Ephesus was burnt the Asiatic Magi saw a bright star shining, from which they prophesied evil for their country.[3] This proved to be the birth of Alexander the Great, which happened on the same night.

---

[1] Cf. Tacitus, *Hist.* v. 12; Josephus, *Ant.* xvi. 14. 3; *Jewish War*, vi. 5. 4.
[2] Suetonius, *Augustus*, 94.
[3] Cicero, *de Div.* 247. For similar visits of Magi recorded by pagan writers see Pliny, *Nat. Hist.* 30. 6; Suetonius, *Nero*, 13; Seneca, *Epistle* 58.

3. But there is no need to go outside Jewish sources. More recent inquirers incline to see in the Epiphany story all the features of the Jewish 'Midrash Haggada', that is, sacred stories used to illustrate and enlarge on the text of the O.T. There is evidence, as we have seen, of the existence of such Midrashic Targums in the Jewish-Christian circles from which the Gospel sprang, along the international highway to the Euphrates.[1] That Jewish teachers applied astrological ideas to the nativities of their own great men is clear from such passages as Num. 24[17] 'a star shall arise out of Jacob', &c., which some have regarded as having given rise to the present passage. Soon after the time of the composition of Mt. such a star was regarded in Judaea as the prelude to the rebellion of Bar-Kokba, the last false claimant to the Messiahship (A.D. 132–5). Nestlé cites a story of the birth of Abraham from a later Jewish Midrash especially noted for its interest in Arabian legends (see Bacon, p. 153), one of which relates how on the night when Abraham was born, Terah's friends, among whom were councillors and astrologers of Nimrod, were feasting in his house, and on leaving at night they observed a star which swallowed up four other stars from the far side of heaven. Forthwith they hastened to Nimrod and said, 'Of a certainty a lad has been born who is destined to conquer this world and the next'. The story continues with a plot of the Magi to kill the child, which Terah frustrated by hiding his son in a cave for three years. In the light of this and other Rabbinic legends, Zahn concludes that Mt. is drawing an elaborate comparison between the history of Israel at its beginning and the personal story of the Jewish-Christian Messiah which is continued up to the arrival in Nazareth (2[23]). To these parallels must be added another version of the Epiphany story almost contemporary with Mt. in the letter of S. Ignatius, bishop of Antioch (*circ.* A.D. 115), to the Magnesians, in which there is a reference to a Messianic star 'which shone forth in the heavens above all stars whose brightness was unutterable and whose strangeness caused amazement'. Finally, it is impossible to ignore the picture in Rev. 12 of the birth of the Messiah which reflects the Jewish belief referred to in Jn. (7[27]) that the birth of the Messiah is secret. Hence his birth must be divinely revealed. Traces of this idea are obviously present in the nativity narratives both of Lk. and Mt. In the former, shepherds are divinely directed to the crib of the Saviour God, in the latter, the discoverers are astrologers from the

---

[1] See Introduction, p. 21.

East. Hence G. H. Box appears to have good reason for his contention that the stories in Mt. 1 and 2 exhibit in a degree that can hardly be paralleled elsewhere in the N.T. the characteristic features of Jewish Midrashic Haggada;[1] and in the case of the Epiphany story, traces of the influence of Persian ideas, likely enough in a Gospel of which the provenance is most probably to be found in or near Edessa where star-worship was the principal heathen cult.[2] Later Christian tradition, beginning with Tertullian, pictured the Magi as three kings, Caspar, Melchior, and Balthasar, whose remains are said to rest at Cologne. This idea is obviously based on such texts as Ps. 72¹⁰, Isa. 60⁶.

4. Assuming that the story is legendary in form must we therefore regard it as not founded in fact? Two main views have been held about the star in the East by those who wish to regard it as something more than a symbol of the coming of the Gentiles to the brightness of His rising (Isa. 60¹). Kepler, the famous astronomer, as long ago as 1605 thought of a close conjunction of the planets Jupiter and Saturn, a rare combination in the constellation of Pisces which takes place only once in 800 years and which occurred no less than three times in the year 7 B.C. Mackinley suggests the Morning Star, from the fact that it was seen in the east and then in the west;[3] Lagrange that the star which is called in Greek *aster*, i.e. a single star, rather than *astron*, must be regarded either as a meteor, which could with difficulty have suggested the nativity of a great man; or a comet, perhaps Halley's, which passed over the perihelium on October 8, 12 B.C. From the sight of this the Magi concluded the approaching birth of a great prince. Of course they may not have started immediately, as Origen long ago suggested; months and even years may have elapsed. The very fact that Herod and all Jerusalem have apparently no knowledge of the star may be considered to support this, because it gives time for the event to have been forgotten.

2¹. *The wise men.* Gk. *Magi*, probably priests of the Persian Zoroastrian Religion. The presents, however, which they bring suggest Arabia, and so it was understood by Justin Martyr, the earliest Christian writer to refer to this passage. But Origen was probably right in thinking that the East means all the country known to Josephus by that name, i.e. northern Syria (see Introduction, p. 21).

---

[1] Box, *Virgin Birth*, p. 19. [2] Bacon, *Studies in Matthew*, p. 36.
[3] Col. Mackinley, 'The Date of the Nativity', *Expositor*, Nov. 1917; cited by Box, *St. Matthew*, p. 82.

2². *In the east.* Gk. ἐν τῇ ἀνατολῇ different from the former phrase and meaning, probably, 'at its rising', an important moment in astrology when the stars are at the maximum of their influence.

Herod the king. The only date explicitly specified by any N.T. writer except Lk. with regard to the birth of our Lord. Herod the Great, son of the Edomite Antipater, the friend of Julius Caesar, became governor of Galilee in 47 B.C., and was given the title of king of Judaea by Antony and Octavius, afterwards Augustus, in 40 B.C. He began to build the temple in 26 B.C., and died in 4 B.C. The date of our Lord's birth, therefore, must be placed some years before the beginning of the era known as A.D. Lk. dates it by the census of Quirinius, which recently discovered inscriptions placed between the years 9 and 8 B.C. But there is not sufficient evidence to determine the question with any certainty (*v.* Balmforth, *S. Luke* (Clarendon Bible), p. 125). Herod's agent and friend Nicholas of Damascus describes him as a master of dissimulation and consummate cunning. His action in this and the following incident has certainly all the characteristic features of the king as described by Josephus (*Ant.* xvi. 11. 7, xvii. 2. 4).

2². *is born,* i.e. must be born in accordance with the sacred writings.

2⁴. *priests and scribes of the people.* This may mean the Sanhedrin, at that time the governing body of the Jewish people, in its three groups of Sadducees, i.e. Priests, Pharisaic Scribes, a growing influence in the reign of Herod, and Heads of families (26³), though the latter are not named in this place, perhaps because they would not be consulted on a purely theological question.

2⁶. *Micah* 5². 'Not least' being substituted for 'though thou be little' of the Hebrew and LXX, because since the birth of Jesus it was no longer possible to speak of Bethlehem as being of little account. But the writer or his source has combined a passage from Micah with one from 2 Sam. 5², 'Thou shalt feed my people Israel'. The passage was understood to mean that the Messiah was to be born at Bethlehem; but all that the prophet himself probably meant was that wherever he might be born he would come out of Bethlehem, i.e. out of the stock of David who was born there.

2⁷. *Then.* Gk. τότε, a sure sign of Mt.'s peculiar style in contrast to Mk. who connects his sentences more usually with καί.

Learned carefully. Gk. ἠκρίβωσεν = to obtain exact information, a word used as a technical term in astrological observations. If it was, as Lagrange suggested, a comet, then the purpose of the king's inquiry would have been to see if the time given by the Magi coincided in all particulars with the appearance of the phenomenon in Jerusalem.

2¹¹. Myrrh and incense are similarly combined in Cant. 3⁶. In the O.T. myrrh is only used as a perfume. It could also be used for the purpose of embalming (Jn. 19³⁹) or mixed with wine as a kind of narcotic for condemned criminals (Mk. 15²³). But offered by the Magi with gold and incense, it conveys the image of a young and brilliant monarch in all the glory of his coronation (Ps. 45⁸).

> Thus aurum myrrham regique hominique Deoque
> Dona ferunt.

2¹². *being warned of God in a dream.* Gk. χρηματισθέντες, a word often used by Josephus,[1] meaning 'to be instructed specially by God'. In classical Gk. the word is a commercial one, 'to pay out money' or 'do business', and is used of officials who transact their business by giving orders, and so transferred to special divine directions of a solemn character, e.g. oracles.

2¹³⁻²². *Flight into Egypt and the Martyrdom of the Innocents.*

This story, like the last, cannot be confirmed by any contemporary evidence. On the other hand, Josephus[2] records the story of an astrologer who warns Pharaoh of the birth of an Israelite who should humble Egypt but exalt Israel. According to Josephus it was the fear of this infant that led Pharaoh to destroy the Jewish babies rather than the desire to control their births as in Exod. 1¹⁶. The story goes on to tell of the miraculous birth of the infant, how he was exposed, rescued by Pharaoh's daughter, and afterwards adopted by her. One day Pharaoh gave the royal crown as a plaything which the child threw on the ground and stamped on with his feet. The astrologer thereby detected the hidden enemy of the royal line and commanded Pharaoh to destroy him. But his daughter hid him. Whether or not the author had in mind the story of Josephus, it is natural to think that he desired to draw some analogy between the Messiah and the great prophet of Israel, and found it in this fact, of which there is no actual reason to doubt the historical truth, that Joseph and Mary lived for a while for reasons of safety in Egypt, which after all was only a short distance from Bethlehem and where they would find many of their countrymen in the well-established ghettos of that country. We may also note an allusion to an old Jewish calumny of the Talmud, that Jesus had been in Egypt and had learnt there his wonder-working power; and that he had been a hired labourer there.[3] This story the author contradicts by his statement that our Lord returned out of Egypt, while still a child, in the reign of

---

[1] Cf. *Ant.* iii. 8. 8.   [2] *Ant.* ii. 9.
[3] G. H. Box regards this as an independent tradition with very early attestation, of which a slightly different form is found in Origen (cf. *Celsum* i. 38).

Archelaus and not later. Egypt had often been a refuge against
the ruling powers at Jerusalem.[1] Onias, son of the high priest
Onias III, fled from the Seleucid king Antiochus Epiphanes and
founded a temple at Heliopolis. But long before that Jews were
very numerous there, coming and going easily either by land in five
or six days or more quickly by boat, like crossing the Channel. By
the end of the reign of Herod Egypt had become a Roman province and was therefore outside the reach of his power.

2[15]. In the prophecy from Hos. 11[1], Mt. reverts to his Aramaic version, for the LXX has 'his children'; but in the Hebrew, God addresses
Israel as 'My Son'. The same thought occurs frequently in the early
books of the O.T. recording the infancy of the nation (Exod. 4[22, 23]).

2[18]. The reference to Jer. 31[15] is not so obvious. It differs from the
LXX; and the writer could hardly have confused the O.T. Ramah
five miles north of Jerusalem with Bethlehem eight miles to the
south. There is nothing Messianic about the passage. In the original
prophecy Jeremiah deplores the deportation into Babylonia of the
tribes of northern Israel by Sargon. The tomb of Rachel stood in the
time of Jesus, as it does to this day, midway between Jerusalem and
Bethlehem. But in Gen. 35[19] and 48[7] the tomb is said to be near
Ephrath, and the words 'which is in Bethlehem' are added. Mt. knowing this gloss on the tradition was therefore able to quote Jeremiah's
words to illustrate his narrative. The martyrdom of the Innocents is
commemorated in the Christian Church along with S. Stephen and
S. John immediately after Christmas—they being regarded as types
of those who suffered for Christ in deed, though not in will, as S. John
suffered in will, but not in deed, and S. Stephen in both.

2[19]. Herod, who died in 4 B.C. at Jericho, bequeathed to his eldest
son Archelaus, Judaea, Samaria, and Idumea, the ancient Edom which
he inherited from his father Antipater who was an Edomite by birth.
Antipas received Galilee and Peraea with the title of Tetrarch; Philip,
Gaulonitis and Trachonitis. Augustus soon afterwards refused Archelaus the title of king until he should have won it by good behaviour.
He had shown himself a chip of the old block by a ruthless massacre
immediately after his succession. His subsequent misgovernment was
such that he was removed by Augustus in A.D. 6, at the instance probably of the Pharisees, who thereby made themselves responsible, as
our Lord did not hesitate to tell them, for the introduction of direct
Roman rule under the first procurator Varius Florus (Mt. 22[21]).

2[20]. *They are dead which sought the young child's life.* A reminiscence
of Exod. 4[19].

2[23]. *He should be called a Nazarene,* Gk. Ναζωραῖος. This obscure reference
gives rise to two problems. (1) There is no prophecy in the O.T. remotely

---

[1] Cf. 1 Kings 11[40], Jer. 26[21], Jos. *Ant.* xii. 8. 7.

resembling it. If it was a proof-text derived from his special source N, the evangelist was no more able to identify it than he could the quotations in 13³⁵ or 27⁹. Tradition from the time of Jerome connects it with the Hebrew word *neser* = branch or shoot in the Messianic passage Isa. 11¹. 'A branch shall grow out of his (Jesse's) roots.'[1] A similar allusion was found in Isa. 49⁶, where the Hebrew word is *nasor*, the 'preserved' or 'preserver' of Israel, a term applied to the Servant of Jehovah. 'It is too light a thing that thou shouldst be my servant to raise up the tribes of Israel, and shouldst be the "*Nazorean*" to restore Israel.' It was this second passage, according to Professor Box, that suggested to the despised Nazarenes, the early name by which Christians were known to the Jews, a means of changing the insult implied in that name into a patent of nobility conferred by the great anonymous prophet of the Exile. In his view the change from *Nazarene* to *Nazorene* was deliberate, being a counterstroke on the part of the Christians against their bitterest enemies. They were the real Israel, the people of the Messiah, the true preserver of Israel.

(2) The name Nazarene or Nazorene, both forms are found, has no connexion with the place called Nazareth. The name Nazorene is not found as applied to Jesus before Acts 2²², and Jn. 19¹⁹, where it appears as a title of Jesus on the Cross. Mark was the first to apply the word Nazarene to Jesus (1²⁴), when it is placed in the mouth of a demon, and Mark it is who appears to have connected the name with the village of Nazareth.[2] In this he was followed by Matthew in this passage, but in the form Nazorene which Matthew prefers (cf. 26⁷¹). Two facts seem to be clear. (1) The name Nazarene was at an early date given to the Christians by their Jewish fellow-countrymen and remained the name by which they were known till it was superseded both in the Gentile and the Jewish world by that of Christians (Acts 24⁵). Both were nicknames, and that of Nazarene survived in remote parts of Syria where Christians were found by Jerome in the fourth century at Beraea-Aleppo still calling themselves Nazarenes or Nazorenes, just as there were others called Ebionites = the poor people. In the Talmud the Christians are called Nozrim and Jesus Nozri. (2) The Jews of Palestine in attaching this nickname to the Christians utilized an *existing* name, perhaps with a contemptuous play upon words, for the despised and rejected sect of Him who was known as the Prophet of Nazareth out of which no good thing could

[1] G. H. Box notes that the Targum on Isa. 11¹ introduces the positive identification of the Branch with the Messiah.

[2] Dalman thinks that Nazarene and Nazorene represented two different forms of the name of the town. Burkitt mentions the suggestion (*Syriac Form of N.T. Names*), that the town where Jesus was brought up was really Chorazin (11²¹), and that the name Nazareth, which is not found in the O.T., Josephus, or the Talmud, was invented afterwards to account for the designation of the Christians as Nazarenes. See, however, Moore's remarks in the *Beginnings of Christianity*, vol. i, p. 426 sq.

come (Jn. 1^{46}). It is known to have been the name of a pre-Christian sect of Syrian Jews akin to the Essenes and known to the Roman historian Pliny in both forms and to the Christian writer Epiphanius, who carefully distinguishes them from the Christians of Beraea-Aleppo whom Jerome knew. The name therefore was, as Box says, a typical Oriental designation of specially religious people in those parts, and its use here is a valuable indication of the place of origin of the Gospel. 'The writer belonged to a Christian community whose members bore the common designation of Nazarenes.' But if the Gospel had originated in Antioch, where they were called *Christians*, the quotation would have lost its point. Bultmann thinks that the name means 'observant', and was early applied to our Lord because He belonged to a group of Observants or keepers of a religious rule. There were, he thinks, two elements in primitive Christianity, one as represented by the Synoptic Gospels (Mt. 11^{19}) and another akin to the Essenes strongly influenced by the Oriental mythology of heterodox sects on the fringe of Judaism.[1] In any case, Lagrange would seem to be right in his judgement that the name was applied to Jesus only after it had become the name of His despised disciples.

PUBLIC LIFE OF CHRIST

3$^{1-12}$. *The Forerunner* (Lk. 3$^{1-20}$, Mk. 1$^{4-8}$).

1. A vivid picture taken direct from the earliest tradition of the Palestinian community: probably from the source Q. There is no clear note of time, but 'by these days' the writer clearly refers to the well-known period when the Christian movement first began, elaborately described by Luke (3^{1}). Like the other evangelists Mt. makes no attempt to invent information as to the intervening time between the childhood and the mature manhood of Jesus. This complete lack of any information whatever is an indication of a late date as well as of dependence upon the first written Gospel, S. Mark.

2. John the Baptist is one of the most clearly historical figures in the history of his time, on which he evidently made a very great impression. What is recorded of him in the Gospels is confirmed in this way by Josephus who regarded John as a man sent from God. 'By his proclamation of the coming kingdom he thrilled the heart of the nation and drew forth the multitude into the wilderness to hear him.' 'He was a good man and exhorted the Jews to exercise virtue by practising righteousness towards one another and piety towards God, and thus to come to baptism. For in this

[1] Lowther Clarke, *N.T. Problems*, pp. 206 ff.

way the baptism also would be acceptable to Him if they practised it not for the passing over of certain sins but for the purification of the body; provided that the soul had been thoroughly
cleansed beforehand by righteousness.'[1] This is not quite the same
idea of John that we find in the Gospels, but we must remember
that it was intended for Roman consumption.

3. The baptism of proselytes as a ceremonial purification from
the defilement of Gentile uncleanness was the usual practice of contemporary Judaism.[2] But it is clear that the baptism of John was
not of this kind. The very fact that this kind of baptism, unlike
that of the Pharisees, required a Baptist, shows that it was something much more serious than anything which had gone before it.
It was in fact a prophetic action, eschatological in character,
analogous to the procedure described in one of the visions of
Ezekiel (9[4]) where the Lord commands the man clothed with linen
who had the writer's ink-horn by his side, to go through the city
and set a mark upon the foreheads of the men that sigh for its
abominations. The same thought is found in writings very close
to the time of the Baptist, e.g. Psalms of Solomon in which it is
said that the Saints of God have a sign upon them which saves
them (15[8]). It seems, therefore, that Streeter, following Schweitzer,
is correct in his view that John's baptism was an *eschatological
sacrament* of this character. At a time when the Messianic judgement was regarded as close at hand the one thought uppermost
in men's minds was how to obtain a guarantee of coming unscathed
through the wrath and being finally saved and received into the
Messianic kingdom. This assurance of salvation in the day of
wrath was offered by John in his baptism as a way of escape to
those who could prove their claim to it by confessing their sins.
Hence the wrath of the Baptist against those who claimed the
sacred passport but were not prepared to substantiate their claim
by a new outlook on life (vv. 7, 8). This view is further supported
by the early description of Christian baptism as just such a
sealing; cp. Eph. 4[30], 2 Cor. 1[22], 2 Tim. 2[19], Rev. 2[17]. In Rev. 16[2]
the mark of the Beast is a sort of spurious imitation of the mark of
baptism which the Christian bears on his head and which S. Paul
probably refers to in his solemn protestation, 'I bear in my body
the marks of the Lord Jesus' (Gal. 6[17]). (For a striking discussion
of the sacramental character of John's baptism see Schweitzer,
Quest of the Historical Jesus, pp. 37 ff.)

[1] Jos. *Ant.* xviii. 5. 2; xxi. 2. 6.
[2] Abrahams, *Studies in Pharisaism and the Gospels*, i, pp. 37 ff.

3^2. *Repent*, Gk. μετανοεῖτε, 'change your minds, your whole outlook'; the true meaning of repentance in the Christian sense.

The kingdom of heaven, Gk. βασιλεία τῶν οὐρανῶν. The phrase usually, but not always, used by Mt.; see Additional Note on The Kingdom of Heaven, p. 187.

3^4. *Locusts*, allowed by the law in Lev. 11^{22}. Honey can hardly have been found in the desert. Lagrange suggests that it is the exudation from the tamarisk tree which abounded in the deserts and which resembles honey in appearance but is very insipid in taste.

3$^{7-10}$. *Pharisees and Sadducees*. The Sadducees, who were the official priestly families of Jerusalem, might well join the Pharisees in scotching a movement that might prove a menace to their policy, which was one of biding their time till a favourable opportunity of revolt from Rome presented itself.

3^9. It is against this flattering dream that John the Baptist uttered his denunciation: 'Your Jewish birth will not save you, for the judgement is the sifting of good from evil. Even if he has to annihilate the entire Jewish people, God is able to create a new Israel.'

3^{11}. *With the Holy Ghost and with fire.* These words do not contrast the two baptisms but unite them. The object of being baptized by John was to secure baptism with the Spirit later. Christian practice ever since has regarded Baptism and Confirmation as two parts of one sacrament.

3$^{13-17}$. *The baptism of the Messiah* (Lk. 3$^{21-22}$, Mk. 1$^{9-11}$).

1. Did John know Jesus? According to Luke he was His kinsman, but there is no evidence that the boys met in Nazareth, though they may have met in Jerusalem and probably frequently did at Passover time. According to the Fourth Gospel John did not know Jesus until the pre-ordained sign of the descending dove warned him (Jn. 1^{33}). There is no objection to the view that John 'knew his character but not his destiny'. The words of John as well as the answer of Jesus are perhaps better explained in the light of the belief of the Church in the sinlessness of Christ. There is an interesting 'Targum' in the Gospel according to the Hebrews which records a conversation between Jesus and his family at the time of John's movement: 'So the mother of the Lord and his brethren spoke to him, "John the Baptist baptizes for the remission of sins; let us go and be baptized of him." But Jesus said to them, "Wherein have I sinned that I should go and be baptized of him? That therefore that I have now said must be sin."' Jesus' answer to John explains the significance of the baptism of Jesus as Mt. understood it, namely that for Him baptism is not the washing away of sin or the seal of salvation for Heaven, but the

anointing of the Servant of Jehovah for his office in accordance with the prophecy of Isa. 61^1, 'The spirit of the Lord is upon me because he has anointed me to preach good tidings unto the meek'. Righteousness in the Deutero-Isaiah means God's faithfulness to what He has foretold, promised, or threatened, and so to 'fulfil all righteousness' means to fulfil all the Messianic prophecy of the O.T.

2. In its original form the story describes symbolically a real spiritual experience of Jesus. As Dalman has pointed out, sonship and Messiahship are not necessarily the same thing, and Jesus was perhaps conscious of the spiritual experience called Sonship before He realized the vocation to Messiahship. It was a unique Sonship to the Father that He became conscious of in the moment of His illumination, as Baptism was afterwards called.

3. The incident of the dove which follows is connected with certain poetical ideas found in the Rabbinical writings. The voice from Heaven was called the *Bath kol* or 'daughter of the voice', and was regarded as one of the vehicles of divine revelation. The 'voice' usually, as here, took the form of a quotation from scripture (cf. Mt. 17^5, Jn. 12^{28}). Abrahams[1] has called attention to the fact that the heavenly voice is often represented as the voice of a bird, and thinks that this association may underlie the present incident. In Gen. 1^2 the spirit of God is represented as a bird brooding on the face of the waters, and in one passage of the Talmud this bird is said to be a dove. Philo used the dove as a symbol of the divine wisdom.

3^{17}. *This is my beloved Son.* Rather as in R.V. margin *my Son, my beloved*; a separate Messianic title (cf. Eph. 1^6). The quotation, as often in the case of the Rabbinic *Bath kol*, is composite; the first part being from Ps. 2^7, the second from Isa. 42^1, which the Targum applies to the Messiah. In Mk. and Lk. the words are addressed directly to Jesus; Mt.'s form implies that the words were addressed to the bystanders and that the proclamation was a public one.

4^{1-11}. *Temptation of the Messiah.* (Lk. 4^{1-13}, Mk. 1^{12-13}.)

The story again is from Q and is, like that just related, our Lord's own description of a spiritual experience. Conscious of His divine Sonship Jesus went into the wilderness to face the temptation to a misuse of powers and functions which He believed Himself to possess.

1. The biblical quotations in this section are all from the book of Deut. which is an inspired commentary of the wanderings of the

[1] *Studies in Pharisaism and the Gospels*, i, pp. 47 ff.

Israelites in the wilderness; and it seems that Jesus identified himself with His people, with their privations and temptations as in some mysterious sense recapitulating or summing them up (Eph. 1^{10}). The narrative was of supreme interest to Jewish Christians. In what sense, it was asked, was Jesus the Messiah? In every respect He seemed to contradict the acknowledged ideas concerning Him. Had not John the Baptist himself doubted? (Mt. 11^3). The great value of the temptation story was that it set to rest any such doubts by showing that contemporary views of the Messiah had been for Jesus an inspiration of the Evil One, far removed from the truth. The whole narrative is omitted by Mk. perhaps as having less meaning for non-Jews.

2. Though like that of the Baptism symbolical in form there is nothing legendary in the event itself. 'The story is a work of art but the artist must be sought in Jesus Himself' (Albertz). Similar experiences are recorded of the Buddha and of the Persian hero Zarathustra which were probably coloured by the Gospel narrative. But the experiences of mystics are the same all the world over and the normal psychological features of such a mystical experience are clearly visible in the poetical imagery of the story; exaltation on the discovery of vocation, retreat into the solitude without thought or care for the body, waning of the ecstasy and resultant hunger and depression which give a fit moment for the intrusions of diabolic suggestion. Our Lord was 'in all points tempted like as we are, yet without sin' (Heb. 4^{15}). The fact that our Lord could not sin, did not, as the story shows, in the least diminish the force of temptation, which consists not in the possibility of the fall but in the painfulness of the struggle in the heart between good and evil. As the Epistle to the Hebrews further states, our Lord was tempted in order that He might sympathize with those who are tempted, and that He might win for them the power to overcome temptation (Heb. 2^{18}).

3. The Temptations summarize the Ministry. They exhibit the refusal to take thought for self, to accede to the demands for a sign, and to seek popularity through the lowering of the moral standard. It has been thought they represent the three possible policies or courses of action that might be adopted by one who believed himself to be the Messiah. They may be said to represent the policies of the three religious parties of contemporary Judaism —the Sadducees with their vested interests in the Temple and its worship, and desire to enrich themselves and secure their own comfort at all costs; that of the Pharisees with their belief in the

Kingdom of Heaven, but only as a form of Jewish nationalism to be attained by the miraculous intervention of God, and the destruction of enemies; thirdly that of the Herodians, with their policy of political compromise at the expense of religious principle. All these policies were at bottom irreligious because they ignored the vocation of Israel to be the religious teacher of the world.

4. It is possible that the last represented the strongest attraction to our Lord and remained a temptation throughout the ministry. It must have been a temptation to any man of consummate ability to place himself at the head of a great Jewish confederacy. There were in the Empire, at that time, six million Jews living in a closely knit organization. Had they combined with the Parthians it would have been serious for Rome, and Rome saw this when the final struggle with Judaism came. They were, as Gwatkin says, the only remaining live nationality in the Roman Empire. Already the Herodian family had risen to unparalleled heights of power through alliance with the Roman Emperors. This they had done by means of a policy of religious compromise, for Augustus and Julius Caesar both demanded that the Jews should not proselytize, and that heathen temples should be erected in cities of Galilee. Our Lord seems to have chafed at the narrow limits of His mission, and there is not wanting evidence that He would gladly have extended it to the whole world, as S. Paul did afterwards. This, however, He regarded as forbidden to Him (Mt. 15²⁴). And He rejects it as He did the other short cuts to success. He is the only reformer who has ever been satisfied to allow the Spirit of God to work in Him unhindered by the slightest self-will. (For further discussions see S. Liberty, *Political Relations of Christ's Ministry*, pp. 19 ff.)

4¹. *the devil*, called Satan by Mark, is in O.T. the sworn enemy of Israel and the personal opponent of the Messiah who is Israel's Prince (Zech 3¹⁻⁸). In the Book of Job he appears as one of the 'Sons of God' and casts suspicion on Job whom God allows him to prove (Job. 2¹⁻¹⁰). Jealousy of Adam was the motive of his action, which brought death into the world,[1] and according to an ancient Apocalypse, the Book of Jubilees, it was Satan who tempted Abraham to sacrifice his son. In 1 Chron 21 it is Satan who tempts David to number Israel to their own undoing. It is probably due to the influence of Persian Mazdeism, with its dualistic contrast between Ahriman and Ormuzd, that the figure of Satan grew into a kind of principle and embodiment of all evil. In apocalyptic Judaism and early Christianity the process is completed.

---

[1] Rev. 12⁹, 20².

S. Paul speaks of Satan as the 'god of this world' (2 Cor. 4⁴), and S. Peter traces to his evil influence all the trials of the infant Church. (Cf. 1 Pet. 5⁸, Rev. 2¹⁰,¹³, &c.) Above all, he was the implacable enemy of Jesus, the instigator of the act of treachery (Lk. 22³, Jn. 13²). He accomplishes in the end the Crucifixion of Christ. It was the Messiah's work to destroy the dominion of Satan, and to restore the world to the spiritual sovereignty of God (1 Jn. 3⁸). Consequently it was natural for the earliest 'writing' Q to place at the outset of the public life of Christ a struggle with the Kingdom of Satan.

4⁴. *every word that proceedeth out of the mouth of God.* The quotation is from Deut. 8³. 'The mouth of God' is a common expression for the will of God, and the meaning of the whole phrase, and its point for Jesus is, (*a*) that His experiences as unique Son of God ought to be those of His people; and (*b*) that those whom God wishes for His own purposes to keep alive must be kept alive, bread or no bread, even as Israel had been miraculously preserved by God in His purposes for mankind in the Wilderness.

4⁵. *pinnacle of the temple,* Gk. πτερύγιον. It was expected that the Messiah would appear on the topmost tower of the Temple over a porch, perhaps the Royal porch on the south of the Temple overlooking an immense precipice.¹ Ps. 91, which is quoted from the LXX was regarded as Messianic by the Rabbis. The Messiah could come to no harm. The reality in the Temptation, apart from its Messianic connotation, is as follows. In the first temptation Christ had declared His absolute trust in God. Let that trust be now put to even greater test, let Him cast Himself down. Our Lord replies again in the words of Deut. 6¹⁶, that to put God to the test is not to trust Him. That quotation is a reference to the striking of the rock by Moses, 'Ye shall not tempt the Lord your God, as ye tempted him in Massah', when the people murmured against God because there was no water to drink, 'and they tempted the Lord, saying, Is the Lord among us or not?' (Ex. 17⁷).

4⁸. The third temptation is placed last by Mt. and rightly because it is the climax. The symbolism of the mountain, and the levitation to the summit of some high place is a commonplace of apocalyptic writing. Cf. also Ezek. 3¹², 11¹; 2 Esdras 13⁶. Lk. makes no mention of a mountain. The quotation this time is again from Deut. 6¹³,¹⁴, the word 'worship' being substituted for 'fear'. 'Thou shalt fear the Lord thy God, and serve him, and swear by his name. Ye shall not go after other gods.'

I will give thee. According to apocalyptic teaching of the time, the devil possessed the world by gift of God. So in S. Jn. 14³⁰ he is called the prince of the World. Hence he is regarded, quite correctly, in this passage as giving that which he has a right to dispose of.

---

¹ Apocalypse of Baruch. Cf. Joseph, *Ant.* xv. 11. 5.

4^{12-25}. *Mission in Galilee* (Mk. 1^{14-39}; Lk. 4^{14-15}, 5^{1-11}.)

The synoptic accounts of the commencement of our Lord's public ministry do not rule out the possibility of an earlier Judaean Ministry as described by S. John ($2^{12\text{ ff.}}$). Mt. describes the arrival at Capernaum in such a way as to bring it into connexion with the prophecy, but follows Mk. in dating the beginning of the public ministry of our Lord from the arrest of John the Baptist by Herod, which is dated by Josephus in the year A.D. 29. Mt. relates the calling of the first disciples but compresses the rest of the Marcan narrative into three verses, 23–25, in order to pass without further introduction to his first book.

4^{13}. *leaving Nazareth.* A reference to a ministry there, perhaps that described in Lk. 4^{16-30}.

Capernaum = the village of Nahum, probably to be identified with Telhum, on the north shore of the Sea of Galilee. It was at this time a flourishing commercial city, a centre of travel and populous. The Synagogue, a very fine one, referred to in Jn. 6^{59}, has been recently excavated. (For further information about the Geography of Galilee see Sanday, *Sacred Sites of the Gospels*, 36 ff., and Hastings, *D.C.G. Capernaum.*)

4^{15}. The quotation is from Isa. $9^{1,\,2}$. The original prophecy referred to the devastation of northern Palestine by the Assyrian armies, which captured Samaria under Sargon in 730 B.C. (2 Kings 15^{27}, $17^{5,\,6}$).

4^{23}. *the gospel of the kingdom*, i.e. the good news that the Kingdom was near. For the Kingdom of Heaven see Additional Note D.

4^{24}. *Syria.* Introduction, p. 20. An indication of the place of origin of this Gospel.

4^{25}. *Decapolis.* The name given to a confederation of Greek cities, originally ten in number, liberated from Jewish control by Pompey in 60 B.C. It included various towns on the east of the Jordan, such as Damascus, Gadara, and Gerasa, and one on the western side, Scythopolis.

5–7. FIRST BOOK OF MATTHEW

THE NEW ETHICS OF THE CHRISTIAN CHURCH.

(1) The Sermon on the Mount is the first of the group of five discourses into which Mt. has divided his Gospel. It is clearly intended to be regarded as an authoritative system of ethical principles binding upon all Christians in the same way that the old Law was binding on Jews. The first Christians did not in any sense regard themselves as free from the law but as under a new law

which S. Paul calls the 'law of Christ' (1 Cor. 9²¹), S. James the 'Perfect law of Liberty' (Jas. 1²⁵), and S. John 'the new Commandment' (1 Jn. 2⁸).

(2) Although the Sermon, as it stands in Mt., is a composite collection of sayings not all of which were delivered at the same time, it is probable that Mt. and Lk. are correct in placing a sermon and what is in substance the same sermon where they do, i.e. at the point at which Mk. places the ordination of the Twelve on a mountain in Galilee (Mk. 3¹³, Lk. 6²⁰). The time had come in the public life of our Lord when it was necessary for Him to delegate some of the work of preaching and healing to men specially chosen for that purpose and afterwards called 'Apostles'. Opposition had begun to grow (Mk. 2⁶) and Jesus had either been excommunicated or had withdrawn of His own accord from the Synagogue (Mk. 3⁶). It was now necessary to give some cohesion to the numerous and unorganized body of His followers in Galilee and elsewhere. He must give them leadership and above all principles of action to take the place of those which His teaching had plainly declared to be inadequate. Some such situation must be presupposed in order to account for the opening beatitudes which are cast in the form of 'paradoxes' aiming at sharp differentiation— in Mt. between the disciples of the Kingdom and the disciples of the Synagogue, in Lk. between the disciples of Jesus and the world. The original Sermon doubtless consisted of the outline which it takes in Lk., beatitudes, the command to love enemies and the warning against empty profession, which would be appropriate to the occasion.

(3) The Sermon both in Mt. and Lk. is recorded with considerable editorial modifications. Even if, as Streeter thinks, the Sermon circulated from the first in two widely different forms, the setting is in either case the work of the Evangelist himself. Luke's purpose is clearly biographical; he is describing what is in effect the first Ordination Service. He therefore omits the contrast between the Old and the New Law which probably stood in Q. Matthew's purpose is entirely different from that of Luke. He represents Jesus as promulgating a Law as Moses did. He therefore gives it a mountain scene, like Sinai. He makes use of the multitude which he has found in Mk., adds greatly to its extent, and makes it the audience of the solemn utterance which he has placed in the forefront of the Gospel. This audience is clearly intended to represent the Christian community, and, as in the other discourses, it is not long before Mt. has passed far beyond the

context with which he began and is addressing the entire Christian Church. In other words, his purpose is to compose a comprehensive guide to ethical and religious practice for the use of all members of the Christian Church.

(4) For this reason Mt. has inserted into the discourse certain passages which we know to have stood elsewhere. The following passages stood elsewhere in Q:

5^{13-16}. The parables of the salt and the lamp (Mk. 9^{50}, Lk. $14^{34, 35}$).

5^{18}. The permanence of the law (Lk. 16^{17}).

5^{25-26}. On reconciliation (Lk. $12^{58, 59}$).

5^{31-32}. On divorce (Lk. 16^{18}).

6^{7-15}. The institution of the Lord's Prayer (breaking the rhythm of the original discourse (Lk. $11^{2\,ff.}$)).

6^{19-34}. On worldly goods (Lk. $12^{33\,ff.}$, 18^{22}).

7^{7-11}. On instant prayer (Lk. 11^{9-13}; cf. 18^{1}, Mk. 11^{24}).

7^{13}. The two ways (Lk. 13^{24}).

(5) Subjoined is an analysis of the Sermon for the purpose of making its contents more easily remembered.

(I) 5^{3-12}. The beatitudes or dispositions which will be rewarded in the coming Age.

(II) 5^{13-16}. Warning to the disciples to take the fulfilment of their vocation seriously, in the interests of others.

(III) The main body of the Sermon with its twofold theme.

(1) The relation of the teaching of Jesus to the old Law and the Prophets, 5^{17-48}; of His spirit to that of the hypocrites (6^{1-18}).

(a) The fulfilment of the Law by bringing it to a greater perfection than before, so as to constitute a righteousness greater than that of the Scribes and Pharisees. (b) The enumeration of six points in which the new righteousness will be more perfect than the old: Homicide (vv. 21–2), Adultery (vv. 27–29), Divorce (vv. 31–32), Truth (vv. 33–37), Retaliation (vv. 38–42), Sentiments towards our enemies (vv. 43–48). (c) The indication of certain points which throw into relief the new righteousness, especially the spirit of interior devotion and religion which is occupied with the thoughts of God alone, as exemplified in Almsgiving (6^{1-4}), Prayer (6^{5-15}), Fasting (6^{16-18}).

(2) The second theme includes (a) sundry counsels on detachment from worldly goods in the search for the Kingdom of Heaven and of Righteousness (6^{19-34}). (b) Conduct to be observed when we are occupied with the spiritual good of others (7^{1-6}). (c) The spirit of hopefulness and trust (7^{7-11}), (d) the Golden Rule (7^{12}). (e) Lastly, Christian prudence in relation to the counsel of the Two Ways (7^{13}); the discernment of spirits (7^{15-20}) and the importance of good works (7^{21-23}).

(IV) Epilogue. The Sermon ends with the final command to act after one has heard.

It is possible in this way to trace a beautiful order and arrangement in the Sermon, which is then seen to constitute a kind of spiritual exercise for the moral perfection of the disciples of Jesus looking steadfastly towards the kingdom of God and determined to do His will. (Lagrange.)

5²⁻¹². *The Beatitudes.* (Lk. 6²⁰⁻²⁶.)

The beatitudes constitute the theme of the whole teaching of Jesus which has been described as a 'transvaluation of all values'. Some believe themselves to be happy and the public declare them to be happy. Jesus proclaims who ought to be called happy.

Mt. has probably expanded the beatitudes into ten for liturgical reasons as the new Decalogue. They are even in their original form a code, but not of behaviour or of works, but of moral dispositions out of which right action will follow, like S. Paul's list of the fruit of the Spirit (Gal. 5²²) and the Hymn of Charity (1 Cor. 13). Lk., who has added corresponding woes on the model of Deut. 28, has only four beatitudes, those relating to the social position of the disciples over against the world, 'the poor', 'the hungry', 'the sorrowful', and 'the persecuted'. To these Mt. has added six others, two of which are taken from the Psalms. The remaining three bear Mt.'s hall-mark, the reward of the kingdom. While it is impossible to say which version of the beatitudes was the original as uttered by Jesus, the more probable view is that Mt. is nearer the original than Lk. Many passages of a strongly ascetic character in Lk. make it probable that it is he who has modified the original sayings of Jesus in the Sermon in a rigorist direction, and added the words against the rich and prosperous not for any misuse of their riches but by virtue of possession alone.

5³. *The Poor in Spirit.*

The words as they stand in Mt. clearly describe not the poor in earthly goods but the poor in the sense in which the word is so often used in the O.T., i.e. the persecuted and down-trodden remnant of the people of God (Isa. 61¹ and frequently in the Psalms). In this beatitude it is applied accordingly to those who have inherited the blessings as well as the sufferings of the ancient people of God, the remnant of Israel, the community of the Messiah, the Christian ecclesia. It is the poor in this sense who have the Gospel preached unto them (Mt. 11⁵) and therein experience all the powers of the promised Kingdom.

It has, however, been suggested that the meaning is even more clearly defined than this and that the word translated 'spirit' means, as in the O.T., the inward wisdom of a man, that portion of the divine Spirit which dwells in him; in which case poor in 'spirit' will mean 'lacking in wisdom' as in 1 Cor. 1²⁰ 'God has chosen the foolish things of this world to confound the wise'. In the N.T. the bad meaning attached in the O.T. to the 'fool' and 'folly' has given place to the sense of 'childlikeness', 'unworldliness', while the 'wise' and 'learned' have become the professional and usually irreligious representatives of piety. The first beatitude will in this case mean 'Blessed are those whose minds lack the legal wisdom of the Pharisees and their Rabbinic Schools'. This would be specially applicable to the Galileans who were despised by the Pharisees as being 'people of the land', the *'Am ha'arez*, who through ignorance and lax observance of the law were regarded as beyond the pale (Jn. 7⁴⁹), but who gladly listened to the preaching of Jesus.

Whichever of these interpretations is adopted, the essential meaning of the beatitude is the same, 'Humilitatem non penuriam' (Bengel); or as in the Magnificat 'Exaltavit humiles'.

5⁴. *They that mourn*, the role of the anointed Servant of Jehovah (Isa. 61²ᶠᶠ·) is to 'comfort those who mourn for Zion', i.e. for its ruins, the fixed attitude of Israel after the exile, and to this day of the Jews in Jerusalem. Jesus, however, speaks not only of Israel and its hope, but of all who are in sorrow, which is bound to be the lot of the servants of God, because here on earth evil outweighs good. The fourth gospel gives the name of Comforter to the Spirit of Christ in the Christian Community.

5⁵. *Blessed are the meek*, Gk. πραεῖς. The third beatitude is little more than a repetition of the first and refers to the same class of persons. It is not an original saying of our Lord but a direct quotation from Ps. 37¹¹ and in the best authorities it stands second. Meekness is the name given to the attitude of those who are poor in spirit towards others. Those who do not stand on their dignity nor make claims for themselves. The vice opposed to meekness is hardness, the ordinary accompaniment of covetousness which is the desire to acquire and possess for ourselves. It is the meek who are always ready to yield even their just rights, who will possess the true riches. The reward is the same as in the first beatitude. The poor and meek will share God's glory in the same way that Israel is to share God's throne in the vision of Dan. 7²⁷. Hence the next beatitude.

5[6]. *Blessed are they that hunger and thirst after righteousness.*
By righteousness Jesus probably meant the divine vindication of
the good cause, as so often referred to in the latter part of Isaiah,
e.g. 45[13], 51[1,5]. Cf. Lk. 18[1-7]. But God's righteousness is never to
be seen in its perfection on earth, therefore there must always be
a hunger and thirst for 'the righteousness of God which is by faith'
(Rom. 3[21-22]).[1]

5[7]. *Blessed are the merciful.* Those who refuse to judge others by
a narrow or superior standard are themselves in a condition to
receive mercy in the great judgement of God which is so often
referred to in this Gospel, and forms the subject of the last of the
five great discourses into which the Gospel is divided.

5[8]. *Blessed are the pure in heart*, the purity of heart to which
is attached the promise of the vision of God does not merely refer
to cleanness of mind and body, supremely important as our
Lord regarded such purity (cf. vv. 27–32) but rather to that single-
heartedness which had already been accounted blessed in the O.T.
'Blessed are they that are undefiled in the way' are the opening
words of Ps. 119. The words mean those who are single-hearted in
the service of God and man and unprejudiced in their judgement of
their fellow men. The 'beatific vision' promised in the beatitudes
has been the supreme object of Christian hope and aspiration
throughout the history of the Church. 'Gloria Dei vivens homo;
vita hominis visio Dei' (S. Irenaeus).

5[9]. *Blessed are the Peacemakers*, not those who avoid war at any
cost but those who 'seek peace and ensue it' (Ps. 34[14]), and who by
the harmony and control in which they habitually live are a source
of peace wherever they are. 'Eirene', peace, is a characteristically
Christian word which together with love and joy forms the first
strophe of the hymn on the fruit of the Spirit in Gal. 5[22]. It occurs
no less than twenty-five times in the N.T. which records the first
moral experience of the Christian Church.

Children of God, rather *Sons of God*, in the O.T. of the Angels,
as in the hymn of creation when all the sons of God shouted for
joy (Job 38[7]). Who will have a better right to belong to the inner
circle of the Angels of God who surround His throne than the Sons
of Peace, for God is a God of peace (Phil. 4[7]) ? But Peace is the fruit
of Justice (Isa. 32[17]). In that sense only the reign of the Messiah
is the reign of Peace, which Christ by reconciling the world to the
Justice of God has made possible for mankind.

[1] For the meaning of righteousness in this sense and as used by S. Paul
see Prof. C. H. Dodd, *Ep. to the Romans*, i. 17.

5^{11}. *Blessed are ye when men shall reproach you and persecute you ... for my sake.* The change to the second person plural paves the way to the apostrophe 5^{12} which forms in Mt. the tenth beatitude. The tone becomes at this point more personal and intimate than in the other beatitudes; the suffering for righteousness will become a suffering for MY sake, Gk. ἕνεκεν ἐμοῦ. Lk. at this point has 'the son of man's sake', the Sinaitic Syriac has 'for the sake of the name', while D has repeated 'righteousness' from the previous verse. These variants are interesting as reflecting the history of persecution in the early Church. Beginning with the social ostracism in Palestine for the sake of the 'new righteousness' it has become actual persecution for the sake of belief in Christ, and even for the name of Christian as we see it already in the first Epistle of Peter, A.D. 70 (I Pet. 4^{16}), and in the famous letter of Pliny to the Emperor Trajan in the early years of the next century. Lk. has 'Their Fathers' limiting the reference to the persecution of the Palestine Jews; Mt., here as elsewhere, has a far wider horizon. The persecution by the Jewish people will become that of the whole world against the Christians (Mt. $10^{22\,ff.}$).

5^{13}. *Salt of the earth.* The disciples have the same task, that of witnessing against the world and its false religious and ethical standards as had the prophets of the O.T. The function of Christians is to act as a preservative, as salt does, and to arrest the processes of corruption inevitable in human society if left to itself. The same task is illustrated by the parable of the lamp which S. Paul echoes in the Epistle to the Philippians (2^{15}). At the same time they must beware lest their own standard deteriorate, like bad salt, or be allowed to grow dim like a hidden lamp, through failure to live the Christian sacrificial life or to spread the light of the Gospel by missionary activity. In an early Christian writing known as the Epistle to Diognetus the Christians are described as the 'soul of the world'. We may compare Pliny's proverb (*Nat. Hist.* 31. 102) 'Totis corporibus nihil utilius sale et sole'.

Your father which is in heaven. This phrase, so characteristic of the first Gospel, does not appear to have been wholly original in our Lord's mouth. It is frequent in Rabbinic Literature, cf. also Isa. 63^{16}, Wisd. 2^{16}, Ecclus. 3^{1-4}.

5.$^{17-20}$. *The Law of Christ the perfection of the Law of Moses.*

The first and the last of these verses form a suitable introduction to what is to follow. But the sequence of thought in the intervening verses is difficult. The meaning would be quite clear if verse 17 were followed directly by verse 20, but the words in vv. 18 and 19 appear to revert to a Judaistic legalism inconsistent with the 'fulfilment' of the law which Jesus came to achieve. Verse 18 is found in a different context in Lk. 16^{17}, and verse 19 seems to refer to certain definite but unspecified commandments. It is probable that Mt. has in this case followed his usual practice of conflating two or more sayings which had originally no connexion with each other.

NOTE A. JESUS AND THE LAW OF MOSES

Clearly Mt. wishes to imply that our Lord did not make a revolution nor let loose on mankind the disorder which is bound to follow from a sudden rupture with the past. All reformers have been faced with this alternative. But Mt. is at pains to show that Jesus made His position in this regard unmistakably clear. He has not come to make a rupture in the Law or the Prophets, the old Dispensation, to which he gives its true weight; but the Law once reinterpreted and understood in its proper sense, He is to demand from His followers an obedience to it much more exacting than was in fact required in the old Dispensation. In other words, to fulfil the Law does not mean to 'make additions to it', which is precisely what the Christians were accused by the rabbinic writers of doing when it suited their purpose, but to *perfect* it in conformity with the intentions of the Supreme Legislator. Jesus was not abrogating nor amending the Law but restoring it to the meaning which God intended it to have: S. Paul uses the word 'fulfil' in the same sense, probably quoting actual words of Jesus, in Rom. 13^{10} 'He that loveth hath *fulfilled* the law'. The process of development will inevitably involve the virtual abrogation (implied in the following verses) of many of its provisions, which either contradict the spirit of the Law, or have no further application. Nevertheless, as Jesus says with more than usual emphasis, there is no point in the divine revelation, no matter how small, which, so long as it *is an organic portion of the whole*, will not have its own proper place and reason when the whole design of God's purpose is brought to completion.

Thus neither Jesus nor his great interpreter S. Paul regarded

[1] On the position of the Law at this time as an instrument of moral progress, see Montefiore, and Bousset, *Die Religion des Judentums*, pp. 87–120. Bousset points out the remarkable power of the Law as an instrument binding together a widely scattered people, as closely as does modern Roman Catholicism, to a spiritual centre.

the Law itself as a bad thing. To Jesus himself it was a revelation of the will of God though not a complete nor final one. No one could deny that it had been a great civilizing power raising the moral standards of the Jewish people far above that of any other nation. Nor does our Lord ever speak of it as a dead thing or a drag on progress, for by a skilful process of adaptation the Rabbis had succeeded in keeping it, like English case-law, a living and a growing thing; with the result that it had been a wonderful bond of union among a widely scattered people, giving them a national self-consciousness and a sense of vocation to the rest of the world. No one reading Ps. 119 could doubt that the Law had been to countless religious Jews a real mirror of perfection and a spiritual means of grace.

But it had certain fundamental weaknesses on which Jesus puts His finger with unerring touch. (1) Its manifest imperfection. The Law needed constant reinterpretation until it bore little relation to the original commandments. 'The Law made nothing perfect' (Heb. 7^{19}). (2) Its *natural* character. In spite of exalted claims it commanded love but restricted that love to one's neighbour. (3) Its *national* character, involved in the 'covenant' relation. The Jew kept the Law as a member of his nation not as personally responsible to God and hoping for Him hereafter. The idea of a covenant established in his mind a claim to God's intervention on behalf of himself and his nation, hence the extreme anxiety about the minutiae of the Law, lest God should take offence, and the rise of a bad sort of casuistry which aimed at keeping the Law with the utmost completeness for the national advantage that could be obtained thereby. (4) It was negative rather than positive; concerned with prohibitions and external conduct rather than with the heart. This was already clearly seen by the prophet Jeremiah who spoke of a new covenant written in the heart (Jer. 31^{31}). What our Lord did in the Sermon on the Mount was to reclaim the fundamental principles of morality from the external character which they had temporarily assumed in their Jewish guise and environment, and to establish them once more on their fundamental divine basis, the disposition of the soul toward God Himself. S. Paul worked out this idea to its logical conclusion in the Epistle to the Galatians.

5^{18}. The Law of Moses was regarded as a divine and immortal thing by the Rabbis who almost personified it. The apocalyptic work, called the Assumption of Moses, held that God had created men for the sake of the Law. 'Everything hath its end, the heaven and earth have their

end, only one thing excepted, which has no end, and that is the Law'
(Philo, *Vit. Mos.* vi). If therefore a Liberal Jewish Philosopher of
Alexandria used the same language about the eternity of the Law
while at the same time advocating an extreme allegorical interpretation of it, it may safely be inferred that our Lord in using the same
kind of language did not mean to imply that the ceremonial details of
the Law were of the same importance and value as the moral precepts.

5¹⁸. *one jot or tittle.* Gk. ἰῶτα ἢ κερέα. 'Jot' was in the A.V. originally
spelt *iote*, the smallest Greek letter, used here to represent *Yodh*,
the smallest Hebrew letter. *Kerea* (horn) was translated in the
A.V. 'Tittle' from the Vulgate 'Titulus', which in medieval MSS.
signified the stroke made above a word to indicate an abbreviation,
hence it is used for any small stroke or mark. The actual meaning of
Kerea is doubtful, but it probably means a small apex ∧ which distinguishes certain pairs of Hebrew letters. Burkitt suggests that it
is the Hebrew letter *Waw*, the hook, which like *Yodh*, could be omitted
from a word without alteration of the sense.

5¹⁹. *Whosoever shall break.* Gk. λύσῃ, the same word as is used in
verse 17 = dissolve an existing authority. The same word is used
later of Peter and all the Apostles in their capacity as Church rulers
(Mt. 16¹⁹, 18¹⁸), and refers not to transgressions of the Law but to
dispensations from its regulations. As it stands here it is a warning
to Apostles and others exercising the powers of dispensation not to
use that power in a loose or wrong way. The later Jewish Doctors
recognized a distinction between the lesser and weightier precepts of
the Law, but no form of dispensation as residing in their Church. Cf.
Jas. 2¹⁰ for a similar rigorist view in the Christian Church.

5²⁰. *scribes and Pharisees.* The *Scribes* were not all Pharisees
(Acts 23⁹). They were a comparatively small body of men who ex-
pounded the Law, taught it in school, and administered it as assessors
in the courts of justice.

The *Pharisees* or Separatists, as the name implies, were the whole
body of orthodox believers who lived the separated life, i.e. kept
themselves by observance of a thousand precautions from any possibility of contamination by surrounding heathenism, thereby failing to
realize or fulfil the vocation of Judaism to be the divinely appointed
teacher of the true religion to the world (23¹⁵). The Pharisees were
the spiritual descendants of the Chasidim, the pious supporters of the
purity of the Jewish Law, who were the first to throw in their lot with
the noble family of the Maccabees in their fight against the paganizing
measures of the Seleucid kings, the successors of Alexander the Great.
So long as the Maccabees' policy was resistance against the totalitarian
ideas of the Greek State, they were supported by the Pharisees, but
when those aims became aggressive and ideas of conquest and Jewish
aggrandisement began to take their place, the Chasidim withdrew and

'separated' themselves from the main body of the people, and became a sect or party within the Jewish nation whose influence persisted with varying fortunes during the Hasmonaean age, until in the time of our Lord they were beginning to become the most influential element in the Sanhedrin.

5^{21-48}. *Six illustrations of the perfection or fulfilment of the Law.* Throughout this section it must be remembered that Jesus is speaking as a Prophet with a prophet's right to announce truth, not as a casuist interpreting a law. By 'they of old time' is meant the old Dispensation, not as some hold the Rabbinic Commentators.

(1) 5^{21-26}. *First Perfection of the Jewish Law: The Christian Rule of Self-Control.*

The new commandment forbids the indulgence of passions of which the result may be murder.

5^{22}. *in danger of the Judgement,* liable to legal proceedings. But as no court, civil or ecclesiastical, can take cognizance of evil thoughts the judgement in such a case can only mean God's Judgement. The sanction of the Commandment is to be found in Exod. 21^{12}.

Raca = empty, an expression of contempt so gross as to be regarded as libellous and therefore actionable. The survival of this and other Aramaic words indicates that we have to do with a Palestinian source rather than a Hebrew Gospel.

The Council, Gk. *Sanhedrin,* again a Palestinian word meaning probably not the supreme court that sat in Jerusalem and tried our Lord, but the court which met in the local Synagogue. Such inferior Sanhedrins are known to have existed in Palestine at the time of Christ, consisting of thirteen persons in every town with a population above 129 and were competent to try even capital charges. (Schürer, *History of the Jewish People,* ii. 1. 153.)

Thou fool, Gk. μωρέ, the word, though an offensive one in Greek literature, could hardly be regarded as morally worse than *Raca.* It is therefore difficult to regard it as the climax in an ascending scale of moral wickedness. According to Bacon and Charles (*The Decalogue,* p. 200) the most probable explanation of this difficulty is to be found in a dislocation of the text. Verse 22 consists of three sentences; and if the first two are transposed we get, not a climax, but a parallelism in the manner of Jewish poetical composition; *Raca* and *Fool* being the same word in two languages. The words 'Whosoever shall kill', and the words 'Whosoever shall say unto his brother Raca', both represent the current Jewish teaching to which Jesus opposes His own teaching respectively, that (1) 'the Rabbis say that murder is liable to judgement, but I say that anger is liable to the

Divine judgement'; (2) the Rabbis say that abusive language such as *Raca* is actionable in the law court, but I say that abusive language such as *Raca* or *More* is punishable with Gehenna.

The Gehenna of fire. The valley of Hinnom, a ravine to the west of Jerusalem, the supposed site of Moloch worship introduced by Ahaz, afterwards for that reason defiled by Josiah (2 Kings 23^{10}). It was long afterwards used as the rubbish dump of the city and hence became on account of its continually smouldering fires a symbol of an eternal punishment, a doctrine held by contemporary Jewish teachers.[1] It would, however, be rash to assume from this allusion that our Lord taught a doctrine of penal and unending punishment in a future world.

5$^{23-26}$. The next three verses give two reasons for the necessity of restraining anger. (1) Anger hinders prayer and makes any true worship of God impossible. It makes no difference in our Lord's view who started the quarrel. It is otherwise in the Talmud. (2) Once allowed to get out of control anger may lead to consequences to which it is impossible to set any limit, involving, it may be, not only friends but families and communities and even at last whole nations in irreconcilable antagonism.

5^{23}. *thy gift*, the Jewish worshipper at the temple after he had performed the ceremonial ablutions prescribed in the Mosaic Law had to bring his sacrifice to the inner court where it was received by the priests. Our Lord says that a further purification of the heart may still be necessary before proceeding with the service.

5^{25}. Stood originally in Q (Lk. 12$^{54-59}$) as a solemn denunciation of impending doom on the apostate race.

5^{25}. *the officer*, Gk. ὑπηρέτης, an apparitor, as we should call him, of the Court, who was probably the Janitor of the Jewish synagogue, or the local *Greffier* or village scribe called by Josephus (*Ant.* xvi. 7. 3) κωμογραμματεύς.

(2) 5$^{27-30}$. *Second perfection of the Jewish Law. The Christian law of Purity.*

Jesus, in accord with the best Jewish opinion of his day, understands adultery to include any kind of sexual intercourse outside marriage. Our Lord gives no reason for the stern prohibition of sexual impurity other than the Law of God. Better live a life which is physically imperfect and unexpressed than sin against God and our neighbour who is also His child. For Jewish teaching on this subject supporting this view, see Montefiore, *Rabbinic Literature and Gospel Teaching.*

[1] Oesterley and Box, *Religion and Worship of the Synagogue*, pp. 250 ff.

(3) vv. 31.-37. *The third perfection of the Jewish Law. The Christian law of marriage.* Lk. 16^{18}.

Whosoever shall put away his wife. A similar saying in Lk. follows that upon the permanence of the Law (Mt. 5^{18}), hence both sayings probably stood in Q but not necessarily in the Sermon. But Mt. appears to conflate the Q logion with that in Mk. 10$^{11-12}$ = Mt. 19^9. Whether all three logia stood in Q, or are from different sources, it is evident that our Lord on one or more occasions uttered solemn sayings about marriage and divorce which must be considered in a separate Note after we have come to the later passage (Mt. 19^9).

5^{31}. The reference here is to Deut. 24$^{1-4}$ or rather to a current scribal interpretation of that passage which had converted an original permission into a positive command. For the Deuteronomic enactment does not *institute* divorce but treats it as a custom already in force and lays down regulations tending to limit it and preclude its abuse. Later Rabbinic writers carried the process still further and added other restrictions, the famous Doctor Shammai maintaining that the only ground for divorce was adultery on the part of the wife. There can be no reasonable doubt that our Lord intended his disciples to take the final and heroic step and pronounce marriage for Christians indissoluble. Otherwise there would have been no advance in this respect upon the Old Law as interpreted by the best religious thought of His day. Why then have introduced the matter at all at this point?

5^{32}. *Saving for the cause of fornication*, Gk. παρεκτὸς λόγου πορνείας. This famous exception (on which see note F) has been too easily understood to mean the same thing as the phrase in Mt. 19^9 (Gk. μὴ ἐπὶ πορνείᾳ) and has therefore usually been taken to mean 'except on the ground or for the reason of fornication'. But, as Lagrange points out, *parectos* does not mean *except* but *not having regard to,* and *logos* does not mean a *cause*, except in the legal sense of the word, i.e. a *charge*. In other words the strict meaning of the phrase is '*apart from or reserving a charge of adultery*'. Whether therefore they are a genuine saying of Christ or, as most critics seem to think, an insertion of the Evangelist from Mt. 19^9 or from some other source, the words in themselves do not give an innocent party in a divorce suit a general permission to remarry but merely reserve the case of an adulterous wife for special consideration. Jesus does not in this place say what ought to be done in the case of adultery. He certainly could not have recommended mere complacency.

5[32]. *Maketh her an adulteress*. This is an alteration of the Q logion of Lk. 16[18] and may be from another source altogether. It appears to mean 'drives her into the arms of another man' as the only alternative to destitution. Against this oriental claim to unrestricted repudiation our Lord opposes the responsibility of the husband for the 'wife of his youth' as the prophet called Malachi, three hundred years before, had done. (Mal. 2[14].)

5[32]. *Whosoever shall marry her*, &c. The words are omitted by the western text D and are probably an assimilation to 19[9]. In any case the words add nothing to what has been already said. Nor have they anything to do with the question of the remarriage of an innocent party to a divorce, because a person of either sex who initiates divorce proceedings is not *compelled* to marry again. The present context is solely concerned with a repudiated and destitute wife.

(4) 5[33-37]. *Fourth perfection of the old Law. Christian law of Truth.*

Our Lord here, as elsewhere, is making a positive command to speak the truth on all occasions rather than laying down a law respecting the use of oaths. This is clear from the concluding words 'Whatsoever is more than this cometh of evil' (*v.* 37). Oaths are the result of the untruthfulness of men and society. It is that which has to be attacked. Many teachers, including some of the greatest of the Christian Fathers, and modern bodies like the Society of Friends, have regarded these words as forbidding the use of oaths even in Christian courts of law. But the teaching of Jesus has always to be viewed in relation to His own practice. He Himself, according to Mt., accepted the oath offered to Him by the High Priest at His trial (26[63]) ; S. Paul frequently makes use of the adjuration (Gal. 1[20]; 1 Thess. 5[27]). Moreover the words 'yea, yea', 'nay, nay' solemnly uttered are indistinguishable from formal oaths. In the interests of reverence and truth our Lord forbids (1) the common practice, not confined by any means to the Jews, of the use of the name of God to add strength to a statement. This, whether done lightly or in earnest, is, like lying itself, an act of irreverence to God's Majesty; (2) the casuistical distinctions which the Rabbis drew between the different degrees of oaths, the hollowness of which our Lord exposes, on the ground that as soon as the words 'I swear' have been uttered a sacred engagement is contracted which involves God whether His name is actually invoked or not.

5[33]. The reference is here to Exod. 20[7], 'Thou shalt not take the name of the Lord thy God in vain', i.e. use it lightly in an oath, cf. Num. 30[2] and Deut. 23[21].

5^{35}. Jesus means that it is impossible to distinguish between such terms and God Himself. Better, therefore, not to bring them in at all.

5^{37}. *Yea, yea, Nay, nay.* S. James (5^{12}), followed by the Didache, understood these words in a slightly different sense as an exhortation to truth. 'If you mean "Yes" say yes, if "no" say no.'

(5) 5^{38-42}. *The fifth perfection of the Mosaic Law. Christian renunciation of rights.*

(1) Jesus is enjoining non-resistance not as a feeble yielding to wickedness but as a positive principle of action with the definite purpose of obtaining a certain end, namely the reconciliation of an enemy. Without that motive, for which a man must be prepared to make, as Jesus says, any sacrifice of property or rights that may be demanded, such a principle would become one of mere cowardice. History has proved the almost unlimited power of the endurance of martyrdom and the refusal to take action against enemies, when undertaken in the belief in the ultimate triumph of love over evil. S. Paul has caught the full meaning of the teaching in his quotation of the old Jewish proverb, 'If thine enemy hunger feed him, if he thirst give him drink, for in so doing thou shalt heap coals of fire on his head' (Rom. 12^{20}). The Jews had forgotten this teaching and the tragedy of their history was the implacable character of their national and international feuds. The application of this, as of all other precepts and counsels of perfection must remain a matter of casuistry. An enlightened and well-informed conscience can tell an individual Christian where his duty lies in any particular case, so long as he is pursuing the command at all times to exercise reconciling love.

(2) The passage has sometimes been used to deny the right of magistrates to exercise their proper rights and functions, and even of parents to punish their children for their own good. This, however, is a confusion of thought. For the use of force which is here normally denied to the individual Christian is by the Law of God an attribute of the civil power. S. Paul who has an exceptionally clear grasp of Christian ethics makes this perfectly plain (Rom. $13^{1\text{ff.}}$) and the Christian Church early recognized this right.

(3) *The lex talionis.* Ancient custom among Semitic peoples gave the individual a particular assurance that he would be avenged by his clan, but, to limit the terrible repercussions of the vendetta, the right of vengeance was limited to reciprocity. In this respect the Law of Moses, expressed in Exod. 21^{24}, Lev. 24^{20}, Deut. 19^{21}, was at one with the ancient Babylonian Code of Hammurabi and that of

the XII Tables at Rome from which the term 'Lex talionis' is derived; 'si membrum rupit talio esto'. At the time of Jesus the Rabbinic jurisprudence probably followed the practice already sanctioned in the code of Hammurabi, to compound the actual infliction of the penalty for a money payment. But as our Lord points out, the Law remained; that had never been authoritatively abrogated. Nor does Jesus seek to abrogate it, for as it stands the law in question is a matter of civil jurisprudence rather than of moral conduct, and however much the principle is modified in its application in the direction of humanity by Christian teaching, the principle of punishment remains; and even if the individual renounces his rights under the civil Law, as he may well have to do as a Christian, the civil authority has not the right to renounce its duty to preserve good order, which involves the punishment of delinquents. Jesus does not attack the principle which inspired the Law, the principle of Justice; for he is addressing himself only to those who wish to be His disciples. As to the power of public authorities, Jesus at no time gave either advice or command, leaving His teaching to penetrate with its gentleness and humanity the exercise of that force which it is their duty to employ where necessary.

5³⁹. *him that is evil*, Gk. τῷ πονηρῷ. A.V. *evil*. For the R.V. translation ἀνθρώπῳ would be necessary especially in the singular. The statement is quite general.

Coat, Gk. χιτῶνα, undergarment.

Cloak, Gk. ἱμάτιον, outer garment necessary in cold weather.

Compel thee, Gk. ἀγγαρεύσει, 'requisition you, press into the state service.' The 'Aggaros' was the name for the mounted courier in the Persian state service who conveyed royal messages (cf. Herodotus 8⁹⁸ and Esther 3¹³). The word is used by Josephus for the compulsory military transport service, and even of the postal service in Egypt (*Ant.* xiii. 2–3). It frequently happened, as we learn from the Talmud, that the requisition was for the only ass in a village, which our Lord himself on one occasion may Himself have demanded. In that case his owner would have to go with him or lose him altogether.

Mile, Gk. μίλιον, a latinism, the Roman mile, the thousand double paces.

(6) 5⁴³⁻⁴⁸. *Sixth perfection of the Law. The Christian law of Love.* Lk. 6²⁷⁻³⁶.

Christ declares Himself against all particularism or discrimination between persons or groups as recipients of love. Christian love has no narrower limits than God Himself who bestows His loving care upon all, on the unjust as well as the just. In their original form the words presuppose a state of persecution.

5⁴³. *Thou shalt love thy neighbour.* Lev. 19¹⁸, 'thou shalt not take vengeance nor bear any grudge against the children of thy people, but thou shalt love thy neighbour as thyself.' The remainder of the verse, as in other references to the Mosaic Law, is not found in any part of the O.T. but is an inference which a Rabbi might draw from such passages as Deut. 23²⁰. The Law itself draws a distinction between Israelites and non-Israelites which, however, does not constitute a *command* to hate enemies. Indeed, the contrary is the case. For Lev. 19³⁴ recommends charity to a stranger, though it is true to say that the stranger in this case is the 'ger' or proselyte who has joined himself to Israel and it is in this sense that we must interpret the famous saying of Hillel, 'Love all men and bring them to the Law.'

love, Gk. *Agape*, consists not in feelings, still less in counterfeit feelings, but as Jesus Himself says, in doing good to enemies and praying for them. The word 'agape', together with joy and peace, was the new coinage of the Christian movement, expressing something different not only in degree but in kind from the human passion of love, Gk. *Eros*, which reached its highest point of perfection in the love of beauty and goodness such as Plato describes in the *Symposium*. Actually in the N.T. it always signifies the love of God for man unconditional and undeserved, and which alone gives value to the human soul (1 Jn. 4⁷). It is this love which we have undeservedly received from God that we are commanded to pass on to our brothers, not for anything good or lovely in them but because it must be our nature, as it is God's, so to love. For this reason love is always regarded in the N.T. (with faith and hope) as a theological or supernatural virtue which is the gift of God. It is not, therefore, a question of mere good nature which we can with a certain amount of education and self-control exercise every day, but of supernatural or heroic virtue.

5⁴⁶. *publicans*, Gk. τελῶναι = customs officials, not the *publicani*, who were far more exalted persons, usually Romans of equestrian rank, while the humble *telonai* were subordinate officials, usually Jews, in their pay. The *publicani* leased the toll or customs on exports of their several districts for a fixed sum and made what profit they could, which led their underlings to exercise gross oppression. For this reason, and because they took money from an alien power and had dealings which brought them into contact with foreigners, the 'telonai' were regarded as outcasts from Jewish society, a sort of 'depressed class'.

5⁴⁷. *Gentiles.* The old Syriac version has 'hypocrites' which would give the link with the next section.

5⁴⁸. *perfect.* Lk. has 'merciful'; this may be the original word as it stood in Q, but the idea of perfection is undoubtedly the key-note of the sermon as it was understood by Mt. and of Christian ethics as a whole. It is because the ethic of the Sermon on the Mount is an ethic of perfection that it cannot be reduced to rule or general principle. It regards every situation as new and as a possible extension of its principles.

6¹⁻¹⁸. *The Christian Rule of Prayer. True and false religion.*

The Sermon passes on to consider a particular aspect of righteousness, viz. as expressed in the three exterior acts of religion, Almsgiving, Prayer, and Fasting. Our Lord does not condemn such exercises in themselves, only the display of them before men. Certain important MSS. (א B D S) have a variant reading in verse 1, 'Almsgiving' instead of 'righteousness', the reason being that among the Jews righteousness, from the derivation of the word *ṣedeq*, had come almost to be identified with almsgiving; which not being definitely ordered by the Law was regarded as a work of supererogation to which special merit was attached. The book of Tobit in the Apocrypha is a good illustration of this characteristic mark of Jewish piety. Cf. 12⁸, 'Good is prayer with fasting and prayer and righteousness' (in the sense of almsgiving). The same teaching with its accompanying doctrine of works of supererogation and of merit passed later into Christianity.

6². *sound not a trumpet*, a proverbial phrase for attracting notice, cf. Juvenal xiv. 152, 'buccina famae'. It has, however, been suggested by G. H. Box that the reference is to the custom of sounding trumpets on the occasions of public fasting in the time of drought. On these days services of prayer were held in the streets, and almsgiving was of course an important part of these exercises. This would provide a great opportunity for ostentation if desired. This explanation affords admirable background for the section as a whole and links it up with what is said about fasting in verse 16.

hypocrites. The word means first of all an interpreter of riddles, a dreamer, then an actor, but it had no moral significance in antiquity. In the Gospels, however, it is used to represent an Aramaic word which can mean hypocritical or flattering, but in the earlier Hebrew meant only profane or impious. The most interesting example of the use of the word by Jewish contemporaries of Christ occurs in the Psalms of Solomon where the charge of hypocrisy in the sense of profane impiety is brought by the Pharisaic author against the worldly governing class known as the Sadducees. Thus our Lord in the Sermon on the Mount turns the reproach against its own authors, the Pharisees, in the sense of insincerity. Piety had become for the Pharisees a bargain with God, the worst form of irreligion.

6³. *let not thy left hand.* A proverbial expression for secrecy, also found in Stoic writings. The desire for glory exercised an astounding fascination over the ancient world. The Stoic was conspicuous in that he did not act with the vulgar desire to be seen of men, but for the satisfaction of his own feelings, or as Epictetus, the most religious of philosophers, adds 'for God'. The disciple of Jesus should not even know that he has done a charitable action.

6⁵. *They have received their reward*, Gk. ἀπέχουσι. The word occurs frequently in the papyri as the commercial formula for a receipt.

6⁵⁻⁸. *Prayer.* Standing was the usual attitude for prayer which in the Synagogue was uttered by one member of the congregation who passed in front of the chest containing the roll of the Law. The Synagogues were the theatres where reputations for sanctity were made. But the Jews were not singular in this respect.

6⁶. *inner chamber*, Gk. ταμεῖον, suggests not so much vocal as mental prayer or meditation, 'the ascent of the mind to God', the kind of exercise which was developed to perfection in Christianity. Our Lord does not, however, condemn private prayer in a public place such as a church, but tacitly approves of it as shown in Lk. 18¹⁰ᶠᶠ. It is in fact the only place possible for the vast majority of people in modern conditions of life, who have no privacy for prayer or any other practice, by day or night.

6⁷. *vain repetition*, Gk. μὴ βατταλογήσητε or βαταλογήσητε, the word was from the first uncertain and is translated differently in the versions; that in the R.V. being from the Vulgate '*multum loqui*'. In this case the Gk. word must have been connected with the Gk. βάτταλος, the nickname given to the orator Demosthenes, 'the gabbler', because of the torrent of words at his command. This is by far the most probable meaning here, for it corresponds with 'much speaking' in verse 7. On the other hand, the Sinaitic Syriac translates 'Do not say idle things', representing an Aramaic word meaning to stutter and so to utter meaningless sounds, the Greek in this case being derived according to Herodotus from the name of Battos, king of Lydia, who stammered (Her. 4¹⁵⁵). Others connect it with a Hebrew word meaning to 'speak thoughtlessly', as in Ps. 106³³, where Moses is said to have 'spoken unadvisedly' with his lips.

as the Gentiles do, the prayer life of the pagan world at the time consisted very largely of a number of incantations and magical formulae, many of which have survived in the papyri recently discovered. The object of magic is to control the powers that govern the world of nature, the exact opposite of Christian prayer, the object of which is to learn and to be conformed to the will of God.

6⁹⁻¹⁴. *The Lord's Prayer* (Lk. 11²⁻⁴).

1. A digression in this place because it intercepts the rhythmical

structure of the strophe, which is resumed in verse 16. The Lord's Prayer is not so much a new prayer as a fresh idea of the meaning of prayer, as the outward expression in the simplest terms that we are dependent upon God. Private prayer assumes in Christianity the character of a personal conversation or colloquy with our Father; an earnest calling on and longing after God rather than mere petition, in which we may bring before God the various needs of our life, become more clearly conscious of our sonship to God, and exercise that relationship. In public, Christian prayer tends to assume the form of thanksgiving; for which reason the Lord's Prayer has always been accorded a leading place in the Christian Liturgy, the Eucharist, or Service of praise and thanksgiving.

2. The Lord's Prayer is Jewish in language and thought. In the *Shemoneh esreh*, or eighteen Benedictions, known as the 'Tephillah', which is found in the Talmud and somewhat later than the time of our Lord, there occur the words 'Thou art holy and thy name is holy; Forgive us, our Father, for we have sinned'. Similarly in the Jewish Liturgy called the Ḳaddish, a late collection of older prayers, we find 'magnified and hallowed be Thy great Name; may His kingdom reign'. And again the Jewish morning prayer has the clause 'And cause us not to come into the hands of temptation'.

3. The prayer has come to us in two main forms: (1) the Matthean, intended for public worship; in which it is also found in the ancient Christian liturgical manual called the 'Teaching of the twelve Apostles'; and (2) a shorter form, with some variant readings, in Lk. 11¹⁻⁵, more suited for private use, as its context, a quiet moment with the disciples, indicates. The variations in the text, which are many, are probably not due to the individual evangelists but indicate the various 'uses' of the 'paternoster' in different neighbourhoods. Both in its Lucan and its Matthean form, however, the Prayer is the clearest example we have of the 'form-history' of the sayings of Jesus (see Appendix, p. 264); for it has been preserved and to some extent shaped by the deepest needs of the Christian Church, that of Mt. representing perhaps the form used in the Eucharist and Lk's that used in Baptism. The Doxology (v. 14) is not found in any of the ancient MSS.—it is plainly a liturgical addition which rounds off the prayer in a powerful and well-sounding phrase.

6⁹. *Our Father which art in heaven.* Luke has simply 'Father', our Lord's own word, as also that of the first Christians who used the Aramaic word Abba = father (Rom. 8¹⁵). The addition 'who

art in heaven' is used in Mt. no less than twenty times with slight
variations, and was widely prevalent in Rabbinic circles. There is,
however, all the difference in the world between the use of 'Father'
as a title of honour (of Jupiter or Zeus) in Greek and Roman
religion, and in Judaism of Jehovah the nation's father (cf. Isa. 63¹⁶)
and the 'our Father' of the Christian Community, which has lost
all the national exclusiveness of the Jew and the mythological
ideas of the heathen. 'He who calls God his Father confesses
thereby his belief in the forgiveness of sins, the remission of punishment, in the justice, the sanctification, the redemption, the adoption, and the title of inheritor of the Kingdom as well as that of
brother of Him who is the unique Son of God, and in the guidance
of the Holy Spirit' (S. Chrysostom).

Hallowed be thy name. 'Holiness' in the O.T. signified
transcendence, inaccessibility, and separateness from men, that
which used to be called in English 'awfulness' (Lev. 10³, Isa. 6³,
40²⁵). In Ezekiel this concept of holiness develops into that of
absolute moral perfection (36²¹⁻²⁵) and it is in this sense that it is
found everywhere in the N.T. The only possible attitude towards
such transcendent holiness is reverence, the atmosphere in which
alone the soul can grow. The petition, therefore, is a prayer for the
reverent recognition of God's sovereign rights over all things by
ourselves and all men.

The *name of God* means God Himself Who, though transcendent,
reveals Himself to men and permits them to enter into personal
relations with Him. Thus God is said in the O.T. to put His name
among His people (Deut. 12⁵⁻¹¹) and they are said to be called by
His name (Jer. 14⁹). In the N.T. the word is used for the revelation of God in Christ, the disciples are said to have asked nothing
hitherto in Jesus' name, i.e. they have not yet come to realize in
their prayer the new and wonderful revelation which God has given
of Himself in His Son Jesus Christ (Jn. 16²⁴).

6¹⁰. *Thy kingdom come*, see additional note **D** (p. 187).

Thy will be done. This petition, rather than the preceding
one, is a prayer for the enlargement of the area of the world under
God's acknowledged government. It is possible that it is a conscious adoption on the part of the community of our Lord's own
prayer in the Garden. In any case the phrase '*Thy will be done*' is not
a formula of resignation as it is so often found on tombstones, but a
prayer for the full accomplishment of God's purpose. The phrase
'*as in Heaven, so on earth*' belongs to all three preceding clauses
which thus descend by this link from God and His attributes to

the social order in which they are to be realized in man, who thus becomes the centre of the remaining petitions.

6¹¹. *Our daily bread*, Gk. τὸν ἄρτον τὸν ἐπιούσιον. According to Origen the adjective was unique in Greek literature and a coinage by the Evangelists to represent an Aramaic word meaning 'of the day' (Prov. 27¹). 'Daily', therefore, is probably right and is supported by Mt.'s insertion of the word 'today' in place of Lk.'s 'day by day'. The phrase would naturally mean 'belonging to the morrow' (ἡ ἐπιοῦσα), but this can hardly be the meaning here, for that would contradict the spirit of the prayer which is to let the morrow look after the things of itself. But there is no reason why it should not mean 'the day which lies before us', for which there are good parallels in classical and later Gk. Jerome, translating it literally into Latin, is responsible for the Vulgate's *panem nostrum supersubstantialem*, i.e. our sacramental food; but the same writer translates it by the word *cotidianum* in the corresponding place in Lk.

6¹². *Our debts*. The idea of sin as a debt was thoroughly Jewish and passed into the currency of Christian thought. 'To pay the price of sin' has been a very common interpretation of the Atonement in Christian thought, pre-eminently in that of S. Anselm according to whose teaching the work of Christ was to discharge a debt due to God which no human being would ever have been able to pay. So in Aramaic the word for 'debt' (*hôbā*) is often used for 'sin'.

6¹³. *Bring us not into temptation.* As the fifth petition presupposes a feeling of unworthiness, so the sixth assumes a sense of weakness and a need of watchfulness, as Jesus enjoined on his disciples in the Garden (26⁴¹). The petition is a truly human one, suitable for disciples who realized that the last difficult time through which they must pass would be a sure test of their faithfulness. This does not mean that God puts temptation in our way (cf. Jas. 1¹³), but that the possibility of falling away from God is necessarily involved in our position as men whom God has created with free will, that we may offer Him a free and not an enforced service. On the truth of this thought hangs the whole Christian doctrine about the existence of Evil and Suffering, and ultimately the entire Christian teaching about God and His purpose for the world.

Deliver us from the evil one, Gk. ἀπὸ τοῦ πονηροῦ. See note on verse 5³⁹. This petition is found in Mt. only; and is more than a repetition of the sixth petition, for it asks for complete and final deliverance; not only for help against falling away, but as the

Didache puts it 'from all evil', or, as in the Jewish prayer, from the evil *yeṣer*, or impulse in our own heart; and for translation into the kingdom of God's peace and love. It is a noble ending, and it is difficult to believe that if Lk. had known it he would have left it out. (For further discussion of the Lord's Prayer see Bp. Gore, *Sermon on the Mount*, pp. 128 ff.; Bp. Chase, *The Lord's Prayer in the Early Church*; and F. D. Maurice, *The Lord's Prayer*.)

6$^{16-18}$. *Fasting.* Our Lord assumes that His followers will practise fasting as a natural act of piety though he excuses its omission for so long as the bridegroom is with them (Mt. 9^{15}). It is certainly true that all great masters of the spiritual life, whether Christian or non-Christian, have felt the necessity of at least a certain amount of ascetic practice especially in the matter of food, which it is most difficult for a man to deny himself. At the same time, in Christianity asceticism has never been regarded as an end in itself or as conferring a title to merit, but always as a discipline and a means of serving God better. In the Christian Church 'fasting' has been restricted to the technical meaning of one full meal only in the day, and that usually towards the evening. Anything less, such as meatless days, is known as Abstinence. From the time of the Didache at least the Church on the authority of this verse has enjoined on its members days and seasons both of fasting and of abstinence.

6$^{19-34}$. *The Christian Rule with regard to creatures* (Lk. 11$^{34-36}$, 12$^{22-31}$, 16^{13}).

After speaking of the relation of the Christian towards God as summed up and expressed representatively in prayer and religious observances, our Lord turns to the second great element in human life, all those things which do not come under the category either of God or our neighbour, those external things which God has given to man for his use or enjoyment: food, drink, clothing, health, position, money, all that it can buy, property, all those things which are included under the name of 'creatures'. The Christian attitude towards creatures expressed in the Sermon on the Mount may be summed up in the word 'detachment'. Christianity has never condemned any of these things. It has warned men against their abuse, and has from time to time declared the use of some particular thing to be against the Law of God or social expediency, but it has never been a religion of mere disapproval. It has acted on the belief that S. Paul has as usual correctly interpreted his Master, and that all creatures of God are to be used with thanksgiving only with due care lest by the selfish or tactless use of any creature we put an occasion of stumbling in the way of our brother (Rom. 14, 1 Cor. 8¹¹, 10²⁵ ff.).

6¹⁹⁻²⁵. *The Christian law of Property*. The Christian is forbidden to amass or hoard wealth. On the contrary, the most complete generosity is required in the words ' If thy eye be single thy whole body shall be full of light, but if thine eye be evil [i.e. *niggardly*], thy whole body shall be full of darkness'. In the same way there must be no question about the true proportions of life. If you make wealth your master it will be your ruling passion, there will not be room for any other. Moreover, any such hoarding of property has for its underlying motive a secret fear of poverty, which is an affront to God who if He has given the greater gift of life will not withhold the lesser gift of what is needed to sustain it. Therefore the Christian is not to make the acquirement of property his end or even a major objective of life. It is not, however, said that he may not hold nor enjoy property. On the contrary, the teaching of Christianity has been that a certain amount of property is necessary to every one for the due development of personality in accordance with the will of God. There have been saints, like S. Francis of Assisi, who have embraced poverty in order to be more like Christ 'who became poor', but it was found necessary even for the mendicant orders eventually to hold property. Prophets, such as Tolstoi who became convinced of the sinfulness of all possessions, have never been accepted by the Christian Church; and for many centuries Christianity, with its doctrine of detachment and of temperance with regard to creatures, fought the heresy of Manichaeism which taught that material things are evil.

6¹⁹. *rust*, Gk. βρῶσις, means the act of eating by mice or vermin of wealth stored up in barns. The precept is illustrated by a vivid picture of oriental wealth in the form of garments or carpets stored in barbaric abundance too numerous for use. Jesus is not only thinking of man's impotence to protect his property against the depredation of insects and robbers, or as one might say his capital from depreciation in an economic world that is beyond his control; but of the fact that possessions draw the heart after them.

6²⁰. *break through*, Gk. διορύσσουσι, i.e. dig through a wall of mud or plaster. Aristophanes (Plut. 565) uses the same word of thieves and burglars.

6²¹ *your heart*. In Jewish phraseology the heart includes the intellect as well as the emotions.

6^{22}. *The lamp of the body is the eye.* Like the heart, the eye in Hebrew was the symbol of the intelligence. Just as a sound eye (Gk. ἁπλοῦς, single) lightens the body, so the heart, if it is in heaven with God, places a man and all that he does in communion with God and with His blessing. But the contrary is also the case— as the destruction of the eye deprives the body of light so also the heart when it is apart from God and filled with selfish desires which Nature offers, plunges the whole man in darkness. It is doubtful, however, if we have in Mt. the original context of the saying. It is placed in an equally unsuitable position in Lk. 11^{34}. But interpreted in the context in which Mt. has placed it, the meaning of 'single' can only be 'simple', in the sense of generous; and evil (Gk. πονηρός) must mean niggardly as in Deut. 15^9. The writer of the First Epistle of S. John understood the words in the same way. 'He that loveth not his brother walketh in darkness,' i.e. all his judgements are warped, and by 'not loving the brother' he understands to mean 'shutting up his bowels of compassion from him' and only *wishing* him well (1 Jn. 3^{17}).

6^{24}. *mammon.* The word is not found in the Hebrew O.T. but occurs once in the Apocrypha (Ecclus. 31^8) and is found in the Aramaic Targums as equivalent to various Hebrew words meaning 'property'; not necessarily wealth but possessions of any kind. The personification in the text probably led to the medieval idea that there was a god named Mammon, like Beelzebub.

6^{25}. *Is not the life more than the food?* The words are misunderstood if they are taken as a contrast between feverish activity and care-free inactivity. The contrast of which Jesus is speaking is a very different one. Either the dominating purpose of a man's life is 'survival', in which case his whole concern will be how to earn and increase the means of his livelihood; or a man has got the love of the Father, in which case it is no longer the satisfaction of natural needs which is his prevailing concern; and, while he asks for his needs, he does so in the consciousness that his life is not precious for its own sake but for the service of God and man.

6^{25}. *life,* Gk. ψυχή, the life-principle common to man and beast. It does not mean the soul or the term of life which is given to us on earth.

6^{27}. *being anxious,* Jesus does not merely mean disquietude, which may be a matter of temperament, but the careful calculation of ways and means towards a given end. Hence the A.V. 'take no thought' is really better as a translation. No amount of 'thought' can add a day to his allotted span.

stature, Gk. ἡλικία = age, as in R.V. margin. In the same way *span*, Gk. πῆχυς, can mean equally well a short interval either of space or time.

6^{32}. *After all these things do the Gentiles seek.* No words better describe the deep inner cleavage between Christian prayer and pagan prayer at its best. Even in so highly a developed form of religion as Stoicism in the time of Cicero, we find prayer but a very little distance removed from what it was when it first emerged in the form of magic on to the plane of human history as an attempt to induce whatever powers there were supposed to be to conform themselves to the desires of man and to supply his material needs. 'We do not pray to Jupiter', says Cicero,[1] 'to make us good but to give us material benefits. . . . We must pray to God for the gifts of *fortune* but wisdom we must acquire for ourselves.' The Christian conception is exactly the opposite. It teaches that human virtue is always and everywhere dependent on God's grace; while to attempt to seek to bend His will to our own it regards as blasphemous, so that the Christian is bidden at all times to remember that he is necessarily ignorant as to whether material goods are in accordance with God's will, and so must always pray for them with that reservation. Above all, Christian prayer recognizes that God's love and care for us is manifested quite as much in what He withholds as in what He gives. (For the whole subject of Christian prayer in contrast with pagan religion see Canon A. L. Lilley, *Prayer in Christian Theology*, S.C.M.)

6^{32}. *Seek ye first*: 'ask for and live as looking for' (McNeile). Mt. adds his characteristic idea of 'righteousness' which is absent from Lk., emphasizing, as we should expect him to do, the 'good works' without which the Kingdom is not to be expected, and of which the Sermon on the Mount is the epitome for the Christian.

7. *The Christian Rule of prudence. Precepts for the Christian in the world.* Lk. 6^{37-49}.

7^{1-6}. *Judgement of others.* Lk. (6^{37}) places this saying in close connexion with the command to love enemies to which it naturally belongs, for such heroic virtue can never be attained without cultivation of the more humble and homely virtue of charity in our judgements of others. Schlatter sees in the words as recorded in Mt. a direct prohibition to Christians to use the law-courts either against one another or against enemies; in which case Paul's

[1] Cic. *De Offic.*

stern rebuke of the Corinthians for this kind of thing would, as so often, be an echo of the words of Jesus (1 Cor. 6¹). The words which follow indicate that God will judge those who infringe this command. More probably the saying in Mt.'s context is a warning to the Christian missionary against imprudent and tactless denunciations of pagans or any among whom he works.

7³⁻⁵. So also with the more intimate relations of the Christian with his less well-instructed brother. Cure your own blindness before offering treatment to others. For the Christian, it has been said, the sight of sin in others is an occasion not for interference but for intercession.

mote, Gk. κάρφος, a piece of dried wood or straw, Lat. *festuca* or *stipula*. '*Hypocrite*', the brother who so acts is a hypocrite, because his censorious and interfering criticisms usually take the outward form of a kindly action.

7⁶. *Give not that which is holy unto the dogs.* A further warning against indiscreet activity. While he is warned against censorious judgement of others the Christian must use discrimination and reserve in his teaching. The law of reserve in imparting religious knowledge has always been regarded as of the utmost importance in the Christian Church. This interpretation receives support from the use of this logion in the Didache as forbidding the admission of the unbaptized to the Eucharist, and by the Christian writer Tertullian who blames heretics for having so admitted them. The warning 'Lest they turn again and rend you' describes the violence of religious enemies who have learned enough of the teaching to use it as a handle of persecution. For the same reason Catechumens were not taught the words of the Creed until the night before their Baptism to minimize the risk of the *regula fidei* becoming known to enemies. 'Holy things for holy people' is a phrase taken from this saying, which is found in the earliest Church Liturgies. At the same time there is nothing mysterious or esoteric in the teaching of Christianity.

7¹¹, ¹². 'With these warnings go forward optimistically with your missionary work. Expect much and you will receive much.' The words 'ask and ye shall receive' are not *in this context* an encouragement to earnest prayer as in Lk. 11⁹⁻¹³ so much as an exhortation to take the best measure of humanity and place a generous trust in it. Look for good and you will find good.

7¹². '*Whatsoever ye would*'—the Golden Rule sums up the teaching of this section—men expect to be treated with kindness, trust, and decency, and without patronage, and will usually respond to it. The word applies not only to ordinary dealings with men, but also, and even more, to the duty of giving them the 'good things', i.e. the best things, the Gospel, and spiritual religion which God has ungrudgingly given to the Christian himself. Other forms of the Golden Rule were well known. Hillel said, 'What is hateful to thee thou shalt not do to thy neighbour: this word is the whole law and all else is commentary'. The positive form, however, is the highest, and appears to be our Lord's own coinage. It has been restated in the great truth which was announced by the philosopher Kant, 'So act as to treat humanity, whether in thine own person or in that of any other, in every case as an end withal, never as a means only'.

7^13-15. *The two ways. Prudence for your own salvation.* The parallel passage in Lk. 13^23, 24 speaks only of a door well-nigh shut. 'Strive to enter in at the narrow door', in answer to the question 'are there only a few that will be saved?' This is the Q form of the saying. Mt., in his usual way, has conflated this saying with another about a *'way'*. In accordance with the best MS. authority the second 'gate' after 'wide' should be omitted and we then have a clear reference to a way of *life* and a way of *death*. It is not a door, as in Lk., giving entrance to a festive hall, but a gate at the entrance to a road, common in ancient cities like Jerusalem. The saying is not, as in Q, an eschatological reference to the doomed, but an allusion to the facts of life. The number of those who are ready to impose on themselves a serious moral and religious discipline is at any time very small. 'The way', in the sense of a doctrine of conduct, an ethical discipline, is common both in Semitic and in Greek literature.[1] Christianity is called a 'way' in Acts 9^2, and the doctrine of the 'two ways' became a commonplace of Christian ethical teaching in the early Church. (See Additional Note B, p. 150.)

7^15-23. *Prudence in the discernment of spirits in teachers, prophets, and exorcists.* This is one of the passages alluded to in the epistles of S. Ignatius who used the words with reference to the Docetic heretics, i.e. those who denied that Jesus Christ had really come in the flesh and believed that he was in appearance only.[2] The Didache has even more elaborate tests for discerning true prophets from the false. Who were the prophets here referred to? (See

---

[1] Jer. 21^8, Ecclus. 21^10, Ps. 119, cf. Didache, 1-6; Hesiod, *Works and Days*.
[2] Ignatius, *Phil.* 2. Cf. Acts 20^29, 1 Jn. 4^2.

Additional Note C.) The logion in this context is an exhortation to deal energetically with fraudulent and dangerous elements in the Church at the end of the first century. Drastic action is required and enjoined in the contemporary document, the Letters to the Seven Churches (Rev. 2^{20}).

7^{21}. *Lord, Lord.* The invocation of Jesus as Lord (Gk. κύριος) was a feature of the primitive Church, especially in the Hellenistic communities with which S. Paul was familiar. It is he who gives a vivid example of prophecy 'in the Name', 'No one can make the solemn affirmation "Jesus is Lord" but by the Holy Ghost' (I Cor. 12^3). The Aramaic equivalent is *Maran*, which survives as a cult-name in the same Epistle (I Cor. 16^{22}).

7^{22}. *By thy name*, so also with the practice of exorcism in all its forms, e.g. in Christian Baptism. As Professor Heitmuller, who has minutely investigated the cult-formulae of the early Church, remarks, 'we have to do with no mere allusion to the Messiahship of Jesus but with a belief in the real mystical secret potency of the invocation, a real belief in the possession by Christ through the power of the " Jesus-name ", establishing an inner communion with the Owner of the name'. The invocation of the name 'Jesus Christ' over the candidate for baptism stands in closest connexion with the idea of the heavenly 'Lord', and implied that the baptized person passed over into the possession of the Divinity invoked, Who not only bound him from that moment to an unconditional allegiance but also took him under the protection of His divine power, so that he passed from the power of the gods and demons to the lordship and protection of Christ. The invocation was said in a loud voice and may have been uttered by the candidate, as well as by the minister; possibly also facts from the life of Christ were associated with the name, the beginnings of the future creeds (I Tim. 6^{13}). The invocation implied the expulsion of all hostile powers and consecration to a greater power; but in I Cor. 5^4 it appears as a terrible and potent weapon effecting the annulment of a previous baptism. We can imagine the tremendous feeling of assurance and protection, e.g. for a slave, afforded by the Christian 'name' at a time when men and women were at the mercy of every kind of tormenting fear and superstition as well as actual bodily and spiritual dangers on all sides.

$7^{22, 23}$. *I never knew you*, i.e. recognized your right to teach or minister in My name (cf. 2 Tim. 2^{19}).

7^{24-27}. *The two houses.* The sermon concludes with a final warning against the folly of a mere profession of Christianity which has no relation to conduct. Christianity simply is not that sort of religion, and any one who imagines it to be so is a fool.

A wise man, Gk. φρόνιμος. The prudent man, the subject of the whole section.

7[28]. The editorial conclusion after every one of the five books of Mt. is employed as a transition to the next. At this point the writer suddenly reintroduces the crowd, but in reality, as we have seen, it is the Christian community itself that is the audience of the Sermon on the Mount. The Evangelist now resumes his following of Mk. 1[22], to which he returns after having left him in 4[23].

NOTE B. THE SERMON ON THE MOUNT AND THE DEVELOPMENT OF CHRISTIAN ETHICS

To what extent did the Christian Church, especially in the early days, succeed in carrying the principles of the Sermon on the Mount into effect? It has been maintained by one school of New Testament critics that the moral teaching of our Lord, as recorded in the Sermon and elsewhere in the Gospel was what is called an interim-ethic, i.e. an ethical system intended to serve only for the brief interval that remained before the end of the world. It was never, therefore, intended for a normal state of society. This view of Albert Schweitzer and the eschatological interpreters of our Lord's life and teaching was itself a violent reaction from the liberal critics of the nineteenth century who, as Schweitzer said, had fashioned a Jesus out of their own social and political ideals. But in order to do so they found it necessary to 'weaken down many of the great world-contemning claims of Jesus in order to tune his denial of the world to our acceptance of it'... 'Consequently many of the greatest sayings of Jesus are found lying about in a corner like explosive shells from which the charges have been removed.'[1] The arguments by which Schweitzer, Johannis Weiss and their followers sought to maintain their view of Jesus as an apocalyptic visionary, proclaiming the immediate end of the present world order, have not been generally accepted by scholars. But they have drawn attention to an element in His teaching which though deeply embedded in the Gospel records had been very largely forgotten, the stern call to world-negation; the ascetic or rigorist element in Christianity. It was this element that in the early days was most decisive in its influence on all that was most distinctive in the Christian life.

[1] Schweitzer, *Quest of the Historical Jesus*, p. 398.

Attempts have been made to get rid of the ascetic element in the Gospels by dismissing it as an alien intrusion from Jewish or pagan sources into the otherwise gentle and homely teaching of the Master. Now there is no reason to doubt that Jesus did make use of apocalyptic symbolism in which to clothe certain truths for which there was probably no other adequate expression, e.g. the absoluteness of His claim, the need of completeness and decision in response to it, and the absence of all relative standards in His teaching. But the remarkable fact is that the great ascetic sayings in the Sermon and elsewhere, the command to turn the cheek, to take no thought, not to lay up treasure, to forsake parents, home, and possessions and to bear the cross are seldom in the gospels directly connected with the apocalyptic or Rabbinic background. Asceticism finds no place in the apocalyptic literature and its spirit is wholly alien from that of Rabbinic Judaism, which has always believed too much in the goodness of all God's creatures to be in any marked degree ascetic in outlook. Still more difficult is it to discover any relationship between the spirit of heroic renunciation which breathes in the gospel and the taboos and ceremonial abstinences of the pagan religions based on the doctrine that the body is evil. The ascetic element in the teaching of Jesus remains an enigma, inexplicable on any other ground than that it represents His own authentic teaching.[1]

In contrast with this aspect, and equally impossible to eliminate from Gospel records, is a world accepting or 'humanist' element in the teaching of Jesus. It is expressed in the love of nature and all God's creatures, of home, family, friendship, and of children and the common things of life which exists unmistakably in the gospels and especially in the Sermon on the Mount and in parables. It was this element which impressed itself on the minds of our Lord's contemporaries; 'the Son of Man came eating and drinking', and the contrast with the rigorism of John the Baptist was made a popular reproach against Him (Mt. 11[18]).

The problem involved by the presence in the same Gospel of these two apparently contradictory elements is reflected, as Dr. Kirk has shown, in the whole history of Christian ethics. 'It set going two streams of interpretation in the Church from the outset, one of which sought its ideal in the temperate use of all

[1] For the historical view of Christ, represented for instance by St. Mark's Gospel, which lies at the root of the ascetic side of the Gospel see Bishop Blunt's commentary on St. Mark's Gospel in this series, Introduction, pp. 49 ff.

God's gifts, and the other which demanded their absolute and their whole-hearted renunciation.'[1]

(1) In Catholicism an attempt was made to reconcile the two divergent aspects by means of the doctrine of the dual standard, that is, the division of the moral teaching of Christ into the *counsels* intended only for the ascetic few and the *precepts* binding upon all. It was regarded as possible for a Christian, without loss of status, to aim as it were, at a 'pass degree' in the spiritual life, without seeking honours. It is possible to see the beginning of this doctrine in Mt.'s version of the story of the Rich Young Ruler, in which a distinction is drawn between keeping the commandments or 'precepts' for which the reward is eternal life, and the 'counsels' of perfection for which the condition is total renunciation (Mt. 19[20-21]). It is not probable that this distinction goes back to our Lord Himself, but it has been remarked that the distinction probably saved Christianity because it was the only way to reconcile the ascetic minority in the Church to the presence in it of those content with a good though moderate standard, and so preserve within the Church the element of other-worldliness so necessary in times of acute secularism. Historically this distinction has taken the concrete form of the 'two lives', the *religious* or monastic life with its vows of poverty, chastity, and obedience, and the vocation to serve God in the world, called the *secular* life. There is nothing wrong in the doctrine of the dual standard, provided that it is clearly understood that *all* have an equal vocation to the higher standard, though not all have an equal capacity to attain it. After the Reformation Puritanism attempted to solve the problem in a different way, by trying to force all, irrespective of their capacity, on to the rigorist standard. Puritanism, however, was a religion of disapproval rather than of renunciation of the world. While it has commanded the admiration of mankind and purified and ennobled national life it can scarcely be said to have embodied the attractiveness of Christian asceticism in the way that men like St. Francis of Assisi have never failed to reveal it to all generations.

(2) Whenever Christianity has found itself confronted by a world fundamentally hostile or indifferent, the rigorist element in Christian ethics has prevailed. In the early days martyrdom was not only bravely endured, but eagerly sought. Celibacy was regarded, as early as St. Matthew's Gospel, as proof of a higher stage

---

[1] See K. E. Kirk, *Vision of God*, p. 68.

in the spiritual life and is advocated by St. Paul (Mt. 19¹², 1 Cor. 7).
It was some centuries before any relief was granted in the severity
of the penitential discipline of the Church. At the same time there
is nothing in the teaching of our Lord in the N.T. to justify the
extreme austerity involving a callous disregard of all human relationships which made its way into the Church in the fourth
century, probably under the influence of gnostic Manichaeism,[1] as
illustrated in the famous letters of St. Jerome to his companions.
Genuine Christian asceticism has never, like that of Hinduism or
Paganism, been practised for the sake of self-annihilation, or in
the belief that the body is evil, but always as a discipline of the
soul and as a protest against materialism in the world. Understood in this sense rigorism stands for something without which
Christianity cannot be complete or maintain its freedom. It is
the salt which purifies and preserves, and it has had a decisive
effect in raising the moral standard of the world, though perhaps to-day it has fewer advocates than at other periods of
Christianity.

(3) By far the most constant tendency in Christian ethics has,
however, been neither the rigorist nor the humanist element, but
a type of moral discipline known as formalism, i.e. the legalist
view of behaviour, which delights to prescribe duties as conditions
of membership in the Christian Society, and leaves little if anything to the judgement of the individual conscience. The tendency
to codify and systematize the Christian ideal has been present
from the first. Matthew himself, as we have seen, was a Christian
legalist. But within a few years legalism had become as great a
feature of Christianity as it had been of Rabbinic Judaism.[2] To
a certain extent this was inevitable. Because Jesus Himself had
none of the entanglements of home or of business life to complicate
the problem of morality His ideals needed to be translated into the
terms of ordinary life. This is what is meant by casuistry. And
just as in the face of a hostile world Christianity has always dis-
played its rigorist aspect, so when its interests have been mainly
pastoral it has tended in the direction of formalism and of a

[1] The belief that matter is evil, involving a dualism like that of the
Persian Mazdaean religion.

[2] The only code which can with certainty be attributed to Jesus, the
Beatitudes, is a code not of actions but of dispositions, and the same is true
of the list of virtues in St. Paul's Epistles (Gal. 5²², 1 Cor. 13, Phil. 4⁸). These
however, together with the household codes (Col. 3¹⁸, Eph. 5²², 1 Pet. 3),
appear to be 'catalogues' only, following the practice of the rhetoric schools
of the day, rather than attempts to codify Christian Ethics.

'casuistry designed to keep within the fold as many as by a stretch of charity can be called Christian'.[1] In the sub-Apostolic age the tendency to formalism developed rapidly. Begun in the *Didache* and other sub-apostolic works, like the *Shepherd of Hermas*,[2] which had enormous influence, this process was continued in successive Church orders and Councils, in penitential books and tariffs, in which the peculiar genius of British Christianity was specially conspicuous. It culminated in the tremendous achievement of the Canon Law, both in its eastern and western forms, 'in which the Church is all but assimilated to the model of a secular society.' It can hardly be denied that formalism altered for many centuries the whole balance of Christian theology by putting into the background that emphasis on faith and grace which is the distinctive feature in the teaching of Jesus as understood by His great interpreter S. Paul. It has had a disastrous effect on the doctrine of the Atonement, which has been dominated throughout by legalist and semi legalist theories. It was formalism that led to the two great protests in Christianity, that of S. Augustine against Pelagianism which was nothing else than 'Judaism with a thin veneer of Christian phraseology', and that of Luther against the system of Indulgences. Neither of these protests succeeded in delivering Christian ethics from the bondage of formalism into the freedom of the Spirit. The old formalism survived in the casuistry of the Jesuitical schools which called forth the protest of Pascal at the end of the seventeenth century; while Protestantism in Calvinism became involved in a system of 'combined rigorism and formalism' of which at the present day only the latter survives, and has been on the whole responsible for the prevalent idea in England that Christianity is merely a name for a particular type of moral practice 'in which the external moral life of a man tends to be separated from his religion'.[3]

Perhaps in no respect is the fundamental weakness of the formalist element more clearly seen than in the disruption of the economic system of Europe under the medieval Church, the only organization that has ever sought to control the social and eco-

---

[1] For the views here expressed see K. E. Kirk, *Vision of God*, pp. 7, 55-94, 122-73.

[2] In both of these works, as also in the so-called Epistle of Barnabas, there appears in slightly different forms the Christian code adapted from Judaism called the *Two Ways*, in which there is already found not only complete lists of virtues and vices, but the application in detail of general principles to the conduct of life.

[3] Bp. Strong, *Bampton Lectures*; quoted by K. E. Kirk, *op. cit.*, p. 429.

nomic conditions of the western nations. One of the results of the Reformation was the rise of an economic individualism, which had no relation whatever to the ethics of the Sermon on the Mount, and which developed into the unrestrained competition of modern capitalistic industrialism. The failure of the medieval system to survive has rightly been attributed by Professor Powicke to its formalist character. 'Its weakness lay in its paganism', by which he means 'the acquiescence in a merely professional Christianity unaccompanied by the sustained religious experience of an inner discipline'.[1]

Finally it was the four cardinal virtues of Greek ethics, justice, temperance, fortitude, and prudence, rather than the Sermon on the Mount, which through the influence of the great doctors of the Western Church, Ambrose and Augustine, became the foundation of the ethical education of the barbarian nations, the chief contribution of the Catholic Church to European civilization. Building on this basis, the greatest of the medieval teachers of the Church, S. Thomas Aquinas, sought a reconciliation of the rigorist and humanist elements in Christianity in the idea that the human passions are not to be extirpated, but educated and harmonized by the spirit of Christ; and the Christian life is represented as the perfection by supernatural assistance of every natural endowment rather than as obedience to a formulated code. It is on these lines that Christian Ethics have very largely developed in modern times. (For further discussion of this question see K. E. Kirk, *Vision of God*. E. Von Dobschutz, *Christian Life in the Primitive Church*.)

SECOND BOOK OF MATTHEW

8–11¹. Concerning Apostleship.

The second book of Matthew is addressed to a more restricted audience than the first. It was compiled as a handbook to meet the needs of the ordained Evangelist or prophet, or as he was sometimes called 'Apostle' in that wider sense of the word with which S. Paul was familiar (2 Cor. 11¹³, 12¹¹, Rom. 16⁷). The discourse itself (10⁵–11¹) is prefaced by an introduction consisting for the most part of Marcan material, but so arranged as to show the qualifications for 'apostleship', the chief work of which is the

[1] *Legacy of the Middle Ages*, p. 31; K. E. Kirk, *op. cit.*, pp. 3–5. For another view, R. H. Tawney, *History of Capitalism*, pp. 1–79.

manifestation of the power of Jesus. (1) He must show capacity for that faith which alone can fit him for the task of what we should call to-day a medical missionary, the faith which can work miracles (8¹⁻¹⁷). This, along with exorcism, constituted one of what S. Paul called the signs or credentials of an Apostle (2 Cor. 12¹²). (2) He must be prepared to endure hardship as a good soldier of Jesus Christ (8¹⁸⁻²²). (3) He must be able to pronounce with conviction the 'word' of the Gospel and of forgiveness without doubt or hesitation, so that all men may know that the 'Son of man hath power on earth to forgive sins' (9⁶). Hence we have narrated for the benefit of these itinerant evangelists a series of ten mighty works designed to convey the lesson of a wonder-working faith. These fall into three distinct groups: (1) three typical examples of Jesus' healing mission authenticated by prophetic scripture (8¹⁻¹⁷). (2) A second group consisting of a series of three works of superhuman power manifesting the authority of the Son of man and rising to a climax in the supreme claim to pronounce forgiveness of sins (8²³, 8²⁸, 9⁶). Between this group and the first Mt., as if to call attention to the supernatural character of a vocation to the ministry to which they have been called, has inserted an account of two vocations (8¹⁸⁻²²). (3) The third group, prefaced by the story of a vocation to apostleship given and perfectly responded to, is again designed to show the necessity of faith, but it is here not so much the faith of the worker as of the recipient that is emphasized (9⁹' ¹⁸⁻³⁴). Mt. brings Part I of this book to a conclusion by repeating the words of 4²³, descriptive of the ministerial activity of Jesus, making a tour of the cities and villages, teaching in their synagogues, preaching the gospel of the Kingdom, and healing all manner of sickness and all manner of disease among the people. The order is different from Mk.'s, but the only passages omitted by Mt. are the Sabbath conflicts (Mk. 2²³–3⁶) and the saying about the spiritual kindred of Jesus. (Mk. 3³¹⁻³⁵) which he reserves appropriately for the next book.

A. INTRODUCTORY NARRATIVE.

(1) *First sign of healing,* vv. 1–4 (Mk. 1⁴⁰⁻⁴⁵); as in the other miracle stories of this book Mt. omits all the vivid Marcan details.

8⁴. *See thou tell no man.* Why? if, as it appears, the miracle was done in the presence of a crowd. Clearly Mt. does not know any more than Mk. The command has come down to them as part of an already fixed tradition which they only repeat. Whole theories about a Messianic secret have been built up upon this simple command, which

as the corresponding passages in Mk. indicate (1⁴⁵) was probably only
a precaution to which Jesus was at the time driven merely by the
limits of what is physically possible for one man to cope with in the way
of medical work.

shew thyself, Lev. 14²ᶠᶠ. Our Lord could cleanse but not 'pronounce
clean', which was the prerogative of the priest, to whom our Lord
always showed respect. But at the same time by touching the leper
(v. 3) he allowed the ceremonial law of uncleanness to give way before
the higher law of love and sympathy.

for a testimony unto them, not of the cleansing, that they would have
to investigate for themselves; but to prove that the mighty power of
the Kingdom was present to heal, and that that power was not hostile
to the Law and offered no challenge to it.

(2) *Second sign of healing*, vv. 5–13. Apparently from Q because
not in Mk, but in Lk. 7¹⁻¹⁰. The incident is a good example of
the paradigm or 'pronouncement' saying of Jesus (see Appendix,
p. 266) and is recorded with the minimum of detail because the
whole point of it is to emphasize and preserve the saying of Jesus
in verse 10.

8⁸. *I am not worthy*, Gk. ἱκανός, the word occurs only in Mt. and in
Lk. 7⁶, an indication that both are dependent on a single written
source. The words which follow mean 'I, even I, a non-commissioned
officer, have soldiers under me and know what it is to receive obedience
to a word of command, but Jesus is obviously subject to no human
authority'.

8¹². *sons of the kingdom*, a Semitic idiom = those who should
inherit it, i.e. the Jewish nation.

(3) *Third sign of healing*, vv. 14–17.

8¹⁶. *when even was come*, implying as we learn from the corresponding passage in Mark (1³²) that it was the Sabbath and the people
waited till it was over.

8¹⁷. *Himself took—bare*, Gk. ἔλαβε—ἐβάστασεν, Isa. 53⁴, a citation
from the Aramaic source and differing from the Septuagint. The
passage was regarded by the Jews of a later day as a Messianic prophecy, and understood as referring to real sickness which the suffering
Servant took upon Himself as a substitute for the punishment of
others.[1] Matthew sees in the prophecy a reference to the healing work
of Jesus, perhaps understanding by the words 'taking' and 'bearing'
the removal of them, for which there is evidence in medical Greek.

---

[1] *The People and the Book*, p. 410; Strack-Billerbeck, vol. i, pp. 481 ff.
See also G. H. Box, *St. Matthew* (Century Bible), p. 154, who quotes from the
Gemara of the Sanhedrin references to the work of the Messiah among the
sick.

8^{18-22}. *Vocations given and refused.* These incidents are a good example of the unchronological character of Mt.'s Gospel. Lk. has placed them where they must certainly belong at the close of the Galilean ministry (Lk. 9^{57-60}), in the period of the last journey to Jerusalem at a time when Jesus had literally nowhere to lay His head. At present, according to Mt., He had at any rate the use of a house in Capernaum (9^{28}). Of the two, one offers himself for permanent companionship without a vocation, the other delays to accept a vocation which has been given. Lk. adds a third example with the remarkable logion of Jesus attached to it (9^{62}).

8^{20} *Son of man.* See Additional Note G on eschatology. The writer throughout this section obviously intends us to understand by the expression the divine claim of Jesus; but originally it may have been equivalent to the Aramaic *bar nāshā*, cf. Ps. viii. 4, where the expression = man in contrast with the beasts of the field.

8^{21}. *suffer me first,* an allusion to the pious duty of burial of parents, so sacred that it dispensed from the recitation of the Shema (cp. Tobit 4^3, 6^{14}).

(4) *First sign of power.* vv. 23-27 (Mk. 4^{36-41}, Lk. 8^{23-25}). For a comparison with the Marcan narrative see Introduction, p. 10.

8^{26}. *O ye of little faith,* Gk. ὀλιγόπιστοι, a very characteristic Rabbinic word peculiar to Mt. It has a close connexion with the idea of authority which the whole section is designed to convey.

8^{27}. *the men marvelled,* i.e. the general public, who heard it, for as Mk. says other ships were with them. Mt. avoids putting the amazed question into the mouth of the apostles. They knew who He was.

(5) 8^{28-34}. *Second sign of power, the Gadarene demoniacs* (Mk. 5^{1-20}, Lk. 8^{26-39}). 'A vivid picture of delusional insanity told from the standpoint of the contemporary belief in demons.' (Rawlinson.) In Mk. the story is told with a 'certain gusto' which is wholly absent from Mt. who relates the exorcisms which he finds in Mk. but does not accept his uncanny theory of the evidence which the demons afforded to the Messianic claim of Jesus. For the whole question of demoniac possession in the ancient world see Rawlinson,[1] who remarks that the demonology of the Gospel is one of the specific marks of its attachment to the popular mind of the period. For the modern man the whole apparatus of demons and their work has passed into the region of myth. To the primitive Christians demons were immensely real things and belief in them

---

[1] *S. Mark*, pp. 63 ff.

was the most pressing and insistent of all beliefs excepting only the belief that Christ could conquer them.

Various explanations, none of them very satisfactory, have been given of the story of the swine, and it has been denied that it has any foundation in fact at all, or that there is any connexion between the miracle of healing and the story of the swine, which may well have been a popular tale attached to a rather unpleasant and sinister neighbourhood. Critics who trace an historical nucleus of the story generally assume that at this point the maniac took the disposal of the unwelcome tenants of his personality literally into his own hands by driving the swine into the water. The story of the swine involves no moral problem because, whatever our Lord's belief about demons, He was in no case a dabbler in magic; and the stampede of the swine, regarded as property, was not due to any action on His part, nor was it, in any case, of the slightest importance in comparison with the supreme victory, the restoration of a human being to sanity which was cheap at the price, and rid the community of a perpetual menace to its safety. It may be noted that the spot indicated in the mountain is the deep gorge of Jarmuk to the south of which lay Gadara, an inland Greek town of Decapolis, about thirty miles south-east of the lake. The whole district is called Gadaritis by Josephus. It was a spot admirably adapted to an uncanny legend of the kind attached to this story.

8²⁹. *torment us before the time*. According to the apocalyptic writings evil angels and demons while awaiting judgement were already imprisoned, but some were set free at times on earth to tempt men (Enoch 10¹²⁻¹⁴, 15¹⁶, Book of Jubilees 10⁸, 2 Pet. 2⁴).

Son of God. A title used of Jesus by the 'demons' (Mk. 3¹¹, Lk. 4⁴¹). It means one possessed with divine power, but was not a usual designation of Messiah.

8³⁴. *depart from their borders*, from superstitious fear of the presence of magical powers.

(6) 9¹⁻⁸. *Third sign of Power. The absolution and healing of the paralytic.*

At this point Mt. resumes the *order* of Mk. after a very long departure from it (Ch. 4). Mt., however, again changes the Marcan story which is intended to be a great example of the *faith* of the man and his friends, into a 'paradigm' designed to embody the unique saying at the conclusion 'the Son of man hath power on earth to forgive sins'. These words imply a claim beyond that of wonder-working power, and in consequence arouse the opposition of the Scribes to the point of attributing even the latter to demoniac agency. It was common ground that the forgiveness of sins was an exercise of a prerogative belonging to God alone. The Rabbis were quite accustomed to pronounce the forgiveness of sins in the name of Jehovah. But our Lord does so in His *own name* and authority; just as He does not *receive* power to perform miracles as the Rabbis claimed to do, but, as they were now beginning to realize, performs them *in His own name* (Mt. 12²⁷⁻²⁸). Hence His work must be either the Kingdom of God already present among them or that of the devil; there is no alternative; they chose the latter (9³⁴). This miracle, as recorded in Mt., is clearly intended to exhibit the authority of the Son of man not only in Himself, which he takes for granted, but as transmitted to His representatives on earth (Mt. 9⁸). For this reason he carefully alters Mk. 2¹², who merely remarks on the amazement of the crowd.

9². *Son of Man.* This recurring phrase, used here for the first time in Mt., is a literal rendering of the Aramaic words 'Bar Nāsha', which would simply mean 'the man', Gk. ὁ ἄνθρωπος. Actually in certain passages in the Gospels it was not so translated, because it had acquired an 'apocalyptic' meaning. In the Book of Daniel (7¹⁵) it is used as a kind of ideogram for the 'Saints of the Most High', who should 'possess the Kingdom', while in the Book of Enoch (Similitudes 37–71) it refers to a mysterious pre-existent Being (see Note K, p. 241). Our Lord probably adopted it from the latter source to express the mystery of His Person, and His supreme authority over men; and St. Paul confirms this in his description of the Lord as the 'second Adam' and the 'Man from Heaven' (1 Cor. 15⁴⁵ ᵃ·, Rom. 5¹⁶).

9⁸. *such power unto men*, Gk. ἐξουσία, 'authority', cf. Jn. 20²³. The clause, 'I believe in the forgiveness of sins', would not have appeared so early in the Christian baptismal Creed had it not been for the conviction of the Apostolic Church that its messengers and stewards have this power. S. Paul undoubtedly claimed it (1 Cor. 5⁵, 2 Cor. 2¹⁰).

9⁹⁻¹⁰. *A vocation to Apostleship.* Mt. here substitutes the name of Matthew for that of Levi, the son of Alphaeus, in Mk. 2¹⁴, Lk. 5²⁷; for the problem involved see note on p. 163.

9⁹. *place of toll*, Gk. τελώνιον. The great road leading from Damascus to the Mediterranean skirted the northern end of the lake and it is at this point that there was a frontier-station between the territories of Antipas and Herod Philip where customs were levied on exports, chiefly of fish from the lake.

9¹⁰⁻¹³, a paradigm attached to the call of Matthew.

9^{11}. *sinners*, with reference to Gentiles, as in Gal. 2^{15}, and to people like the 'publicans' who were forced to incur defilement by association with them. The final and authoritative answer to this vexed question in the early Church is given, as Mt. saw it, in his Fourth Book (15^{10-15}).

9^{13}. *I desire mercy*. 'Study Hosea's words for they contain the principle on which I work.' From Hos. 6^6 agreeing with the Hebrew against the LXX, as in Mt. 12^7, where the words are again ascribed to Jesus.

9^{14-17}. Two further 'paradigms' attached to the vocation of Matthew.

Fasting was unnatural for the disciples of the Messiah during His days on earth when He was actually exercising the powers of the kingdom, the manifestation, as Paul called it, of righteousness, joy, and peace in the Holy Ghost (Rom. 14^{17}). On the other hand, with the Baptist in prison, or already dead, the feeling of his disciples was natural. The parable of the old coat and wine-skins suggested to the early Church not only the incongruity between the old and new, as represented by John and Jesus, but the danger, very real at the time, of *schism* in the Christian movement occasioned by the dispute between the Gentile and the Jewish Christians. The point of the saying, therefore, is that the old Jewish practices were to be respected while not forced upon the Gentile; thus will both be preserved within the fold of the Church. Our Lord's words evidently imply the necessity of some bounds for the new wine even though they may not be the same as the old. Hence the interest of such a saying to a writer like Mt. in compiling a manual for evangelists. After the example of the Lord they are to exercise the widest tolerance in the problem that confronts them. As we have seen, there is reason to believe that the Church, for which Mt. wrote, acted on this principle. (Introduction, p. 3.)

9^{14}. *the disciples of John*. We read a good deal about these men in N.T. (Jn. 1^{35}, 3^{25}, 4^1, Acts 18^{24-26}, 19^{1-7}). Probably they played a larger part in the history of the early Church than our records admit (see further on 14^{1 ff.}).

9^{15}. *sons of the bride-chamber*. A Hebrew expression for the wedding guests. As so often in Mt. the days of the Messiah are depicted under the image of a wedding feast.

9^{16}. *a piece of undressed cloth*. Literally a patch of an uncarded strip of cloth, i.e. not cleaned by carding or combing, hence undressed.

rent, Gk. *Schisma*. An ominous word which very soon took on a technical ecclesiastical meaning and is already so used in the epistles of Ignatius.

9¹⁷. *new wine, fresh wine-skins*, Gk. *neos*—*kainos*, both words mean 'new', but *neos* = recently made, *kainos* = of a new kind, such as has not existed before as in Mt. 26²⁹ and Heb. 9¹⁵, 10²⁰.

(7 and 8) 9¹⁸⁻²⁶. *First and second signs of faith. The Ruler's daughter and the woman with the haemorrhage* (Mk. 5²²ᶠᶠ·, Lk. 8⁴¹ᶠᶠ·). The first of these is evidently regarded by Mt. as a case of resuscitation, but the obviously authentic words of Jesus 'she is not dead but sleepeth' forbid any such view.

9¹⁸. *ruler*, Gk. ἄρχων. The word seems to imply any rich or important man, such as a ruler of the synagogue. Mk. and Lk. give his name as Jairus.

9²⁰. *border of his garment*. Gk. κράσπεδον, the sacred part of the garment. The garment itself was a large piece of linen or wool covering the whole body, the loose end of which hung over the left shoulder and the tassel attached to the end was the border or hem which the Pharisees were taught to enlarge (Num. 15³⁸, Deut. 22¹²). As in 9², 'Courage, daughter'.

9²³. *Minstrels.* Common accompaniments of a funeral in Palestine, where a great deal of money was spent on funerals even among the poor, as in England to-day.

(9) 9²⁷⁻³³. *Third sign of faith. Two blind men*, Mk. 8²²⁻²⁶, Lk. 18³⁵, duplicated as in the case of the demoniac of Mk. 5¹. See Introduction, p. 11.

9³⁰. *strictly charged them.* Gk. ἐνεβριμήθη, a much stronger word than the English implies, used of the snorting of horses and the raging and fury of men. Our Lord sternly rebukes the men for taking upon their lips a popular cry with the idea perhaps that it might flatter without realizing or accepting its implications.

Mt., as usual, conflates two distinct stories. It is, however, odd that while the narrative as a whole is similar to that in 20³⁰ᶠᶠ· (Mk. 10⁴⁵), the last part, vv. 30 and 31, is clearly a reminiscence of Mk. 1³³⁻⁴⁶, the healing of the leper.

(10) 9³²⁻³³. *Tenth and last mighty work. A dumb demoniac.*
This miracle provides a setting for the saying in 9³⁴.
As they went forth, i.e. the blind men.

9³⁵⁻10⁵. *The ordination of the Twelve* (Mk. 3¹³ᶠᶠ·, Lk. 6¹³ᶠᶠ·).

According to Mk. this belongs to an early date in the public life of Jesus and was due to the necessity of delegating work which was now beyond the power of a single individual. The importance of the step as implying the foundation and authority of a permanent ministry by our Lord as His gift to His Church is plainly indicated by the solemnity with which in all three Synoptics the occasion is surrounded and of which Luke is thinking when he speaks of the Lord making choice of the Apostles through the 'Holy Spirit' (Acts 1^2).

Little is known of the majority of the Apostles or of their subsequent history. The Fourth Gospel shares with the apocryphal Gospels the desire to record something more of them as personalities. But even the identity of some of them is doubtful, notably that of Matthew himself, who is here identified with the publican of 9^9. In Mk. 2^{14} the name of the publican is Levi, the son of Alphaeus, who appears to be called as a fifth Apostle after Andrew, Peter, James, and John, and yet in the list of Apostles a few verses farther on, 3^{14-19}, Levi does not appear. Lk. follows Mk. without commenting on this strange phenomenon. On the other hand, the ninth Apostle in Mk.'s list is called 'the son of Alphaeus', of whom nothing further is said. Desiring to correct this apparent confusion the 'Western'[1] text of Mk. 2^{14} has substituted 'James' for Levi as the name of the tax collector. This is an evident piece of harmonization, for the same Western text adopts a similar reading in Mt. 10^3. On what authority then has Mt. substituted Matthew for Levi, the son of Alphaeus, as the tax collector, and added to the name of Matthew in his list of Apostles the title of 'the publican'? The Alexandrian scholars, Clement and Origen, refused to accept this identification, and in spite of the decisive influence of Mt. on all subsequent versions, it is difficult to justify. According to Bacon, no examples exist of two Jewish names such as Levi and Matthew being given to the same person. Zahn does give examples of such double names, but Mt. would surely have recorded, as he always does, such a surname if it had existed. Accordingly, it is possible that the ascription of the name *Matthew* to the tax collector was based on the list of the Twelve in Mt. 10^3. This list differs in important particulars from Mk.'s, especially in the addition of the title '*the publican*' to the Apostle Matthew. This may originally have been inserted in the margin by a scribe; and while, intended to belong to *James the son of Alphaeus*, was gradually taken into the

---

[1] The name given to the readings of the MS. D. (Codex Bezae) at Cambridge, which appears to have much in common with many of the Latin versions of the N.T. and what is called the Heraclean Margin, a correction of the old Syriac version with similar characteristics.

text and attached to the wrong name. Bacon conjectures that this mistake was the ultimate cause of the strange identification. Ever afterwards it was supposed that the Evangelist was, as it were, whispering in the reader's ear, 'I am the real Levi of whom Mark relates this; I had two names, one Levi, the other Matthew.' The Gospel of the Nazarenes made use of this identification by suggesting that Matthew wrote that Gospel because from his profession he alone of the Twelve could write and was therefore given the task of delivering 'the testimony to Israel'. If this explanation is correct then Matthew is no more than a name to us. (For the bearing of this statement on the ascription of the Gospel to Matthew see Introduction, p. 18.)

A similar obscurity surrounds the name of *Thaddaeus* for which the D text, together with Origen and Augustine, reads *Lebbaeus*. Other MSS. combine both and make another double name. The Sinaitic Syriac, however, reads instead of Thaddaeus, 'Judas the son (or brother) of James,' i.e. the Judas, not Iscariot, of Jn. 14²² (cf. Lk. 6¹⁵). Again an unauthorized identification has been made; but Christian tradition knows of Thaddaeus (in connexion with the story of the conversion of Abgar of Edessa, see Introduction, p. 22), as one not of the Twelve but of the Seventy. In the same way Mk. 14¹⁰ speaks of Judas Iscariot as 'one of the Twelve' as though to distinguish him from a Judas called Thaddaeus (or Lebbaeus), who was not one of them. Origen indeed speaks of 'Lebbaeus the publican', which J. Weiss thinks represents an early attempt to bring Levi within the number of the Twelve. It is odd that there should not have been a reliable list available anywhere of so important a body as the Twelve. That in itself is evidence that the name 'apostle' was not from the first confined merely to the number of the Twelve (see Additional Note D).

10². The name apostle, Gk. ἀπόστολος, Heb. *shaliach*, does not mean merely one who has a message or news to bring, but a plenipotentiary who in virtue of the powers imparted to him represents in person his superior's authority. 'A man's shaliach is as it were himself' (Talmud).

Simon Peter. See Additional Note E.

James and John, surnamed Boanerges, sons of Thunder with reference to the incident in Lk. 9⁵¹ (cf. Mk. 3¹⁷).

Philip, like Peter and Andrew, was of Bethsaida, in the north-east corner of the sea of Galilee (Jn. 1⁴⁴).

Bartholomew, a son of Tolmai. Nothing whatever is known of him, but he is said by Eusebius to have brought the Gospel to the Nazarenes of north Syria. His identification with Nathanael, Jn. 1⁴⁵, if it had ever been suggested, would have been certain to have found its way on the analogy of Levi and Matthew, Thaddaeus and Judas, into lists of the Twelve. His body is said to rest in the church of that name in Rome.

Simon the Cananaean. Lk. has 'called Zelotes'. The word Cananaean is connected with the Hebrew word *Kana* = to be zealous. Thus Phinehas, the hero of the incident in Num. 25, is called in 1 Macc. 2^{54} 'zelotes'. It may, therefore, only indicate a feature in his character. Dalman, however, thinks that the original form was *Kannaios* = a Zealot in the sense of a member of the political party. But it is not certain that the party known by this name to Josephus was in existence in the time of our Lord.

Iscariot = a man of Kerioth.

B. THE ADDRESS TO THE BEARERS OF THE APOSTOLIC COMMISSION

10^{5}–11^1 (Mk. $6^{7\,ff.}$, Lk. 9^{1-6}, 10^{1-16}).

The composition of this discourse illustrates even more than the Sermon on the Mount Mt.'s *topical* arrangement of his material. He has lost sight at the end of the discourse of the occasion with which he began it. The nucleus is the original charge to the Twelve, vv. 5–14, which stood in Q. But a totally different situation is presupposed in the verses which follow. The first of these interpolated passages warns of persecution (vv. 16–25), the second encourages martyrdom and fearless confession of the Name (26–33). The horizon 'extends temporarily to the second coming and geographically to the end of the earth' (Bacon). The compiler of the Gospel has ceased to be an historian and has become the preacher of his own age using certain well-known and authentic sayings and predictions of Jesus uttered on many different occasions. Among these some were undoubtedly uttered at the Last Supper as the parting words of Jesus to his disciples. According to Luke and John, Jesus did then give just such warnings, predictions, and promises to Apostles, notably (in a highly detailed form in Jn.) the promise of the Comforter (Jn. 14, 16, Lk. $22^{28,\ 32}$, cf. Mt. 10^{19-20}). Others have been taken from the great eschatological discourse on the Mount of Olives in Mk. 13^{9-13}, where Mt. in the parallel passage 24^{4-11} condenses and paraphrases Mk., refusing to duplicate material which he had already used in this discourse. No reference is made to the return of the Apostles because at verse 16 Jesus is no longer addressing the Twelve but all who should be their successors in the work of evangelization. The outlook of the Christian missionary, as Mt. sees it in this discourse, is in every respect identical with that enjoined in the Pastoral Epistles for the work of an Apostle or Evangelist; cf. 2 Tim. 1^6–2^{13}, with its exhortation to 'stir up the gift' that 'is in thee by the laying on of my hands'; to endure hardship, to rebuke false teachers, to emulate the fortitude of those who like the Lord and His Apostles had given their faithful witness before governors and kings.

10^5^. *Go not into any way of the Gentiles.* The origin of this logion, which is peculiar to Mt., is unknown, but it seems to come from the same source as the cryptic saying of verse 23 with which it would appear to be closely connected. Like that, it may have been part of that valedictory address to the Apostles at the Last Supper and may refer to the expected *parousia* of Jesus in or near Jerusalem. The saying explains the strange hesitations on the part of the Apostles, very imperfectly concealed in the records of Acts 8^14^ and 11^22^, towards the Samaritan and Gentile Missions, and the words were probably a weapon in the hand of those who wished to oppose them. The apocryphal work called 'The Preaching of Peter' has a saying which forbids a mission to the Gentiles until after twelve years from the date of the crucifixion.[1]

way of the Gentiles = roads leading to the circle of Hellenistic towns which surround Galilee, Scythopolis, Ptolemais, Tyre, Hippos, Gadara.

10^9^. *Get you no gold*, Gk. κτήσησθε = gain by earning, cf. Didache 11^1^. 'If he, the prophet, ask for money he is a false prophet.'

10^10^. *food*, Gk. τροφῆς, but Lk. has μισθός = pay, a word which Mt. has good reason to avoid because of the well-known abuses (cf. also 1 Tim. 5^18^). The Didache (c. xiii), as usual, follows Mt.

10^13^. *your peace.* The Apostolic benediction is no mere friendly greeting, but is regarded as having an effective existence like the ban in 1 Cor. 5^4-5^. It would settle on a house worthy of it, otherwise, like the 'curse causeless' in Proverbs, it would return and remain available for future use.

10^17^. *councils.* The local Sanhedrins of Palestine, as in 5^22^. The flagellation which was inflicted by them, usually with option of a fine, for breaches of discipline such as associating with Gentiles, consisted of a maximum of 40 stripes. It was five times suffered by S. Paul (2 Cor. 11^24^).

10^18^. *kings.* Herodian princes as in Acts 12^6^ and 25^23^; but the word could mean the Emperor himself before whom Paul, whose experiences the writer seems to have particularly in mind, was brought (2 Tim. 4^16^). The vivid description of a bitter persecution here given recalls the description in Tacitus (*Annals*, 15. 44) of the outbreak of the Neronian persecution in Rome in A.D. 64. He records that a great multitude was arrested on the information given by those who were first seized, the accusation, being hatred of the human race, of which the words 'ye shall be hated of all men' is a strange echo. This persecution made a tremendous impression on the minds of Christians. But the words 'for my name's sake' indicate that the persecutions

[1] M. R. James, *Apocryphal Gospels*, p. 17.

that Matthew had in mind were those of a date later than Nero and nearer that of Trajan, whose letter to Pliny refers explicitly to the charge of the *Name* of Christian only. 'I investigated whether they were *Christians.*' This is the whole burden of Tertullian's great apology on behalf of Christianity, that no other crime than 'the bare name' was ever preferred against the Christians.

10^{23}. *This city,* i.e. *Jerusalem.* Another strange oracle, like verse 6, peculiar to Mt. and of unknown but certainly Jewish-Christian origin. But, as J. Weiss remarks, this saying is not meant for the missionaries but for the Church as a whole, the community of the disciples. The two verses together prove that there were oracles current in the early Church attributed to Jesus or to the Spirit which warned the community not to desert Jerusalem as the head-quarters of the Christian movement; and if compelled by persecu-tion to leave Jerusalem temporarily to choose only a Jewish city. Another such oracle, known to Eusebius,[1] forbade the Apostles to leave Jerusalem for ten years after the Ascension. The strange fact that they remained there after the persecution that arose about Stephen may have been due to the existence of such an oracle. It was in obedience to yet another oracle that the Christian community deserted Jerusalem in A.D. 67 after the martyrdom of S. James, the Lord's brother, and fled to Pella, a Greek city, thereby escaping the horrors of the siege (see Mt. $24^{15,16}$, Mk. 13^{14}). But as Bacon remarks, whatever the temporary refuge permitted, the only interpretation of this strange verse which seems to do full justice to its implications is that which regards Jerusalem itself converted and purified as the permanent centre in view of the impending return of the Son of man. That is the reason why it is still for Mt. the Holy City, the city of the Great King as he calls it, with a world-wide position, the Mother and Mistress of Churches. In a real sense Jerusalem is still the centre of Christianity as its cradle and first home.

For Schweitzer's use of this logion in support of the eschato-logical interpretation of the public life of Jesus see *The Quest of the Historical Jesus,* pp. 357–63.[2]

[1] Eusebius, *H.E.,* 3. iv. 5.
[2] A variant in the D text has, 'when they persecute you in this city, i.e. Jerusalem, flee unto the other, and if they persecute you in that other flee unto another', that is to say, the head-quarters of the Church may pass from city to city as a temporary measure to avoid persecution, but only a Jewish city may be considered for the capital. This text would seem, according to Mt., when combined with verse 6, to rule out such Gentile and Samaritan centres as Antioch, Caesarea, or Rome.

gone through. Gk. τελέσητε, meaning 'exhausted', as possible head-quarters of refuge in Palestine.

10²⁵. *Beelzebub*, Gk. *Beelzebul*, this term of reproach is variously spelt and its meaning is doubtful. In the time of Jesus the form was Beelzebul = Lord of the lofty mansion, i.e. of the nether regions, as in 12²⁹, or the name of some powerful and important demon. But the lord of evil spirits in the Jewish literature of the time is called Beliar, not Beelzebul. The form Beelzebub or Baalzebub, which found its way into the English versions from the Vulgate, means 'lord of flies'.

10²⁶. *for there is nothing covered*. A challenge to open profession and proclamation of Christianity, 'bear witness bravely and publicly, for every thing that in your obscurity you have undergone shall be made known', 'preach fearlessly in spite of persecution for everything that I tell you in secret I wish you to proclaim openly and it will in any case become known'. (Cf. Lk. 8¹⁷.)

10²⁸. *soul*. Gk. ψυχή, has three meanings in N.T. (1) the life principle common to man and animals as in 6²⁵; (2) the seat of thought and feelings, sometimes expressed by *kardia* or *pneuma*, as in Mt. 10³⁹, Lk. 14²⁶; (3) the soul, something higher than either, as in 16²⁶ and in this passage. For the whole idea, see the striking parallel in Wisd. 16¹³.

10²⁹. *a farthing*, Gk. ἀσσάριον, from the Latin, = one-sixteenth of a denarius, which in the time of Nero, who depreciated the coinage, was equivalent to about ninepence halfpenny of our money, so that the farthing would be rather more than a halfpenny.

10³⁴, ³⁵. Probably in contrast to the words of Malachi 4⁶ describing the reconciling work of the returning Elijah. The division created in the Jewish nation by the apostolic preaching was the first example of the truth of our Lord's words. Social strife, however, was a common-place of apocalyptic literature in describing the last days.

10³⁷. *He that loveth*. Lk. has an even stronger expression, Lk. 14²⁶.

10³⁸. *take his cross*. It was doubtless a common sight, for a con-demned criminal had to carry the cross beam (Lat. *patibulum*) to the place of execution. A Rabbinic writing says that Isaac took the wood for the offering 'as one who bears his cross upon his shoulders' (Gen. 22⁶).

10⁴⁰. *He that receiveth you*—the address reaches a conclusion no less sublime than that which ends the eschatological discourse in Ch. 24. The words themselves are a solemn asseveration of the divine authority of the apostolic ministry. It is these words that Clement, Bishop of Rome, A.D. 95, had in mind in a famous passage in his Epistle to the Church of Corinth which had dared to eject its presbyters from their office (xlii. 1–4):

'The Apostles received the Gospel from the Lord Jesus Christ, Jesus Christ was sent from God. Christ therefore is of God and the Apostles from Christ.'

10⁴¹. *He that receiveth a prophet in the name of a prophet.* 'In the name of' = *as such*. The meaning is that the motive of the action must be to desire to honour the prophet or righteous man with the honour which is their due and not to secure the reward. In the teaching of Jesus it is only those who are prepared to follow Him from some other motive than that of reward, 'for My sake and the Gospel's', who are promised any further reward.

10⁴². *one of these little ones*, obscure believers engaged in missionary work, not children. As Schlatter remarks, 'if one reads this chapter, all disparaging talk about Jewish Christianity ceases'. There is a moral greatness in the type of Christianity here depicted which was manifested not only in the great missionaries of the Church, the Apostles, Prophets, and Confessors, but in the simple and obscure believers, the little ones of Christ, of whose weakness much is said in the N.T. but of whose great and single-hearted heroism little is elsewhere recorded. Cf. Mt. 18⁶ and S. Paul's words in Rom. 14.

NOTE C. THE APOSTOLIC MINISTRY

Who are the persons addressed in this discourse, who appear in the N.T. under the various names of Apostles, Prophets and Evangelists, and Teachers? If we read only the Gospels and the Acts of the Apostles we find the word 'Apostle' used exclusively for a member of the college of the Twelve chosen by Jesus to be with Him and to act as His delegates in the Galilean Mission and afterwards in the carrying on of His work after the Ascension, especially in the witnessing to the Resurrection and in the government of His Church. Generally speaking the dominant conception at the end of the first century of what was meant by an Apostle was that which is expressed in the *Apology* of Justin Martyr (A.D. 150), 'from Jerusalem men twelve in number have gone out into the world and though uneducated and without facility of speech, by the power of God have made known to the whole human race that they were sent by Christ to teach all men the Word of God'.[1] To which may be added the famous passage of S. Clement already quoted, and the words which follow, 'Both therefore came of the Will of God in the appointed order'. 'So after they had received their credentials and were confirmed in the faith by the Resurrection of Jesus Christ they went forth and announced the Kingdom of God.' The word 'apostle' itself is a Jewish name for the diplomatic agents

[1] *Apology*, i, 39.

of the High Priest, who received the contributions of the dispersed Jews for the maintenance of the temple, or conveyed his letters to the synagogues. We find S. Paul acting in both these capacities, either before or after his conversion (2 Cor. 3[1], Acts 9[2], and 28[21]).

Side by side with the Apostolate in the strict sense of the word, there is evidence of a wider use of the term in S. Paul's epistles and in the ancient Church writing, called the 'Teaching of the Twelve Apostles' (the Didache), a document either of Antioch or of some Syrian church. While claiming the name of apostle for himself, in the narrower sense, as in every respect an equal of the Twelve, S. Paul names several others as apostles, e.g. James, the Lord's brother, Barnabas, Silvanus, Timotheus, Andronicus, and Junias.[1] Thus it is probable that the name was used in a wider sense for any duly accredited missionary, and in this sense doubtless Barnabas was so named after his separation and ordination as a missionary by the Prophets in Acts 13[1].

Alike in S. Paul and in the Didache the Apostles in this wider sense are found closely associated with the 'Prophets'. In Eph. 2[20] the Church is said to be built upon the foundation of the Apostles and Prophets, and in 1 Cor. 12[28], together with the teachers (as in Acts 13[1]), they form the leading trio in the list of the *charismata* or gifts of the Spirit to the Church. This seems then to be the case also in Mt. 10[41]. At first the Prophets who are frequently mentioned in Acts (11[28], 13[1]) appear like the Apostles to be a separate category of ministers, having power to ordain others and presumably themselves also ordained. But the term is used in a wider sense again by S. Paul in 1 Cor. 14 where the term is applied to any one exercising the gift of tongues or of preaching. By the time of Mt. (7[15], 10[41]) the meaning of the word has gone far beyond that of the Acts and has come to mean travelling missionaries, who appear to exercise a sort of universal ministry in the Church, as we find them doing in the Didache, which applies many strange tests in order to distinguish the true and false prophets (c. 3). If, for example, such a travelling missionary stays longer than three days or in an ecstatic trance says anything about a 'table' being prepared for him, he is no prophet but a *'Christ-monger'* and to be sent packing. Some prophets, according to the Didache, which is our only contemporary evidence, were allowed to 'give thanks', i.e. to celebrate the Eucharist or the Agape, of course to preach, but there is no evidence that such prophets or apostles ever exercised

---

[1] 1 Cor. 9[5], Gal. 1[19], 2[9], 1 Thess. 2[6], Rom. 16[7].

discipline or administered the Church except when authorized to do so, as Timothy and Titus were given by S. Paul such power in his own churches of Ephesus and Crete.

For some years after the discovery of the Didache, which created a great stir at the time (1883), it was thought by Harnack and other eminent authorities that in the primitive Church two kinds of ministry existed side by side, one belonging to the whole of the Church and only in part and occasionally localized, and another which was never anything but the local executive of a particular community. Of these, the first was thought to be a charismatic ministry or a ministry of grace of direct divine appointment—the latter an ordained ministry chosen by the community to administer its own affairs. It was thought that the Didache represented a most important movement in the development of the Church's constitution, when the charismatic ministry, consisting of Apostles, Prophets, and Teachers, was on the point of 'passing on its ancient and supreme authority and bequeathing it to the administrative classes of Bishops and Deacons'.

Now it is clearly a fact that there was in the primitive Church a ministry with a kind of roving commission, which even in the second century still looks like a sort of rival of the regular ministry, as the 'Confessors' afterwards came to be regarded;[1] but, as Dr. Armitage Robinson has pointed out, to imply that the local ministry was not a gift or charism of God to the whole Church and so to depreciate it in comparison with the prophets and other teachers is to go beyond anything of which the N.T. gives any hint. Nor is there any reason to suppose that these 'prophets', other than S. Paul and the Twelve and those authorized by them, in any way superseded the regular resident ministers in any place whither they had gone. Their duty was to go from place to place confirming the Churches (Acts 15[41]). And this is what we find them doing in the Didache. Nor is there any reason to assume that they were not, like Barnabas and Paul, 'ordained', in addition to exercising whatever gifts of the Spirit they might happen to possess.

How far were any of these ministries permanent? The apostolic differed from the prophetic office in that it could be handed on or delegated to others, as S. Paul did in the case of Timothy and Titus. There is no evidence that the expectation of the end of the world prevented the early Church from making permanent provision

[1] Confessors were Christians who suffered imprisonment for their faith.

for the continuance of the ministry. In the dark years which followed the close of the N.T. canon, it is known that Christians everywhere turned to the apostolic churches, i.e. those believed to have been founded by the Apostles in the belief that all that was essential to the apostolic ministry would be provided by them. It was always believed that the Apostles themselves had provided for its continuance. We find evidence for this in the Epistle of Clement of Rome who wrote a letter to the Christian community at Corinth, which had recently ejected its senior presbyters from their office. After the sentence which has been already quoted on p. 169, Clement goes on to say that the Apostles went forth preaching the Gospel. 'As they preached up and down the countries and cities they appointed their first-fruits, after having tested them by the Spirit, to be trusted as bishops and deacons of those who should come after them. . . . For this reason, therefore, they appointed the aforesaid officers and made further provision that if they fell asleep other proved men should succeed to the ministry of the presbyters in question.'[1] But in fact all the essential forms of the ministry were from an early date already to hand, and like many other things in Christianity were taken over from Judaism. There is no reason to doubt that an order of ministers, not essentially different from those afterwards known as deacons, was early instituted by ordination at Jerusalem (Acts 6[6]). At the same time or a little later we find already existing at Jerusalem, without any explanation offered, officers called presbyters who sit with the Apostles in council (Acts 15[2]), and afterwards are found in every place where a Christian Church has been founded. S. Paul ordained such in every city and gives an important address to those at Ephesus (Acts 14[23] and 20[17]). In the latter place they are named 'bishops', which looks very much as though that were the Hellenistic equivalent for the Jewish term Elder. J. Weiss, however, suggests that these presbyters at Jerusalem were originally elected and ordained as representatives of the Jewish population as a counterpoise to the deacons who represented the interests of the Hellenistic element. Whatever the exact facts about their origin, this order of Presbyter-Bishops was continued everywhere in the Church and there is no question that it was the element from which the permanent ministry was universally

[1] Ad Cor. xlii. 1–4, xliv. 1–3. A statement which shows that the Roman Church, at any rate in the first century, believed that the foundation of the Ministry was due to the instruction received from Christ by his Apostles.

and in unbroken succession derived. (For the evidence and discussion of the questions involved see Swete, *Early History of the Church and Ministry*.)

THIRD BOOK OF MATTHEW

THE MYSTERY OF THE KINGDOM OF HEAVEN: ITS HIDING AND ITS REVELATION

The third book of Matthew is intended for a wider circle than the last. Its purpose is to instruct Christians about the nature and the ground of the promises made to them in that faith. The Christian Church now possesses both the 'Spirit and the gifts' formerly vouchsafed to Israel alone. At the close, therefore, of the proclamation of the Gospel by Jesus throughout all Galilee and its further dissemination by the mission of the Twelve, the Evangelist naturally proceeds to an account of the rejection of that message by Israel 'after the flesh', which has 'stumbled' at the word, and of its reception by the 'remnant', the true Israel, afterwards to receive the name of 'my Church', the people who prove themselves to be of the true kindred of Jesus by hearing and doing the will of God (12^{50}). The evil generation seeks only for a sign, and no sign will be granted to it save the sign of the Prophet Jonah, i.e. the same preaching of repentance in view of impending doom and judgement (Mt. 12^{38-45}). In other words Mt.'s third book is apologetic just as the second is evangelistic. Its object is to give assurance to the members of the Church now separated beyond hope of reconciliation from Judaism, and to enable them to 'be ready always to give an answer to every man that asketh a reason of the hope that is in them' (1 Pet. 3^{15}).

Naturally Mt. begins with the defence of Jesus against those who impugned His authority and blasphemed His word, for which purpose, deserting Mk. (except for the two anecdotes about the Sabbath held over from the last book), he utilizes a passage from Q in which the claim of Jesus to be the supreme revelation of God reaches a sublime climax unsurpassed in the N.T. (11^{25-30}). Meanwhile the question which all the Synoptics place at this point in the narrative, 'Art thou he that cometh or do we look for another?', reveals the real issue involved in the Christian preaching. At a later stage Mt. will return to ask the further question which so much troubled Mk., Why did not all believe at once in so wonderful a teacher? Why did some stumble at the word? (13^{1-23}.) But before adding the second part of the Book, the discourse in parables, Mt. brings out the full meaning of the claims of Jesus in three decisive pronouncements. (1) The doom of the unrepentant cities of Galilee, 11$^{20\,ff.}$, in the same way as he concludes Bk. V with a pronouncement of doom on unrepentant Israel (25^{46}). (2) The sentence of spiritual death on those who wilfully call light darkness and good evil (12$^{22\,ff.}$). (3) The solemn transfer of Israel's privileges to a people bringing forth the fruits thereof (12$^{46-50}$). We note in this book the deeply rooted belief common to Israel and Christianity that God gives, and man is able to receive, a Revelation; Christianity adds that the Revealer and the Revelation must be alike divine if they are to reveal the character of God to man (11$^{25\,ff.}$).

A. Introductory Narrative.

11$^{2-10}$. *The relation of the Baptist to Jesus* (Lk. 7$^{18\,ff.}$).

According to 3^{14}, Mt. must have understood by this question that the Baptist had become once more doubtful about the Messiahship of Jesus, because His public appearance did not accord with the idea which he had formed of His office. Jesus accordingly administers to him a serious rebuke for which He afterwards compensates in the face of the people by words of exalted praise.

There is, however, probably more than meets the eye in the question. The disciples of John, who appear to have been a numerous and to some extent organized sect of Judaism, and even John himself evidently held aloof from the movement of Jesus and His disciples. Wellhausen thinks that here and elsewhere in the N.T., especially in Jn. 3$^{22-36}$, Acts 19$^{1-6}$, we have a glimpse of an early dispute and gradual estrangement between the two sects of Judaism, one destined to increase and the other to decrease: the followers of John claiming priority both in time and importance for their master, and the disciples of Jesus maintaining that John was only the forerunner. Jesus in His reply announces the presence of a time of healing predicted by the great anonymous Prophet of the Exile which has already broken in upon men (Isa. 61$^{1-3}$), but He adds significantly 'not the time only, but also the man', with whose lowly appearance they must not be offended.

11^{2}. *in the prison.* According to Josephus (*Ant.* xviii. 5. 2), in the fortress of Machaerus on the east of the Dead Sea. For the cause of his imprisonment and death see 14$^{3-12}$.

11^{3}. *he that cometh.* Not so far as is known a recognized title of the Messiah; but used here, as Klosterman suggests, with a secret application of apocalyptic language, such as that of Dan. 7^{13}. In the primitive

Church it became a regular title of the Christ, perhaps owing to our Lord's own words 'I am come'. (Mt. 9¹³, Jn. 10¹⁰.)

11⁵. *the blind—the deaf.* The challenge of the Book is here disclosed, the contrast between Israel after the flesh, the Servant of Jehovah who is both blind and deaf (Isa. 42¹⁹), and the poor who hear the word of God and receive the blessings of the kingdom.

11⁷. *What went ye out into the wilderness to behold?* Obviously the masses had not gone out into the wilderness, the ancient scene of Theophanies, to look at an everyday occurrence. Nor did they go to look for manifest impossibilities, so great an ascetic become a courtier. Indeed it was on account of his rigorous attitude to Herod that he was actually at that moment an inmate in a king's palace.

11¹⁰. *Mal. 3.* In the LXX and Heb. the words are 'before my face', where it is a question of a messenger whom God will send before His own face to prepare the way, i.e. a Messiah or Messianic figure.

11¹¹. *he that is but little.* John is by far the greatest of mankind in virtue of his prophetic office, but the standard of comparison has been altered by the entrance into the world of a new thing. We do not know what the context of the saying originally was, but it can hardly be likely that Jesus intended to exclude John from the benefits of the kingdom now already in His own Person and Power present among men.

11¹². A very difficult passage and like the last can hardly have been spoken by Jesus in the present context, or in the lifetime of the Baptist. Three explanations have been suggested: (*a*) That of J. Weiss who takes the words as a sort of 'aside' on the part of the Evangelist, meaning 'the old saying of Jesus "the kingdom of heaven suffereth violence", always so hard to understand, has indeed proved true from the days of John the Baptist until now' (A.D. 90); and the reference is to the persecution which the Church is still suffering at the date of writing. (*b*) That the kingdom is being violently seized by those who think that the Messianic blessings are political in character and hope to obtain them by a rebellion against Rome such as that of Judas the Gaulonite in A.D. 6 (Acts 5³⁷). This is the most probable meaning of the original saying, the occasion of which is lost beyond recovery. It referred to some Zealot rising of which we have no knowledge. Jesus had such politically minded men among his immediate disciples, one of whom was Judas Iscariot (Bacon). (*c*) The reference is to the Galilean multitude who by their enthusiasm are storming their way as it were into the Christian movement, breaking violently down the barriers of Judaistic particularism. But there is no evidence that they ever were doing this: rather there are signs of doubt and disillusionment on the part of the crowd, which perhaps since the arrest of John has undergone a subtle change.

11¹³. *all the prophets*. Their line ended with John who heralded the kingdom which they only foretold. Hence the reference in the following verse, for the prediction about Elijah in Mal. 4⁵ forms the conclusion of the portion of the O.T. called the *Prophets*.

11¹⁶. The picture of the children playing alternately at weddings and funerals, with the usual quarrels that follow any suggestion as to what they should play, suggests a change in the temper of the people who now react neither to John nor Jesus but are indifferent to both. But the application of the parable either in this or the Q context (Lk. 7³²) is doubtful. The words in themselves suggest an antiphonal song game among the children themselves, the point of which is now lost.¹

11¹⁹. *Wisdom is justified by her works.*

(1) What is the meaning of this expression and (2) what is the reason for the change from or to Lk.'s 'of all her children'? (Lk. 7³⁵). As to (1) the 'Wisdom' is clearly the personified Wisdom of the poetical books of the O.T. and Apocrypha known as the Wisdom literature (cf. Job, Prov., Eccles.) in which it appears as a designation of God Himself in His divine purpose and action as disclosed in creation and history. The meaning of the words will then be 'God in his purpose and action for man as revealed to Israel through the prophets and now still more in his Son is justified, as against the growing opposition of the Pharisees, by works of power of which so many wonderful examples have been given and which are the standing condemnation of the cities of Galilee which witnessed them'.

As to (2) Lk.'s version is probably the genuine one, if only because of the O.T. use of the expression 'Sons of Wisdom' (Prov. 8³², Ecclus. 4¹¹), i.e. those who are obedient to her words and share her nature. Mt. may have substituted 'works' for 'children' because his whole argument is directed to the mighty works as evidence of the divine claim of Christianity.

11²¹. *Woe unto thee, Chorazin*. The fact that in spite of this severe judgement not a single event in the Gospels is recorded as taking place at Chorazin and very few at Bethsaida, illustrates the fragmentary character of the records and the uncertainty as to the place where any particular event happened. Chorazin is the modern Korizon or Cherazeh. Burkitt however suggests that it is a concealed form of the name Nazareth. (See note on Mt. 2²³.)

Bethsaida, house of fishing or game, the modern Et-Tell. Herod Philip gave it the name and dignity of a city and called it Julias after

¹ See G. H. Box, *Century Bible*, p. 197.

the name of Caesar's daughter (Joseph. *Ant.* xviii. 11. 1). It stood on the east side of Jordan about a mile north-east of the point where it runs into the Lake. The old town may, therefore, have stood on the shore of the lake which probably at that time extended farther north than at present.

Tyre and Sidon, two cities in O.T. times full of wealth and wickedness, and denounced by Isaiah and Ezekiel under the image of a gallant ship (Am. 1⁹, Isa. 23, Ezek. 26).

11²⁵⁻³⁰. *The Ecstasy of Jesus*.

A great Christological passage (Lk. 10²¹, ²²). 'Mt.'s Pearl of Great Price' (Lagrange). 'In striking contrast with the sentence of doom upon the unbelieving cities, rings out the triumphant note of Jesus' thanksgiving for the revelation of the mystery of the Kingdom to the Son' (Bacon). Lk. places the ecstasy appropriately after the return of the disciples from their successful mission but omits the 'comfortable words'. But we are indebted here, as in other cases, to the editorship of Mt. who has added a third strophe from an unknown source. (1) The 'Ecstasy' is the climax of the self-revelation of Jesus, and the point at which the Synoptic Gospels' tradition approaches most closely to the doctrinal outlook of the Fourth Gospel. We do not know the original context of this sublime utterance, but as placed by Mt. it appears to be closely connected with what we have seen to be the subject of this book, viz. the hiding of the mystery of the Kingdom from the chosen nation, and its revelation to the little ones of Christ on whose behalf Jesus rejoices in the Holy Spirit, the Agent of revelation, in God's elective decree. (2) But it is also probably connected with the allusion which has just been made (in v. 19) to the Wisdom, which, rejected in the world, is often spoken of in later Jewish writings as having taken refuge in Israel like Noah's dove in the Ark. The enlightenment of Israel by a revelation hidden from the heathen world is a commonplace of this literature, and in the late Apocalypses and in Philo it may be said to have become a dogma of the Jewish religion. This doctrine is itself a development from the Servant poems of the second Isaiah, in which it is the mission of Israel as Jehovah's Servant-Son 'to sprinkle many nations' and bring them to a knowledge of the true God. In virtue of this unique revelation Israel is regarded as the hierophant of the divine Wisdom, and as such claims the august title of *Son of God*. It is this thought of Israel as the Son, and organ of revelation which supplies the key to the meaning of the poem as it stands in Mt.; for it is this claim, with all its antecedents, that Jesus is in this passage represented as transferring absolutely to Himself in His own Person as unique Son and Revealer of the Father. Through it S. Paul and the Christian Church were led to make use of the conception of Wisdom as the expression of what they believed about Jesus as the mediator of a new revelation superseding that to Israel, and as the Person in whom the plan and purpose of God not only for Israel but for the universe has been fully and finally expressed, and who is, therefore, called in the Fourth Gospel, the Logos or Word of God. Eventually the Church in its Creed dropped the Wisdom phraseology in favour of that of Sonship.[1]

Norden[2] and Easton, have thought that they have discovered in this passage a close affinity to the central theme of the theosophical mysticism of the East which is best known to us in the form of the Hermetic Literature; the idea that the true knowledge of God is hidden and comes mysteriously to a clearer form by a semi-divine mediation. But as we have already seen there is no need to go outside the area of Judaism. A far more striking parallel to the whole passage, which Norden himself notices, is to be found in the last chapter of the Book of Ecclesiasticus (51), in which we find the same threefold arrangement. (1) Thanksgiving for the revelation of Wisdom to Israel, vv. 2 ff. (2) The seeking of Wisdom, vv. 13–22, and (3) the concluding appeal to accept the yoke of the Torah, vv. 23 ff. It is not improbable that our Lord had such a passage in mind when He uttered these words; and it was a wonderful inspiration by which Mt. was led to add a third stanza to the two already existing in Q, even though our Lord may not have uttered all three at the same time.

It seems, therefore, best to accept the view of Bacon and Lagrange that Jesus adapted a theme well known among His people as the medium of a new teaching. The saying surpasses in fact as well as in mystery any known parallel. It is, as Bishop Gore says, authentic beyond question, it cannot have been derived. Jesus, who is conscious of Himself as the Son whom the Father alone uniquely knows, appropriates to Himself the unique relation

---

[1] I Cor. 11^{12-16}, 2 Cor. 1^{25}, Eph. $1^{8\,ff.}$, $3^{2\,ff.}$, Col. $1^{4\,ff.}$

[2] *Agnostos Theos*, p. 287. The passage which Norden quotes from the Poimandres, one of the documents in the Hermetic Collection, is a beautiful apostrophe addressed by the initiate to God as Father, somewhat analogous to the thanksgiving of Jesus to His Father for the Revelation given to Him as Son. The date, however, of all this literature is most uncertain.

which Scripture had already established between the Wisdom and
God, placing Himself thereby in a sphere as transcendent as the
Father Himself. If the saying were not genuine it would be difficult to find a plausible point of departure for the greater part of the
Pauline and Johannine Christology. It is, as Johannes Weiss[1] remarks, the utmost that the earliest Church was able to assert of
the earthly Jesus. (For the best discussions of the whole passage
see A. E. J. Rawlinson, *N.T. Doctrine of the Christ*, pp. 251 ff., and
B. W. Bacon, *Studies in Matthew*, pp. 202 ff.)

11²⁵. *answered*, like 'opened his mouth' in Mt. 5² to prepare the
reader for a solemn and weighty pronouncement.

I thank thee, Gk. ἐξομολογοῦμαι, as in Ecclus. 51¹. As Jerome remarks, 'confession' of God is made not only by penitence but also by
giving of thanks, as in the opening words of psalms 105, 107 where
the same word (Lat. *confiteor*) is used.

these things, the same as 'all things'; not only the mysterious facts
named in verse 27, but the whole revelation of God's nature and
kingdom which has been the subject of His preaching to the cities of
Galilee.

wise and understanding, see note on Mt. 5³. How different was
the view not only of the O.T. writers but of the greatest heathen
thinkers of the time! According to the Stoics the wise man only
is religious, because he alone has the right knowledge of the true
nature of God.

seemed good unto thee, Gk. εὐδοκία ἔμπροσθέν σου the same word as
occurs in the angels' song in Lk. 2¹⁴, 'men of good pleasure'. It is a
literal rendering of an Aramaic original. The corresponding verb is
found again in Lk. 12³². 'It is the good pleasure of the Father to give
you the kingdom', and it is twice used in reference to our Lord Himself at solemn moments, e.g. the Baptism, Mt. 3¹⁷, and the Transfiguration, Mt. 17⁵. Here it means the divine decree by which the
babes have been chosen to be the recipients of God's latest and fullest
revelation of Himself.

11²⁷. *All things have been delivered unto me*, Gk. παρεδόθη, here in the
sense of revelation rather than of power as in Mt. 28¹⁸ or 1 Cor. 15²⁴.

11²⁸⁻³⁰. *The yoke of Christ.*

In spite of McNeile's objection Norden was right in emphasizing
the close parallel of Ecclesiasticus 51 with the Comfortable Words
especially in the Hebrew version of the former, as will be seen by
the following comparison.

---

[1] *Das Urchristenthum*, p. 87.

Ecclus. 51²³ ff.	Mt. 11²⁸ ff.
(v. 23) Draw near unto me, ye unlearned,	(28) Come unto me, all ye that labour,
(26) Put your neck under the yoke, and let your soul bear her burden:	(29) Take my yoke upon you, and learn of me;
(27) Behold with your eyes, how that I laboured but a little, and found for myself much rest.	(29) For I am meek and lowly in heart: and ye shall find rest unto your souls.

As Lagrange remarks, even more striking parallels with the thought are to be found in Prov. 8³² and Ecclus. 6²⁴, ²⁸, in both of which Wisdom makes her own act of praise.

11²⁸. *labour and are heavy laden.* Not to be identified with the babes of the previous stanza. The words refer to those burdened with the heavy weight of Pharisaic legalism (cf. 23⁴) of which the writer is about to introduce two examples from the Marcan narrative.

11²⁹. *meek and lowly in heart.* S. Paul could appeal to the meekness and gentleness (2 Cor. 10³) of Christ as a recognized fact. But as in all really gentle people, who are also strong, His wrath could blaze out with terrible fierceness when He saw cruelty or hardness, infliction of unnecessary suffering, and neglect of God and His rights.

11³⁰. *easy,* Gk. χρηστός, meaning 'kindly', when used of persons, 'good of its kind', when used of things.

12¹⁻²¹. *Two examples of the lighter yoke* (Mk. 2²³–3⁶)

Mt. here returns to the Marcan order at the point where he had left it in 9¹⁸. Each of these is a perfect example of the paradigm (see Appendix). The defence of Jesus or of His Church in both these examples is clear and is a direct challenge to the Rabbis. It is impossible to understand the following section of Mt. in which He hands down to Peter and the Twelve this same power of binding and loosing unless He had already duly claimed to exercise this power Himself. In the pronouncement 'the Son of man is Lord of the sabbath', which is the crux of the paradigm, our Lord claims the same right that the doctors of the Law themselves exercised 'to bind and to loose' (see Mt. 16¹⁹). Christ claims it both for Himself and His disciples for the same reason that He has just employed in His answer to John, namely that a greater *thing* than the temple, or the whole Jewish establishment, is here, the very presence and nearness of God and His kingdom.

12⁴. *shewbread.* Exod. 25³⁰, Lev. 24⁵. According to Deut. 23²⁴ to pluck corn in another man's field was allowed, but forbidden on the sabbath by the Rabbis as being a form of reaping.

12⁵. Our Lord refers to an exception allowed by the Rabbis them-selves and based on Num. 28^{9, 24–27} and Lev. 23²⁵.

12⁶. *one greater than the temple is here*, Gk. μεῖζον, i.e. a greater thing or occasion.

12⁷. Hosea 6⁶.

12⁸. This logion may have originally referred either to Jesus Him-self as Messiah or to the principle embodied in the quotation which precedes it, the supremacy of human need, a principle admitted at any rate in later Judaism. It does not, however, mean that man as such has a right to override the Law of God. Our Lord is not likely to have allowed any such principle, but as it stands here the phrase 'Son of Man' can only refer to Jesus Himself as Lord. See Mt. 9⁸ note.

12^{10–15}. Mk. 3^{1–6}. A paradigm of the same type as the last but containing a miracle story.

In the Mishna or codified law book of Palestinian Judaism it was laid down that every case where life is in danger supersedes the Sabbath. This could hardly have been such a case and, therefore, like the first example, was a direct challenge.

12¹⁴. *counsel*. Mk. has 'with the Herodians', indicating, as Professor Burkitt suggests, that they informed Herod's police against Jesus. This seems to have involved a virtual excommunication of Jesus from the synagogue and His withdrawal to the seaside, with the commence-ment of an open-air mission and the adoption of a method specially suited to it, namely the teaching by parables.

12¹⁷. The point of the prophecy from Isa. 42^{1–3} lies in the thought that the opposition of the Scribes and Pharisees, the climax of which is about to be related, was about to draw upon Israel after the flesh its doom, namely the forfeiture of the right to be called the children or the Son of God, in favour of the new people, those who, under the leadership of the Chosen Servant of Jehovah, once more as of old rejected by His own people, would proclaim true religion to the Gentiles and so fulfil the vocation of Israel to the world. The quotation is once more from the N source.

12^{22–37}. *The 'Beelzebub' incident* (Mk. 3^{22–30}, Lk. 11^{14–23}).

The doom of spiritual deafness and blindness. This incident is recorded by all three evangelists. Mt., as usual, conflates the two (Mk. and Q) with some slight variations of his own. It is a good example of 'the synoptic problem', for the variations in the three versions are difficult to account for. It also illustrates one of the principles of 'form-criticism' (p. 265). A miracle is used without any apparent interest in such a tremendous occurrence, but only for the purpose of a peg on which to hang an important saying of Jesus, which is intended to be the climax of the subject of Bk. III. Many are offended because they cannot distinguish between the work and the apparently humble agents of the Kingdom. Many oppose their work and ascribe it to the devil. So they did in the time of Jesus. Such blasphemy is not a matter of concern to the Son of man, but it matters deeply to the disciples because the work is God's work and, like all good work, performed in the name of God and by the power of the Holy Spirit. To deny that is to call good evil and evil good, and this is to commit moral suicide. There is no forgiveness possible for such sin, because none is desired. The saying in verse 31 indicates a period of discipline in the early Church when sins were already divided into 'mortal' and 'venial', cf. I John v¹⁶⁻¹⁷.

12²². *blind and dumb*, as 'my servant' in Isa. 42¹⁹.

12²³. *the son of David*. The 'incredulity' is here transferred by Mt. from the friends of Jesus (Mk. 3²¹) to the people. In either case it is the contrast between the greatness of the work and the poverty of the agent.

12²⁷. *sons*, i.e. your fellow Jews. Exorcism was a common practice among the Jews and in the adjoining Mediterranean world generally.

12²⁸. *The Spirit of God—kingdom of God.* See Additional Note D.

12²⁸. *come upon you*, Gk. ἔφθασεν = has come unexpectedly, as in classical Greek.

12³⁰. *He that is not with me is against me*—identical in Lk. 12¹⁰, but absent from Mk. Here the meaning is, 'you have thrown down a direct challenge to My work; from this time forward I warn you that all neutrality is impossible.'

12³¹. *Therefore I say unto you.* There are many Rabbinic parallels to this tremendous saying (cf. Num. 15³¹, I Sam. 3¹⁴), but none which claims a power so absolute to remit and retain sins as is claimed here by Jesus. It is undeniable that the words as recorded had a far-reaching and serious influence upon the ethical and penitential system of the first few centuries of the Christian Church (cf. Heb. 6⁴⁻⁸). But it is obvious, as Mk. saw, that the words as originally spoken could not have referred to any one particular sin, even that of blasphemy, on which the Rabbis were specially severe, but to the spiritual condition into which rancour, especially religious rancour, can reduce the best men, so that they lose all sense of moral values.

12³⁴. *Out of the abundance of the heart the mouth speaketh*; that is, the blasphemy against the Holy Ghost could not be accounted as mere idle words which those who uttered them did not mean. These words of the Pharisees were spoken out of the abundance of the heart, i.e. with the fullest consciousness of their meaning and after the most prolonged examination by the religious and moral experts of the nation.

12³⁸⁻⁴². *The adulterous generation.* Proceeding from this vantage point Jesus now takes the offensive Himself. His opponents demand a sign from heaven, i.e. fire, or some other portent in the sky, of the truth of His claim, such as was suggested by the Devil in the second temptation. This is refused, with the example of Jonah, whose warning of doom to the unrepentant was humbly accepted by the Ninevites without further attestation.

12³⁹. *adulterous*, as often in the O.T. sense of unfaithfulness to Jehovah and his religion. Cf. Hos. 1 and 2.

12⁴⁰. *The sign of Jonah.* What is the meaning of this expression? It seems to be different in Mt. and Lk. Lk. (11²⁹) has ' Jonah became a sign to the Ninevites', i.e. by the preaching of repentance. That was sufficient for the Ninevites and this generation must not expect anything more. There is no reference to the story of the whale or to the Resurrection. In Mt. the whole analogy seems to turn on the story of the whale as a parable of the Resurrection. The probability is that both sayings are genuine and that Mt. has in his usual manner conflated them. He has the repentance of the Ninevites in verse 41. But he has added a characteristic remark of an eschatological character to the effect that the sign of Jonah was the impending judgement; i.e. if the Ninevites had not repented Nineveh would by its destruction soon have been taught that Jonah was a true messenger of God. But, according to the Pharisaic teaching, judgement involves a previous Resurrection (cf. Dan. 12²). Hence the cryptic allusion in verse 40 to the Resurrection, a doctrine which, we must remember, is always in the New Testament regarded as an eschatological event preceding judgement, of which the Resurrection of the Messiah is the preliminary stage or first-fruits. (1 Cor. xv. 20; Col. i. 18.)

12⁴⁰. An allusion, whether original or not, to the descent into Hades, a very ancient doctrine in the Christian Church (cf. 1 Pet. 3¹⁸ ff.).

12⁴². *greater*, Gk. πλεῖον, neuter again as in 12⁶, the repentance evoked by the preaching of John and of Jesus was a greater occasion than Jonah's mission at Nineveh; even as the miracles attendant upon

Jesus' glad tidings were a greater matter than Solomon, whose wisdom reached 'to the uttermost parts of the earth'.

12^{43}. The meaning of this parable is that Israel is God's dwelling-place now being purged of demons and evil powers by His intervention. He must, therefore, be received to dwell among His people, or the evil powers will return with sevenfold virulence. Lk. places it where Q presumably did, after the Beelzebub incident, to illustrate the futility of the multitude of the Jewish exorcists. They only made matters worse.

12^{43}. *waterless places*, the abode beloved of demons (Isa. 13^{21}, Rev. 18^2). So in the Book of Tobit the spirit Asmodæus when he smells the burnt fish liver flees in terror to the uttermost parts of Egypt (Tob. 8^3).

12$^{46-50}$. *The spiritual kindred of Jesus* (Mk. 3^{31}, Lk. 8^{21}). Mt. deserts Q at this point and goes back to Mk. 3 where the saying is found in the same context. Verse 47 is omitted by the best text ℵ.B, as well as by the Latin and Syriac versions.

12^{49}. The words do not in the least imply repudiation by our Lord of His Mother and His brethren; they indicate an extension of His family by adoption of believers into the circle of the home at Nazareth, which is the hearth and cradle of Christianity (for the brethren of Jesus see note on 13^{55}).

B. 13. The Discourse in Parables.

The word parable, Gk. παραβολή, is the LXX rendering of the Hebrew *māshāl* usually translated 'proverb', and denotes various kinds of utterance, proverbs, wise sayings, riddles (Ecclus. 39^3), dark sayings of a prophetic character like those of Balaam in Num. 22 ff. ; Ps. 78^2 ; 'Taunt' sayings which 'curse' as in Mic. 2^4, Jer. 29^{22} ; fables like that of Jotham in Judges 9^8, or of Nathan in 2 Sam. 12. The word is used in the N.T. outside the Synoptic Gospels only in Heb. 9^9, 11^{19}. The Fourth Gospel prefers the word *paroimia*, figure. A vast literature of parables exists in Rabbinic writings, some of which bear a close resemblance to those in the Gospel. Jülicher has rightly emphasized the distinction between the parable and the allegory. Parables illustrate and express in a vivid way some truth or judgement in which details must not be pressed. The point of an allegory lies in the details, every one of which has a hidden meaning.

In many cases the original context and, therefore, point of the parable has been forgotten, and this is probably the reason for allegorizing explanations attached to some, e.g. the Sower and the

Tares. Mt., however, follows Mk (4^{11}) in assuming that the parables, of which the original point was no longer remembered, were intended to obscure truth rather than to shed light on it ; and that this was the reason why people did not at once understand and believe. They were not intended to do so. This is the meaning of the quotation which in all the Synoptic Gospels is put in the mouth of Jesus when asked for a reason why He taught in parables. To Mt. the teaching by parables is simply another example of the hiding of the mystery from the Jews that it may be revealed to the true Israel which has ears to hear. Characteristically Mt. expands Mk.'s list of three parables to seven.

13$^{1-9}$. *The parable of the Sower, or the Receptive and Unreceptive Soils.*

The parable of the Sower in Mt. follows in natural sequence from what has gone before. It was evoked by the blasphemy of the scribes. In it Jesus replies with a vindication of His work and methods addressed to Wisdom's children, by whom He is justified in the abundant harvest, which is the real point of the parable. The great multitude may well have been gathered from those who had been touched by the mission of the Twelve and wished to see something of the Master of whom they had heard so much, and they may also have formed the majority of the multitude which was fed in the wilderness.

13^{11}. *mysteries* = secrets divulged to certain persons which they may in turn reveal to others. This is the constant meaning of the word in the LXX and apocryphal writings, and S. Paul frequently uses the same word to express the truth so astonishing, because so unsuspected, that the Gentiles should be fellow-heirs with the Jews in the Church of God. Eph. 1$^{9, 10}$, 3$^{3-6}$, Col. 1$^{26-27}$.

13$^{14-15}$. Verbatim from the LXX of Isa. 6^9, but not introduced with Mt.'s favourite formula because taken directly from Mk.

13$^{18-23}$. *Explanation of the parable of the Sower.* It does not, however, really suit the parable, the point of which is the assurance of an abundant harvest, not the difficulties that stand in the way, which hinder but cannot destroy the Word. The explanation in fact makes an allegory of what is essentially a parable. Birds, for example, do not obviously suggest the Evil One ; and in any case the clumsy identification of the hearers with the seed sown rather than with the soil does not suggest the clear teaching of Jesus.

13$^{24-30}$. *The parable of the Tares.* The dangers of false teaching. This parable, with its elaboration of the difficulties which beset the administration of Christian discipline, and the dangers of rigorism, speaks, as Bacon remarks, eloquently for Mt.'s environ-ment and special interest.

13²⁵. *tares*, Gk. ζιζάνια, Lat. *lollia,* one of four main species of weeds in Palestine which grow as tall as wheat and are not usually pulled up till close on harvest. The idea is found in the Talmud, and is still said to be held by peasants in Palestine, that tares are wheat that has degenerated.

13²⁹. The words appear to reflect the prevailing opinion in a Church which held that the wicked or heretics must not be excommunicated because Christians may err in their judgement. The separation must be left to God.

13³¹⁻³³. *Parables of the Mustard Seed and of the Leaven* (Mk. 4³⁰ᶠᶠ·, Lk. 13¹⁸,¹⁹). The position of these two parables in Mt. and Lk. indi-cates that they stood together in Q. This is also one of the places where Mt. and Lk. agree in points of detail against Mk. The point of the 'Mustard Seed' is the rapid growth of the Christian move-ment about to overshadow even Judaism itself. The point of the 'Leaven' is the revolutionary working of the movement in society, at once secret and irresistible.

13³³. *measures*, Gk. σάτα. According to Josephus = one and a half of the Roman 'modium' = about a peck.

13³⁵. The quotation is from Ps. 78² and is from the Aramaic translation.

13³⁶⁻⁴³. *Explanation of the parable of the Tares.* Addressed to the Apostolic Body representing those charged with the preservation of purity of doctrine in the Church by the weapon of ecclesiastical discipline. The congregation are carefully dismissed (v. 36). McNeile admits that this explanation stands on a different footing from that of the Sower. Not only does it allegorize to an excessive degree, 'but the style is stilted, the interpretation of successive detail mechanical; the apocalyptic expectation popular and con-ventional, and the use of the title Son of man for Jesus first in his human life and then in his Messianic glory must be due to Christian tradition.'

13⁴³. An allusion to Dan. 12³. The truly pure in heart are assured that their righteousness will be made as 'clear as the noon-day' without the terrible weapons of excommunication and rigor-ism being necessary to emphasize it.

13⁴⁴⁻⁴⁶. *The parables of the Treasure and the Pearl.* In both of these parables, additional to those in Mk., the activity of man illustrates the kingdom of heaven. Having found God through the preaching of Christ, either by a sudden change of heart or after earnest and even lifelong search, man will give all for all.

13⁴⁷⁻⁵⁰. *The parable of the Drag-net* forms, with its doctrine of rewards and punishments, a fitting climax to the Matthean group of parables. As in the 'Tares' the kingdom in this parable approaches nearest to the idea of an ecclesiastical institution or system gathering all kinds of people out of the world. The conclusion is again characteristically Matthean. As in the Tares Mt. again applies a parable to confirm his already decisive attitude towards the question of discipline in the Christian Church.

13⁴⁷. *net*, Gk. σαγήνη, French *seine*—a large drag-net.

13⁵². *made a disciple to the kingdom.* **The** reading is doubtful; if it is the plain dative Gk. τῇ βασιλείᾳ it will mean 'instructed' with respect to the teaching about the kingdom: if 'into the kingdom', Gk. εἰς τὴν βασιλείαν, it will mean 'made a disciple with a view to usefulness in the kingdom'. The saying in either case refers to the twofold relationship of Jesus' teaching to Judaism; which it does not annul but fulfils. But the second meaning best suits the context in which Mt. passes from the instruction to the initiation of disciples into the unity of the Church, according to the apostolic authority, to which he is about to address himself in the Fourth Book.

To this concluding verse might well be applied, as Bacon remarks, the figure employed by Zahn with reference to the curious incident in Mk.'s account of the Passion, of the young man 'who fled away naked' (14⁵). 'It is the artist's signature subscribed in an obscure corner of the canvas.'

NOTE D. THE KINGDOM OF HEAVEN

Mt. alone in the N.T. uses the expression Kingdom of Heaven. It is possible that Mt. himself intended to suggest some distinction between the *Kingdom of Heaven*, which he uses thirty-two times, and *Kingdom of God*, which he uses only four or five times (6³³, 12²⁸, 19²⁴, and 21³¹, ⁴³). Weiss thinks that the latter may have suggested a more personal idea, that God Himself directs the government; the former the idea of its heavenly character and divine origin. The plural 'heavens' which occurs in the Gk. (τῶν οὐρανῶν) is a Semitism, perhaps only a Rabbinic periphrasis for God. Dalman thinks that our Lord Himself employed it (*Words of Jesus*, pp. 91 ff.).

The idea that God has an everlasting kingdom is a familiar one both in the O.T. and the later Jewish literature. In almost every case the Hebrew word *Malkûth* denotes not a 'kingdom' in the concrete sense of a theocracy, but 'kingship', in the abstract sense of sovereignty. For the Jew, the interest in the Unity of God lies in the moral unity of the world, and the interest in the omnipotence of God lies in the sure fulfilment of the great moral purpose which He has revealed by His prophets—the good world that is to be. The idea, therefore, of the sovereignty of God forms part of the hope of Israel and is inseparable from its eschatology. The text, Zech. 14⁹, 'The Lord shall be King over all the earth. In that day shall the Lord be one and His Name one', contains in a nutshell both the idea of the Kingdom and its close connexion with the ethical monotheism of the Hebrew people. Prayer for this consummation is one of the most striking features of later Jewish liturgies and of the private household prayers of the Jewish family. In the time of Jesus the professed aim of the official teachers of the Law, the Scribes, was to make the people fit for deliverance from a heathen kingdom. For the vindication of Israel as the people of Jehovah in the eyes of the nations was the first and indispensable step towards that universality of the true religion, which was, as it is still, the aim and object of the best elements in Judaism, and what they meant by God's Kingdom. Hence the zeal, amounting in the time of Jesus to fanaticism, for the strict observance of the Law. If but two Sabbaths, so it was said by the Rabbis of that time, could be perfectly kept by the whole Jewish people, the Kingdom of God would come.

The idea of God's Kingdom, therefore, appears in the time before the N.T. in two different aspects, both of which are reflected in the teaching of Jesus and His disciples. On the one hand the sovereignty of God is regarded as in a sense always present. In the people of Israel it has its present earthly manifestation so that the man who takes the Law upon himself takes at the same time the 'yoke' of the Kingdom. In this view God is, as we might say, *de jure* king over all the earth in virtue of creation, but *de facto* only for those who acknowledge His sovereignty. Israel alone of the nations did this at Sinai; and individual members of that nation do so every time they recite the 'shema'.[1]

On the other hand, the manifest contrast ever since the Exile, with the exception of the brief but brilliant period of the Maccabean rule, between the ideal and the actual and, from an

---

[1] The recitation thrice daily of the combined texts, Deut. 6⁴⁻⁹, 11¹³⁻²¹, Num. 15³⁷⁻⁴¹, called 'Shema' from its opening word 'Hear'. It contains the central dogma of the creed of Israel in much the same way as the recitation of the 'Angelus' contains the central doctrine of the Christian Church, the Incarnation.

earthly point of view, hopeless situation of the Jew, gave strength to the apocalyptic idea of the Kingdom. At the moment Jehovah does not rule directly, but Satan or other gods under him, and the Gentiles, the nations of this world, have the ascendancy. Nevertheless, at the end of the age, Jehovah's sovereignty will be manifested in a universal catastrophe in which all other world-powers will be annihilated.

Our Lord's teaching, while making use of these and other ideas current at the time, transcends them all. Certain features of His teaching concerning the Kingdom mark it out as original. (1) It was not for Him, as for the Rabbis, merely one among many theological ideas—it was everything. His thought is wholly theo-centric. 'God is the beginning, the middle and the end and the ceaseless presupposition of all Jesus' teaching' (Von Hügel). The Kingdom of God in the teaching of Jesus means *only* God, and its proximity, as expressed in the urgency of apocalyptic language, means God's nearness. It is in this respect that His teaching has the closest affinity with the great prophets of Israel.

(2) Unlike contemporary ideas, it is concerned wholly with ethical religion and not with political and eudemonistic (a good time coming) hopes. There is nothing in the teaching of Jesus which remotely resembles millenarianism, such as that of the early Christians in the Apocalypse, or that of Savonarola in the Renaissance, or Cromwell's Kingdom of the Saints, or modern non-religious Communism, itself so largely Jewish in origin. On the contrary its blessings are spiritual blessings reserved for those who do the will of God, the pure in heart, the poor in spirit, the persecuted, and little children (Mt. $5^{3\text{ff.}}$, $19^{\text{ff.}}$, 19^{13}).

(3) In the parables the Kingdom of Heaven is in every case likened not to an institution or an ideal state of things but to some action or event. The point of comparison is not the field or the treasure, the pearl, nor the feast in itself, but the sower, the royal host, the rash speculation, the brilliant find. The framework of the parables always encloses a piece of living action or happening. The Gospel of the Kingdom in the Synoptic Gospels is the message of Jesus that God's sovereign power and will are here and now present and active among men. For the 'Sons of the Kingdom' that sovereignty takes the form of the divine forgiveness of sins and miracles of healing; but assumes the terrible aspect of judgement upon those that resist His will. When Jesus said, 'If I by the Spirit of God cast out devils, no doubt the Kingdom of God is come upon you', He meant that God, through Jesus as His Christ,

brings His newly revealed power into action in the presence of men; specially manifested in the victory over the demon powers of the underworld, the Messianic struggle with the anti-God powers of sin and darkness.

(4) It is Jesus himself who wields the sovereign powers of the Kingdom. It is in the person and activity rather than in the teaching of Jesus that the revelation of the Kingdom is made. Jesus no longer, like the Rabbis, teaches about the Kingdom, or like John heralds its approach. He actually brings it in His Messianic activity right into the present. In Him the powers of the age to come—the heavenly powers, have broken in upon the present age and taken them by surprise. This is what His contemporaries found so hard to understand, but it was the realization of the fact that the Kingdom had already come in the Person and works of Jesus that was the real meaning of S. Paul's conversion.

(5) The Kingdom of Heaven in the teaching of Jesus and of the N.T. generally is always the gift of God. Nothing is further from the N.T. than the very common idea that the Kingdom of God means the progress or evolution of the world. Any such ideas are based upon a grave misunderstanding of Jesus' teaching, and assumes a view of human nature and progress, which would make this world and not God the centre of man's care and striving. Rather it is man *in his evolution* that according to Jesus needs redemption. Christianity, as von Hügel said, is man in the presence of God. The kingdom is nowhere promised as the reward of human effort. It is this idea of the *givenness* of the Kingdom of God's power and grace which finds expression in the suddenness and unexpectedness and imminence, apart from which Jesus rarely speaks of the Kingdom. For the mystery of the divine operation is so remote from human co-operation as to take place while man sleeps, 'he knoweth not how' (Mk. 4²⁷).

(6) Jesus' teaching about the Kingdom is *eschatological*, in the sense that He identified it to some extent with the Resurrection and the world to come. This is seen most clearly in the story of the Transfiguration which occupies a central position in all the Synoptic Gospels, and is regarded by all three as an exhibition of the Kingdom which in Christ has already broken in upon the present world-order and begun to make an end not only of sin and evil but also of death. The sovereignty of God will not be exhibited in its perfection until it is seen in that reconstitution of the world, and of the entire nature, bodily and spiritual, of man in its integrity, which is the meaning in the N.T. of the Resurrection. The escha-

tology of the N.T. knows of no isolated event at the end of the world, but only of a fulfilment of that which has already begun in the historical activity of Jesus. And just as the present working and power of God was revealed in a wonderful way to the disciples on the Sacred Mount, so will the final event be fulfilled through the action of Christ manifesting Himself in power and great glory—when that which is now invisible will become visible and 'all flesh shall see it together'. It is this aspect of the teaching about the Kingdom of God which is most richly developed in the teaching of S. Paul and other writers of the N.T.

(7) While it is, generally speaking, true that for Jesus the Kingdom of God means the absolute unconditioned working of God's transcendent and sovereign Will, it cannot be denied that in Mt.'s Gospel there are passages which suggest that the expression had taken on an institutional meaning. In Mt. $13^{24\,ff.}$, $^{47\,ff.}$, 16^{19}, it can scarcely have meant other than the Church. But the N.T. usage as a whole is against the view that Jesus ever used it in this sense. (For further discussion see Moore, *Judaism*, vol. ii, and for the Rabbinic doctrine especially Schechter, *Some Aspects of Rabbinic Theology*.)

13^{54}–19^{1}.   FOURTH BOOK OF MATTHEW

THE UNITY OF THE CHURCH.

Mt.'s Fourth Book is intended for those called to exercise authority in the Church. S. Paul recounts some of the difficulties that confronted the rulers of the early Church; difficulties connected with questions of casuistry, the relation of Church to the State and to the world outside, and above all the unity of the Church.[1] As in the other books Mt. introduces his discourse with a section of narrative taken from the Marcan source, which already had a brief discourse on Church government ($9^{33\,ff.}$). At the same time Mt. has managed to find room for all the material between Mk. 6^{1} up to that point. Most of it was in a high degree relevant to his subject. After a brief introduction which outlines the situation, the passion of John the Baptist portending Jesus' own (14^{3-12}) and His final rejection at Nazareth (13^{53-58}) he proceeds to relate the two miracles of feeding, one in Galilee and one in Peraea, in a way that clearly connects them with the Christian ministry and its special function, the administration of the Eucharist (14^{15-21}, 15^{32}): the introduction and settlement by authority of the

---

[1] Cf. Rom. 12, 1 Cor. 12.

great problem of primitive Christianity, the validity of the Law of Moses in its ceremonial aspect (15^{1-20}): the beatitude addressed to Peter who has already been accorded special mention as the object, in his weakness, of Christ's special care and protection (14^{30}) leading on to the great commission to Peter and the terrible rebuke to his presumption upon it (16^{13-23}), and its confirmation in the mystical experience of the Transfiguration (17^{1-13}). After which the fourth discourse begins with the words (17^{22}), 'While they abode in Galilee'. We may note that Mt. from this point onwards follows Mk.'s order to the end of the Gospel.

$13^{55, 56}$. His brothers and sisters, here mentioned, are supposed by Christian tradition to have been the children of Joseph by a former marriage. They are nowhere said to have been the children of Mary. This is the only mention in the Gospels of sisters—two of them were probably Salome and Mary, the wife of James (Mk. 16^1, Jn. 19^{25}). The James named here was the head of the early Church in Jerusalem, surnamed the Just (Acts 12^{17}, Gal. 1^9), who met his death in A.D. 62 at the hands of Zealots in the heat of party strife shortly before the destruction of Jerusalem. Simon became the second Bishop of Jerusalem, the others remained unknown, though descendants of them were mentioned as still alive at the end of the first century by the Jewish-Christian writer Hegesippus, who tells the trustworthy story of their appearance before the Emperor Domitian who dismissed them as harmless peasants. (For full discussion, see Lightfoot, *Galatians*, pp. 252–91.)

14^{1-12}. *The Martyrdom of John the Baptist* (Mk. 6^{14-29}).

This incident must have occurred early in the Public Life because Herod has only recently heard of Jesus. The reason for this may have been that Herod had been fully occupied with his war with Aretas the Arabian king which was the result of the divorce and re-marriage condemned by John. The Herodias here mentioned as the instigator of the crime was the sister of Agrippa I, who afterwards became king, and daughter by Bernice of Aristobulus, son of Herod the Great and the elder Mariamne. She was married to her uncle Herod, son of Herod the Great and the younger Mariamne, who had a daughter named Salome. It was this daughter, not Herodias, who was married to Philip the Tetrarch. It has been sometimes asserted that there were two Herods named Philip; but there is no evidence in Josephus for this, and errors of this kind were all too easy in the complicated marital relationships of the Herod family. Josephus mentions that the imprisonment and execution of the Baptist took place at the fortress of Machaerus, a strong border town in Peraea built against the Arabians with whom he was for many years at war. But Josephus knows nothing of the story in the Gospels. He says that Antipas, fearing that the extent to which John had gained the confidence of the people might lead him to sudden rebellion, thought it much better to anticipate any mischief he might cause by putting him to death. So he sent him as a prisoner to Machaerus and there killed him. He is moved to relate this incident as bearing on the progress of Herod's campaign against Aretas, because the Jews believed that the destruction of Herod's army in A.D. 36 was sent as a punishment upon him.[1] The silence of Josephus, as well as the improbability of a royal princess taking the part of a dancing girl, has led some critics to see in the incident as recorded in the Gospel a story which had lost nothing in the telling in the bazaars and synagogues of Palestine and Syria. On the other hand, the impropriety itself is a good reason for the respectable Josephus to suppress it.

14^{12}. *went and told Jesus,* cf. Mk. 6^{30}. A good example of the way in which the Gospel was composed out of disconnected events. For in order not to lose any part of Mk., Mt. puts these words, which in Mk. refer to the return of the Apostles from their mission, into the mouth of the disciples of John telling Jesus about their master; but with a strange carelessness, for he has forgotten that the story of John's death, to which in this context they refer, is not part of the narrative but inserted to explain Herod's attitude to Jesus and so to account for the withdrawal from Galilee.

14$^{13-21}$. *The Agape by the Lake* (Mk. 6$^{32\,ff.}$, Lk. 9$^{11\,ff.}$).

The description of this miracle in all four Gospels is clearly coloured by the resemblance which the primitive Church saw between the farewell meal of Jesus with His followers in Galilee and the Christian Eucharist. The Eucharistic features, as well as the discourse in Jn. 6, show plainly enough that the miracle of the loaves prefigured for the early Church its communion with the Risen Lord of Whose Presence and Gifts to His disciples the loaves and fishes are already in Jn. 21^{13} regarded as the sacred symbols. In the same way the multitudes in orderly groups (Mk. 6^{40}) recalled the Church's worship under the direction of the Bishop surrounded by his Presbyters and Deacons, so familiar to Christians at the time when S. Ignatius wrote the letters which so often refer to it. To this extent Sanday is right in his remark that an eyewitness at the present day would not necessarily have given the same description of what happened.[2] Schweitzer is on the right

---

[1] Josephus, *Ant.* 18. 1–4.
[2] Article 'Jesus Christ' in Hastings's *Dictionary of the Bible.*

lines in his explanation of the miracle as a 'veiled eschatological
sacrament', one of many rehearsals of the great Messianic banquet
(of which the Last Supper was the chief), to which it was for the
enthusiastic and famished multitude the very passport and pledge
of admission.[1]

14[17]. *five loaves and two fishes.* Bread with fish as a relish was the
ordinary food of the poor people of the district. The loaves were the
flat passover cakes which could easily be broken.

14[19]. *on the grass.* Indicates that the desert place was not the sandy
desert but the 'wilderness' which in Palestine is never very far from
the belt of cultivated land (Ps. 65[12]). The scene suggests springtime
and the Passover season (Jn. 6[2]).

looking up to heaven he blessed and brake. Cf. 1 Cor. 11[24], Lk. 24[30].
Apparently a familiar action of our Lord, not done for the first time
at the institution of the Eucharist. The 'fraction' has ever since been
a most characteristic part of the whole Eucharistic action. (See
Brilioth, *Eucharistic Faith and Practice*; and Dix, *Shape of the Liturgy*.)

14[20]. *that which remained over of the broken pieces.* As Bishop
Westcott remarks, not the crumbs lying about which the people had
dropped in their eagerness or satiety, but that which was *reserved*
of the consecrated food for further use.[2]

baskets, Gk. κοφίνους, a heavy wicker basket used mostly for agri-
cultural purposes.

14[22-33]. *The first Petrine Supplement.* Mk. 6[45 ff.], Jn. 6[17 ff.]. At
this point we meet with the first of four remarkable additions to
the Marcan framework designed to throw into relief the supreme
authority of Peter, as Vicar of Christ on earth (see Additional
Note E). Mt. appears to have worked up to a great height the
mysterious event recorded in Mk. 6[45-52], itself perhaps, as Professor
Turner[3] and others are inclined to think, a reminiscence of a Resurrection appearance of Jesus, restoring the broken faith of the
disciples. But in relating the story immediately before the crucial
decision about the validity of the Law for Christians, Matthew
was clearly interested in a further point which appears again in
Lk. 5[1-11] and Jn. 21, viz. Peter's part in the restoration of that
faith after his denial and subsequent restoration. The fact of the
description in Mt. of the *worship* of Jesus, 14[33] (Gk. προσεκύνησαν),
in contrast with their 'fearful astonishment' in Mk. is an additional
reason for regarding the story in its Matthean form as a post-
Resurrection appearance. Some think that the lost ending of Mk.

---

[1] *Quest of the Historical Jesus*, pp. 377 ff.
[2] Com. on S. John, 6[13].   [3] *New Commentary*, p. 72.

contained such a story, in which Peter appears as the author of the
Resurrection faith of the disciples. Certainly S. Paul knew of and
records an appearance to Peter first of all on Easter Day, and it
would be odd if no account of this appearance was to be found in
the N.T. There is reason to think that in the early Church the
primacy of Peter was in a very real sense bound up with his
pre-eminence as recipient of visions and revelations, especially of
the Risen Lord (Lk. 22³², Jn. 21⁷, ¹⁵, Acts 10 ff., 1 Cor. 15⁵).

14²². *constrained.* The reason, though not given in Mt., is supplied
by Jn. 6¹⁵. when the people are said to have been about to seize Him
and make Him a king, i.e. a Messiah of the political sort rejected at the
Temptation. Jesus remains to frustrate their purpose, evidently with
success, for He is left alone.

14²⁴. *in the midst of the sea.* The lake is nearly four and a half
miles across = 40 stades or furlongs, so that on a moonlight night a
tiny boat might be visible for at least half that distance, as Mt. says.

tossed, Gk. βασανιζόμενον, lit. tortured or distressed, transferred by
Mt. from the labouring rowers, as in Mk. 6⁴⁸, to the boat itself.

14²⁵. *fourth watch.* Between 3 and 6 a.m. The Romans reckoned
four watches, the Jews three.

14³². *the wind ceased*, as in the storm on the lake. There were
evidently several lake stories, and the details were no longer distinguishable (cf. Lk. 5⁷⁻¹¹).

14³⁴. *Gennesaret.* A small triangular plain of great fertility lying
between Capernaum and Tiberias, which sometimes gave its name to
the lake itself (Lk. 5¹).

15¹⁻²⁰. *The momentous settlement of the problem concerning the cere-monial cleanness* (Mk. 7¹⁻²³).

After repeating the Marcan passage about healings in Gennesaret,
Mt. resumes the thread of his introduction to the great discourse on
unity, and approaches the crucial question of the relation of the
Gentiles to Christianity, in which he is about to appeal to the
authority of Peter himself for the supreme decision of the Church
in Apostolic times. The question of ceremonial uncleanness was
from the first seen to involve two larger questions, (1) the distinction between clean and unclean meats, which in no case could be
described as a 'tradition of the Elders', seeing that it was an established principle of the Mosaic law; (2) the position of the Gentile
Christians in relation to the Law, a question which early
threatened to disrupt the Christian Church (Acts 15). Mt. in his
version of this section moderates Mk.'s extreme anti-Judaism by
omitting the clause, 'making all meats clean' (Mk. 7¹⁹); for he

knows that a prolonged and bitter controversy in the Church was not so easily settled as Mk. seems to imply. At the time of writing, however, the main question, i.e. the admission of Gentiles to the Christian Church without the necessity of submitting to the Law, had long been answered in the affirmative, largely owing to the clear insight and determination of S. Paul. Mt. is here mainly concerned to give S. Peter his due position in this all-important step in the founding of a Catholic Church, i.e. universal without distinction of race or caste. Streeter maintains the view that the answer given in Mt.'s version of the incident represents a compromise between those who disapproved alike of the extreme rigorism of James and the Jerusalem Church, and of Paul's too liberal attitude which occasioned the outburst recorded in Gal. 2^{11}. Bacon, on the other hand, regards the words inserted by Mt. in verse 13, as a complete endorsement of Peter's position as recorded in Acts 10–11, before he yielded to pressure from Jerusalem.

15^2. *Tradition of the Elders.* By 'Elders' is meant the great Doctors of the Law, and by their 'tradition' the casuistry or application of the general principles of the Law to particular cases, in view of a more complex civilization. This tradition, supposed by a legal fiction to have been delivered by Moses at the same time as the written Law and handed down orally, was regarded by the Jews ever since the time of Ezra as of equal authority with the written Law. Owing to the numerous and often conflicting judgements of the Rabbis, this oral tradition was codified at a certain date into a system known as the Mishnah, which was itself incorporated at a still later date into a larger code known as the Talmud, which in its Babylonian or Palestinian form is regarded by the modern Jew as containing, with the Law, the final expression of the Jewish religion. Our Lord's opposition was not to casuistry as such but to the bad casuistry of the Scribes and Pharisees of His day, who are accused not of explaining the Law but of explaining it away, even to the extent of transgressing the Law itself.

They wash not their hands. The reference is probably to defilement contracted by the Jew through coming into contact in business with the Gentile. Such ablutions were therefore a daily necessity for all Jews who lived in a heathen town. The question, therefore, concerned the whole relation of Jews and Gentiles with each other. Jesus insists that they were no part of the Law, not being an O.T. requirement. For a long time the obligation was a matter of controversy between the Pharisaic schools and was especially urged by that of Shammai (v. G. H. Box, *Century Bible, ad loc.*).

15^{5}. *given to God*, i.e. 'that by which you might have received advantage from me is hereby dedicated to God as an offering', the words of a supposed vow on the part of a Jewish son. Our Lord's words assume that it was a bogus vow—the actual dedication of the property is not contemplated; it was dedicated only so far as it concerned the person who hoped to receive it, in this case the parent. It is thus an illustration of their casuistry; a vow is a vow and nothing can undo it, even though its fulfilment should involve a direct infringement of the positive commandments of God. On the other hand, by a slight change of reading, authority for which is the Sinaitic Syriac version only, the Greek word δῶρον, meaning a gift (Heb. *Corban*), becomes not a vow but an oath, i.e. 'by Corban, i.e. by the offering on the altar of the Temple thou shalt not be profited from me'. This would be an oath in the mouth of a degenerate son refusing to help his parents, such an oath being regarded on the same principles of casuistry as binding.

The difficulty, however, is that the Jewish scholar C. G. Montefiore maintains that this is a travesty of Jewish tradition, the object of which was actually the annulling and not the upholding of vows, so that while the fifth commandment might conceivably clash with others, it could not be said to be abrogated by the Scribal casuistry. Further he states that according to the Mishnah and Talmud the Rabbis are actually on the side of Jesus and adopt the same view on this very point. It may be that we have here an echo of a Jewish-Christian controversy of a later date, but at the same time it must be remembered that we are concerned in the Gospels with a particular period for which they are in fact almost the only contemporary evidence. We know, however, that the principle of making religion easy for the average man by allowing the wholesale annulment of vows was embraced by the School of Hillel and carried to great lengths after the destruction of Jerusalem. Is it not possible that Jesus' criticism bore fruit in a reform of this particular abuse?

15^{13}. *Every planting*, a common Rabbinic phrase for a branch of doctrine or school of thought. The words were evidently intended to apply not only to ceremonial washing, but to the whole distinction of clean and unclean.

15^{15}. It is interesting to note the three points of view in the primitive Church as to the validity of the ceremonial portions of the O.T. (1) The Alexandrian, as represented by the Epistle of Barnabas, which taught that they were always intended to have an allegorical meaning, the literal sense having been imposed upon the Jews as a punishment for their wickedness. (2) The Pauline view, that believers had been authorized by Divine revelation to regard the Mosaic distinctions as obsolete, and the refusal to act or associate with non-observers as morally reprehensible (Gal. 2^11ff.). This view is endorsed by Mt. and Mk. (3) The view of James and the Jerusalem Church that they remained binding on all *Jews*, and the Gentiles entering the Church must observe at least such of them as were contained in the decree of Jerusalem (Acts 15^20).

15^21-28. *An example of the cleansing of the heart by faith. The story of the Canaanitish woman* (Mk. 7^24 ff.).

Even if in vv. 12–14 Mt. does not mean to go the whole length of Mk.'s position with regard to the ceremonial law, he intends in this section to bring out the positive Pauline principle of the 'heart cleansed by faith'. 'His additions to Mk.'s story of the exorcism are clearly designed to make it apparent that faith is a sufficient reason for abandoning Mosaic limitations in the case of Gentiles. At the same time, Mt. carefully exonerates Jesus from the charge of having Himself violated the ceremonial law in this case. Jesus does not Himself go outside the borders of Judaism, still less into a heathen house. The woman comes out from their borders.' (Bacon.)

15^21. *Tyre and Sidon.* Mt.'s general expression for the country of Phoenicia which bounded Galilee on the north.
   Canaanitish. A dogmatic rather than a geographical expression in Mt. implying that the woman belonged to the ancient uncleanness of the land (McNeile).
   15^22. *thou son of David.* The words imply already a certain faith on the part of the woman. Our Lord invites her to consider the full implications for herself and her religion of a title thus applied to Him.
   15^31. *the God of Israel.* Mt. regards the crowd referred to and subsequently fed as being mainly Gentile in contrast to the five thousand, and as admitted to the Feast on the ground of faith alone.

15^32-38. *The Agape in Peraea* (Mk. 8^1-10).

In this case Jesus Himself takes the initiative. The idea that this miracle symbolized the preaching of the Gospel to the Gentiles as the former did that to the Jews, goes back to S. Augustine but is already embodied in the Matthean view of the incident.

15^{37}. *baskets*, Gk. σφυρίς, Lat. *sportella*, a flexible basket made of mat and used for carrying fish or fruit. It does not differ from the *kophinos* in size but in material and use.

15^{39}. *Magadan*. Mk. has 'the parts of Dalmanutha'. Neither place has been identified. The reading 'Magdala' in the lesser MSS. substitutes a well-known name for an unknown.

16^{1-12}. *The Sign demanded by the Pharisees and the conversation about leaven* (Mk. 8^{14-21}, Lk. 11^{16}, 12^1, and $^{54-56}$).

16^5. We have here the same cycle of hurried comings and goings as in Mk. 6–8, which are suggestive, if they are at all connected, of the life of a fugitive.

Verses 2 and 3 are absent both from the Vatican MS. (B) and the Codex Sinaiticus (ℵ). They are a 'western' reading inserted, according to Westcott and Hort, at an early date into that text. They are an assimilation from Lk. 12^{54-56}.

16^4. See note on $12^{39\,ff}$.

16^6. From the diversity of form and context in which this saying is reported it is clear that the authors of our present Gospels no longer possessed the key to its original meaning. If we assume the Lucan form, which is the shortest, to have been that which stood in Q, it is not difficult to account for the editions of both Mk. and Mt. In the former (leaven of the Pharisees and Herod), the saying must refer in some way to the conspiracy recorded in Mk. 3^6, 12^{13} of the Pharisees and the Herodians and the dangers to Jesus therefrom. In Mt.'s version it obviously refers to the controversy which has just taken place. The Pharisees and Sadducees stand for the formalist element in Judaism. Leaven in the Gospels is usually a symbol for secrecy as in the parable (Mt. 13^{33}), and the saying, therefore, is by him taken as a warning against the hidden and unnoticed recrudescence in the Christian Church of the spirit of Judaistic legalism. As early as A.D. 54 the Pharisaic element was at least large enough to give extreme uneasiness to S. Paul, though it was not large enough to leaven the whole lump. We have, therefore, here a good example of a saying of Jesus applied to an existing situation in the Christian Church, whatever its original meaning may have been.

16^{13-16}. *Peter's confession* (Mk. 8^{27-30}, Lk. 9^{18}).

It has long been recognized that the confession of Peter and the Transfiguration are central, both in time and importance, in the Marcan or Petrine tradition, of which these two peaks, as they have been described, form the watershed. To these connected events the whole of the earlier history of the Gospel leads up, while the thrice-repeated prediction of the Passion begins to usher in, as with a knell, the final stage of the drama now hastening to its end. Mt. characteristically adds two further Petrine supplements. (1) Foreshadowing the foundation of a Church on Peter and defining its relation to the Synagogue, vv. 18–20. (2) Adjusting the relations of the Church to the civil administration, 17²⁴⁻²⁷.

16¹³. *Cæsarea Philippi.* Formerly Paneas, named after Philip the Tetrarch, son of Herod the Great, who had rebuilt it in honour of Augustus, and to be distinguished from the Cæsarea on the coast called Sebastae or Stratonis, the seat of the Procurator of Judaea. It lay at the foot of Mount Hermon where, in a wild gorge of surpassing grandeur, the Jordan bursts out, a fully formed river. On the summit of the rocky gorge stood a temple dedicated to Augustus which some think occasioned the imagery of verse 18.[1]

16¹⁴. *Jeremiah.* Why? Because Mt. is well aware of the Jewish belief in the appearance of the famous dead before the outbreak of the Messianic age, first of Elijah (11¹⁴), then of Moses (17³), and afterwards of many others (27⁵²⁻⁵³), such as Jeremiah (see 4 Esdras 2¹⁸, 2 Macc. 2^{5f.}, 15^{14f.}).

16¹⁷⁻²⁰. *Second Petrine Supplement.* These words are not found elsewhere in the Gospels or referred to in the N.T. and have been the subject of much controversy. It should, however, be borne in mind that there is no reason to suppose that Mt. departs from his usual practice of grouping together sayings which were not uttered at the same time. In this passage he may have wished to improve on the Marcan story of Peter's confession with its abrupt rebuke (Mk. 8³⁰) which, according to Mk. and Lk., was the only answer which it received. For this purpose it has been suggested that Mt. has in vv. 18–19 transferred into the historical narrative a logion taken from one of the post-Resurrection utterances of Jesus. It is equally possible that Mt. is here, as in other places, following a better-informed source than Mk. At the same time, while there is ample evidence of a logion of Jesus designating Simon as the 'rockman' (Jn. 1⁴², Mk. 3¹⁶) (this is in fact, as some think, the actual occasion on which the name Peter was conferred), Mt.'s habitual use of the 'targum' may account for the addition of vv. 19 and 20. At the same time, while it is true that the sequence of thought from 16¹³ to 17¹⁴—the idea of life through death—is

---

[1] For the topography of the Gospels as a whole the best books are: Sir G. Adam Smith, *Historical Geography of the Holy Land*; Sanday, *Sacred Sites of the Gospels.*

rather harshly interrupted by an unexpected reference to the question of Church administration, account must be taken of the poetic unity of the words as they stand in Mt., reminding us of the poem in Mt. 11[25-30]. If we examine closely the structure of the verses we find the characteristic form of a Hebrew poem of two strophes: (a) the line *Thou art Peter*, followed by two others amplifying the theme, corresponding to *Thou art the Christ*; (b) the line *I will give unto thee the keys*, followed by two further lines in the same way. The removal of any part dislocates the whole. (A full discussion of the bearing of these verses on the position of Peter in the Apostolic Church, and the various interpretations of this passage, is postponed to Additional Note E.)

16[18]. *Peter—on this rock*, Gk. *Πέτρος—πέτρα*. In Aramaic there is no distinction of gender so that the play upon the name Peter is quite certain. There can, therefore, be no doubt that the words ʻI will build my church' were understood by Mt. to refer to Peter himself personally. The image of the rock which bears the community, and applied to a particular person, e.g. Abraham, was not uncommon in later Jewish literature. The idea in all probability was derived from the classical passage Isa. 28[16], which is itself a development of the common oriental theme of the sacred foundation or cosmic rock, which is the beginning of creation, the centre of the earth, the keystone of the underworld and the protection of the creation against its powers.[1] Hence the reference to the *gates of Hell*. This sacred foundation had long been identified in its Jewish form with the rock of Mount Zion, still to be seen at Jerusalem in the Mosque called the Dome of the Rock, and which was probably the exact site of the Holy of Holies, but in Christian folk-lore it came to be associated with the rock of Golgotha, where Adam was believed to be buried. Just as the Rabbis, therefore, regarded Abraham as the foundation and keystone of their nation, so our Lord regards Peter as the foundation of the new Israel.[2] If, as some think, this saying is to be regarded as a post-Resurrection utterance of our Lord, the reference then is to the community which

---

[1] Dr. J. Jeremias in his book *Golgotha* has brought together a great deal of interesting information on this legend and connected it with many other references in the N.T., e.g. 1 Cor. 10[4].

[2] An ancient Midrash on Deut. 21 is quoted by Taylor (*Sayings of the Jewish Fathers*, p. 160) to the effect that ʻGod says, how shall I create the world while the godless exist and provoke me? But when he saw Abraham who should be born then He spake, "See! I have found a rock to build on it, to found on it the world." Therefore named He Abraham *Rock*, for it is said, "Look unto the rock whence ye are hewn".' (Isa. 51[1].)

looked upon Peter as the author of its resurrection faith[1] (v. note on 14^22 ff.).

I will build my church, Gk. *ecclesia*, used only once again in 18^17. In LXX it usually represents the Hebrew *qahal* = Israel, as a congregation assembled for a religious purpose (cf. Acts 7^38). The use of the word raises the difficulty that our Lord could hardly have contemplated at that time, the founding of a church in view of the near approach of the end. But probably the word is here equivalent to the Aramaic *k'nishta*, the word used in the time of our Lord for a separate congregation or synagogue, just as S. Peter calls the Christians a 'peculiar' people, with the existence of which Judaism in his time was perfectly familiar. It is the view of Kattenbusch that such a separate synagogue could hold its own special beliefs without being in the least schismatical, and even regard itself as representing, *pars pro toto*, the true Israel. In that case the allusion in this logion is to such a passage as Dan. 7^27, where the Kingdom is given to the *ecclesia* of the saints of the Most High; or even more probably to the apocalyptic work called the Book of Enoch, in which the Messianic community is quite definitely referred to as the *synagogue of the last days*,[2] which, according to Acts, was just what the primitive Palestinian church believed itself to be. The strength of this interpretation lies in its recognition of the eschatological character of the saying, which has escaped the notice of commentators, who have been preoccupied with its dogmatic and ecclesiastical relations.

Gates of hell, Gk. πύλαι ἅδου, a common synonym for the powers of the underworld and of death (cf. Homer, *Il.* 5. 646. The meaning clearly is that the community of the Messiah, whose authority Peter is, will be delivered in the last days when the powers of the underworld will overwhelm mankind. Harnack mentions an ancient Patristic variant which has 'you' for 'it', referring directly to Peter, in which case the words refer either to the Transfiguration (16^28), 'You shall not die before the parousia'; or that his office will, like the Church, be perpetual.

16^19. *The keys of the kingdom of heaven.* A much-disputed phrase, (1) What is meant by the power of the keys? (2) What is meant here by the Kingdom of Heaven?

(1) There are three possible explanations: (a) the authority to

[1] 1 Pet. 2^9.
[2] Book of Enoch 38^1 and 62^8.

admit into or to exclude from the Church—the power of excommunication. (*b*) A more general expression for the position of chief steward or major-domo in the Church of God, the keys being the symbol of the authority entrusted to the householder (Gk. οἰκονόμος, Lk. 12^{42}). In this sense, Peter is Christ's vicar on earth. (*c*) In a protective sense, i.e. Peter holds the keys of the Kingdom as Christ Himself holds the keys of Hell and of Death (Rev. 1^{18}). Of these (*a*) is supported by the words concerning the binding and loosing, which immediately follow and by the phrases in 23^{13}, Lk. 11^{52}, where the Pharisees are said to shut up the Kingdom of Heaven in the face of men. It was this power that subsequent Popes, such as Callixtus, claimed to use in mitigation of the severe penitential system of the Church in the third century A.D.

In favour of (*b*) there is the use of the same expression in Isa. 22^{22}, where Eliakim is given the keys as Steward or Grand Vizier of the Royal Household. In this case the word implies general administrative authority in the Church of God inclusive of the power of the keys in the more technical sense of (*a*).

In favour of (*c*) is the application of the same functions to the Risen and Exalted Christ in Rev. 1^{18}, and 3^{7}, and in the parallel passages quoted by Reitzenstein and others in support of the mythological origin of the passage. If the keys imply 'Wardenship' the words may represent the application to Peter of a Jewish tradition such as that in the Greek Apocalypse of Baruch, where Michael the Archangel is described as the Warden of the keys of the Kingdom of Heaven.

(2) In all these cases the Kingdom of Heaven appears to be identified with the Christian Church. This, however, is not absolutely necessary, because if the argument (Additional Note D) is correct, that the Kingdom always bore in our Lord's teaching a dynamic meaning, the words may be said to give to Peter, as Vicegerent of Christ, the 'powers of the world to come' which Christ Himself exercised when on earth, manifested in the forgiveness of sins and miracles; together with the right to receive into the visible sphere of the Church which is Christ's Messianic Kingdom those revealed to him (e.g. non-Jews) as its true members and alternatively to exclude them. In any case it is the Church regarded as the visible sphere or manifestation of the power of God exercised by Jesus on earth.

16^{19}. *Whatsoever thou shalt bind*, Gk. δήσῃς—λύσῃς = first of all, legislative authority. The Greek words, if equivalent to well-known

Aramaic words, are the usual term for the verdict of a Doctor of the Law, who in the strength of his expert knowledge of the old tradition declared some action bound, i.e. 'forbidden' or 'loosed', i.e. permitted. Many things which the School of Shammai 'bound', e.g. divorce except in case of adultery, that of Hillel 'loosed'. Peter is hereby declared to be the great Rabbi or scribe of the Christian *ecclesia*, who could make infallible and irreformable decisions on the basis not of the tradition of the Elders, but of the teaching of Jesus. This is the view adopted by most commentators, including Streeter, who cites Mt. 23[13] and Lk. 11[52] in support. Kirk, on the other hand, regards the words as an expansion of the saying about the keys and as referring to the question of the admission of the Gentiles. For this reason he regards the passage in Mt. 18[18] as probably the more primitive of the two. Probably there was no reference to absolution in the words, except as a judicial sentence; the word 'bind' (Gk. δέειν) being never used by the Jews for retaining sins in the sense of refusal of absolution.

In heaven, Gk. ἐν τοῖς οὐρανοῖς. Professor Bartlett calls attention to the fact that elsewhere in Mt. the contrast between heaven and earth is expressed by the singular as in 18[18], which he therefore regards as the original saying, and Mt. 6[19-20].

16[21]. Mt. continues the narrative of Mk. with the first prediction of the Passion. Like Mk. he gives no reason for the necessity (δεῖν) of the departure for Jerusalem and the sufferings which will follow arrival there. The idea of a suffering Messiah was probably alien to the Jewish thought of the time, but not if combined with the picture of the suffering Servant of Jehovah.

16[21]. *elders*. Chief Priests and Scribes, the Sanhedrin; Israel in the most formal expression of its mind and sovereignty—a deliberate and considered rejection.

the third day. Is this original? It seems to be an allusion to words in Hosea 6[2], 'After three days he will revive us'; the reference being to the Jewish tradition that death did not finally take hold till after the third day; cf. note on Mt. 12[40], and Jn. 11[39].

16[22]. *Be it far from thee, Lord*, Gk. ἵλεώς σοι Κύριε, an exclamation like our 'good gracious'.

16[23]. *Get thee behind me Satan*. Because the suggestion to evade the Cross was of the same nature as the temptation in the wilderness. This is the only instance recorded of advice being offered to Jesus, and that by one himself only on the outer fringe of the Kingdom. It was not repeated.

mindest not, Gk. φρονεῖς, as translated by T. R. Glover, 'You think like a man and not as God thinks.'

NOTE E. THE POSITION OF PETER IN CHRISTIAN TRADITION

The Primacy of S. Peter is a very real thing to Matthew. In the fourth book of his Gospel every possible occasion is seized to enhance the authority of Peter to bind and to loose. It is idle to deny this; and the attempt to do so has been very largely abandoned by modern critics. Peter, the foundation rock of the Church and, in virtue of his resurrection faith, its chief Under-Shepherd, had in Mt.'s belief been fully authorized to interpret and apply the saying about inward cleanness, so that in due time he might break down the middle wall of partition and carry the Gospel to the Gentiles without that yoke which, as Peter elsewhere himself declares 'neither our fathers nor we were able to bear' (Acts 15[10]).

But it is not Mt. who is alone responsible for the central position of Peter in the primitive church. Peter's leading position already begins to appear in Mk. with the story of his call by the Lake of Galilee,[1] his confession at Caesarea and, above all, in the message of the angel of the Resurrection.[2] This position is greatly enhanced in Lk.–Acts as seen in the incident of the miraculous draft of fishes, Peter's ordination to be a 'fisher of men',[3] the direction to Peter of the words about the trustworthy steward;[4] the task laid on him in the hour of his temptation to strengthen his brethren,[5] and the mention, unique in the Synoptic Gospels, of the appearance to him of the Risen One;[6] to which may be added the more favourable light in which Peter is made to appear in the Garden[7] and, lastly, the role of leadership attributed to him in the early chapters of the Acts, made all the more effective by the shadowy figure of John who appears as a sort of foil to the great Primate of the Church.[8] This tendency was continued in a special degree by the first Gospel, in which is recorded the change from what appears to have been at first a loosely organized community, the life of the Christian brotherhood, to an ecclesiastical theocracy under the primacy of Peter.[9]

[1] Mk. 1[16].   [2] Mk. 16[7].   [3] Lk. 5[10].   [4] Lk. 12[41].   [5] Lk. 22[31].
[6] Lk. 24[34].   [7] Lk. 22[45].   [8] Acts 1–5, cf. 10 and 11.
[9] Mt. 16[19]. On the other hand, the writer of the Fourth Gospel seems to suggest that the Petrine witness, as seen in the Gospel of Mk., was less trustworthy than that of another member of the Apostolic circle whom he called the 'beloved disciple'. In the very first chapter he tells us that an unknown disciple of John the Baptist, together with Andrew, the brother of Peter, became a disciple of Jesus before Peter, while at the beginning of the Passion

Matthew, accordingly, writing at the end of the first century, long after the death of Peter, clearly regarded the primacy and office of Peter—though not yet connected with Rome[1]—as a permanent factor in the Church, while John, writing at the same time, or a little later, placed the Apostolic authority in the Twelve and their successors, as Mt. in another place[2] appears to do.

What have been the most important interpretations of the Petrine passage in ancient and modern times?

1. We may note first of all the claim of the Latin Church that the words of Mt. 16[18-19] are a plain statement of fact, that Jesus gave to Peter and to his successors universal and immediate jurisdiction over the Christian Church and all its members. The further claim that this succession is that of Rome, rather than Antioch,[3] which, according to well-supported tradition, was the first See of Peter, is not of course based on the sayings of Jesus; but in the language of Lagrange, 'the words of Jesus at Caesarea are so manifestly a prophecy which has been fulfilled (in Rome) that it is a powerful argument for its credibility'.[4] This interpretation has the weight of a vast, though never *universally* accepted tradition behind it, and the Petrine authority championed by Mt. remains a factor not to be disregarded in the history of the Church.

2. Next to the Roman, the most widespread and oldest interpretation from the second century onwards, is that the words in verse 19 refer to the *faith* of Peter, then for the first time confessed,

the unknown one appears as the most trusted disciple whose mediation Peter must secure to learn who the traitor is. That other disciple goes in with Peter to the court of the High Priest, but unlike him does not deny his Master, even though he goes farther within the range of danger than the other. While at the foot of the Cross, Jesus, by a last testament, adopts not Peter but the beloved disciple into His own family; and that disciple who took the Virgin to his own home becomes *ipso facto* the true heir and guarantor of the orthodox tradition (**19[35]**). The same order of things is seen again at the Tomb and in the subsequent appearance by the Lake, when Peter is no more than reinstated in the Apostolic office which he had forfeited by his denials; while there can be no question of a place as Over-shepherd of the flock, for that is expressly reserved in the Fourth Gospel to Christ Himself as it is also in 1 Pet. 5[4], cf. Jn. 10.

[1] Cf. Streeter, *Four Gospels*, p. 515.   [2] Mt. 18[18].

[3] There is no need to question Canon Streeter's statement that the primacy of Peter to which Mt. refers was already in his time associated with Antioch, which claimed Peter as the founder of its succession of bishops of which S. Ignatius was the third, and which was for many centuries the acknowledged authority and centre of all the oriental churches, as it is still of the Syrian. Origen (Hom. in Luc. vi) asserts that Ignatius was the second Bishop of Antioch *after Peter*.

[4] *L'Évangile selon S. Matthieu*, p. 327.

in the Messiahship of Jesus. Here at last was a man to whom Jesus was able to commit Himself, and on the strength of whose faith He could now begin to build an institution which would survive amid the fluctuations of time.

The general Patristic exegesis[1] of the passage may be summed up in the words of S. Ambrose, 'primatum egit confessionis utique non honoris—fidei non ordinis', i.e. in making his profession of faith he exercised a primacy of faith not of order.[2] S. Augustine[3] and once even Leo the Great (A.D. 440), who was one of the first of the Popes to make great claims for the Papacy, regard the rock as Christ Himself. S. Cyprian, however (A.D. 248–59), stands out among the Fathers as the contributor of a remarkable interpretation which may still perhaps, when understood, supply the key to the solution of this problem. Speaking of the claims of the Bishop of Rome to exercise authority in the matter of faith, he remarks in the book *On the Unity of the Church*, 'He builds His Church upon one man—and although after His resurrection He assigned equal power to all His Apostles (in the words of Jn. 20[21–22]) nevertheless, *in order that He might make manifest its unity*, He disposed the origin of that same unity as having its beginning under one man.'[4] He proceeds to maintain that the *Cathedra Petri*, or the chair of Peter, is not to be sought in the Apostolic See of Rome only, or any other episcopal See by itself, but in the succession of bishops as a whole. This exegesis which has exercised powerful influence in the history of the Church has the advantage of reconciling the two apparently conflicting passages, 16[18–20] and 18[15–20], while at the same time emphasizing the principle which the Roman See has

[1] The earliest references in Christian literature to this passage are (1) Justin Martyr, *Dialogue with Trypho*, Ch. 100–6, 113; (2) Tertullian, *De Baptismate*, 17, *De Pudicitia*, **21**; (3) Irenaeus, *Adv. Haer.* 3. 21. 8; (4) Clement of Alexandria, *Strom.* vi. 6, 48; 5, 39. But though all show knowledge of the passage in question, all regard *Christ* as the rock and the foundation-stone. The first to attribute the words directly to Peter is the author of the so-called *Kerugma Petri*, the source of the pseudo-Clementine literature (A.D. 220–30) in which Peter is already the first of the Apostles, and on account of the truth of his belief and the trustworthiness of his doctrine the foundation-stone of the Church. His power to place Bishops in various churches is referred back in the Epistle to Clement (1 and 2) at least indirectly to Mt. 16[18-19], and accordingly the Roman bishop is regarded as his successor.

[2] Ambrose, *De Incarn.* 4. 32. Liturgies point to the same interpretation.

[3] Augustine, Sermons 76 and 270; Leo, sermo 15, tom. 5. For a first-rate example of modern exegesis of this text referring it to the faith of Peter see Scott Holland, *Creed and Character, the Story of an Apostle's Faith,* pp. 3–36.

[4] Cyprian *De Unitate Ecclesiae*, Ch. 15. Cf. Ep. **33.**

always put in the forefront of her claim for supremacy, namely the unity of the Church, with which, as we have seen, the book of Mt. where both passages occur is also concerned. To Cyprian the *Cathedra Petri* is the Christian episcopate, whether as a whole or as represented in its individual members.

(3) Modern critics are sharply divided both as to the authenticity of the words and their exact meaning. But there is a strong tendency, especially among German critics, to maintain the substantial historicity of verse 18 and its personal application to Peter, but to relegate verse 19 to the category of 'sayings of the Spirit' like those in the Apocalypse. Even so conservative a critic as the late Professor C. H. Turner was inclined to regard both verses as having originally circulated as a saying of the Risen One.[1] From that position it is only a step to that of Bultmann who regards them as an utterance of the primitive community of Palestine placed in the mouth of the Risen Lord. Streeter, admitting the substantial genuineness of verse 18, regards verse 19 as a saying of the Lord but modified in a Judaistic direction and representing 'the conversation as remembered and repeated and in repetition doubtless not a little modified by those who disapproved alike of the undue conservatism of James and of Paul's too liberal attitude towards the law, but were content to accept the *via media* of Peter a great name at Antioch, in whom by Christ's appointment as the supreme Rabbi, rested the final interpretation of the new Law given to the new Israel'. As we have seen, there were other Gospels like that according to the Hebrews which ignored Peter and recognized only James. (See Introduction, p. 18).

(4) It is perhaps in the uncertain character of the functions attributed to Peter that the secondary character of Mt. 16^{19} becomes most apparent. Power of admission to and expulsion from the Church, of infallible interpretation of Scripture, of definition of doctrine and morals, of legislation, jurisdiction, and, above all stewardship and protection of the community, are all advanced as interpretations of the powers conferred in verse 19, and it is impossible to exclude any one of them. For this reason alone it is difficult not to believe that we have to do here with the expansion or development in the Church of a saying of Jesus about Peter as a 'rock-like man' in some other connexion. For the description of Peter in this verse is not so much that of an apostle as that of a *bishop* in the second-century meaning of the term, i.e. of a

[1] See the Essay on Peter in the N.T. in the posthumous book *Catholic and Apostolic*.

'monarchical bishop', like S. Ignatius of Antioch. Already in the Pastoral Epistles the bishop appears as the 'steward' both of the earthly and heavenly treasures of the Church, and Mt. himself elsewhere refers to the rightly instructed scribe of the Kingdom, as a 'householder' (Mt. 13⁵²). Hence it has been suggested by a recent writer that the purpose of Mt. 16¹⁸⁻¹⁹ is to describe Peter as the archetype of the monarchical bishop at that time beginning to arise in Syria. It is in the monarchical episcopate that we find the same association of powers as are entrusted in these verses to Peter, and it would appear probable that the later exaltation of the bishop to a monarchical position in the Church is not without its relation to this passage. The suggestion that our author has sought in the promise to S. Peter the origin of an institution beginning to emerge in his own day, rather than the glorification of Peter himself, now no longer alive, gives point to Cyprian's exegesis of the passage which saw in it a guarantee of the unity of the Church, the purpose for which the Episcopate, as we now know it, was developed. And if, as Streeter suggests, the monarchical episcopate had its origin in Syria, what time would be more likely for its emergence than when the death of the 'pillars' of the primitive community, to whom Paul attributes such importance,[1] namely James and the other blood-relations of the Lord, had deprived the parent Church of its natural leaders? The place of the Patriarchate of Jerusalem is to be taken by the monarch-bishop under the guise of Peter as representative of the Apostolic authority. In this connexion it is significant that to S. Ignatius, who is usually regarded as the pioneer of the movement towards monarchical episcopacy, the Gospel of Mt. is the Gospel *par excellence*. It is at least possible that it was he who advocated its claim to canonicity at Rome. Did he introduce to that church not only the Gospel of Mt. but the new idea of episcopacy of which it was the advocate? In any case it cannot be doubted that the Gospel of Mt. proved a tremendous stimulus to the movement towards administrative consolidation in the Church as it was to anything which made for unity against its enemies.

17¹⁻⁸. *The Transfiguration* (Mk. 9² ff., Lk. 9²⁸ ff.).

From the beginning 'the Church had fixed upon the Transfiguration as the central moment of our Lord's earthly life. It had surrounded that moment with a glamour of allusion so complex that it cannot now with any certainty be analysed into its

---

[1] Gal. 2⁹.

constituent elements. And it had done this to remind itself that the whole Gospel from beginning to end must be read and regarded as one great vision of God in Christ, divinity breaking through the humanity of Jesus.'[1] If we are to understand its meaning and place in the Gospel story, it is necessary, as in the case of the Petrine passage, to bear in mind its *eschatological* character. It is closely connected (1) with the judgement and coming of the Son of man (16^{27-28}); (2) with the Resurrection (17^9) always regarded in the N.T. as a great act of God in which His invisible power is made visible, as it was in the Transfiguration; the Kingdom of Heaven breaking through the barriers of the visible world. S. Paul works out the implication of the story on these lines in 2 Cor. 3^{18}, where the same word for Transfiguration, Gk. μετεμόρφωθη, is used; and it was probably the Transfiguration which inspired his words in Rom. 8^{19-21}, in which he speaks of the 'adoption, to wit the redemption', of our bodies. It is, however, probable that even in its early surviving form in Mk. the story had already been subjected to some degree of literary elaboration.

17^1. *high mountain.* Tabor in Galilee, the traditional scene of the theophany, could not by any stretch of imagination be called high. The mountain was probably Hermon, 14 miles north of Caesarea Philippi.

17^2. Each Evangelist chooses his words independently. Mk. has the homely comparison of the whiteness of the garments to fuller's work, which Mt. in D and some old Latin versions, has altered to snow; but 'light' is the better attested reading, the symbolical form in which mystics of all ages have attempted to describe their ineffable experiences.

17^3. *there appeared*, Gk. ὤφθη, i.e. a vision occurred—a word almost always used in the N.T. of supernatural appearances.

Moses and Elias. Various explanations have been given for the appearance of these two O.T. Saints: (1) they represent respectively law and the prophets; (2) they were both translated into heaven, Elijah, as recorded in 2 Kings 2, Moses by assumption, according to current belief in the time of our Lord. (3) Each was expected to reappear as a forerunner of the Messiah (Deut. 18^{15-19}, Mal. 4^5). (4) Each had held solemn communion with God (Exod. 20, 1 Kings 19). As a result Moses' face was transfigured so that he was compelled to cover it with a veil while speaking to the people (Exod. 34^{32-35}, 2 Cor. 3^7). Both reappear later as the two witnesses in Rev. 11^3. They are also found together in

---

[1] K. E. Kirk, *Vision of God*, pp. 97–101.

the Midrashim as the forerunners of the Messiah and as his 'immortal companions'. (See Box, *St. Matthew*, p. 270.)

17^5. *a bright cloud*, an allusion to the Shekinah or cloud of divine glory, the ancient symbol of the localized divine presence as in 1 Kings 8^{11}. From it the divine voice, the Bathkol, proceeded (see note on Mt. 3^{17}). Cf. 2 Pet. 1^{17}, Exod. 24^{18}, 40^{34}, where in LXX the same word is used of the cloud overshadowing the tabernacle.

17^5. *hear ye him.* With reference to the prophet of Deut. 18^{18} whom God would raise up after Moses and like unto him, regarded by many as the Messiah.

17^9. *Tell the vision to no man.* It is these words which connect the vision closely with the Resurrection, an event which, according to all Jewish belief since Dan. 12^2, must precede the full manifestation of the Kingdom of God.

17^{11}. *Shall restore all things.* The ἀποκατάστασις or restoration of the world to its primeval perfection was a well-known feature of Messianic expectations (Mal. 3^{1-4}). The disciples had seen Elijah on the mountain; in what relation did this appearance stand to his advent, as understood by the official theologians, and what did Jesus mean by the prediction of His Passion, if all things were already restored? His reply is that Elijah has, in reality and not only in vision, appeared in the person of John the Baptist—but so far from restoring all things they killed him and prevented him from doing anything of the kind. Therefore it is that the prophecies of the Passion yet find room for fulfilment.

17^{14-18}. *The healing of the epileptic boy.* Raphael's famous cartoon brings out, as the Evangelist intended, the striking contrast between the rapt contemplation on the mountain and the frantic scene below.

17^{21}. This verse, when found in MSS., e.g. in Codex Sinaiticus (b), is clearly an assimilation to Mk. 9^{29}.

$17^{22, 23}$. *Second prediction of the Passion* (Mk. 9^{30-32}, Lk. 9^{43-45}).

17^{22}. *while they abode*, Gk. συστρεφομένων = in LXX, to gather together for battle; the word, therefore, implies more than in R.V. and A.V. It means 'while they were collecting at some rendezvous in Galilee', suggesting that the group had broken up during the exile in the north into small parties which mustered at certain points on the route to Judea.

17^{24-27}. *Third Petrine Supplement*, from the N source. The question of Church administration on its external side, i.e. its relation to the religious and civil authorities outside the Church. While the Temple was still standing groups of christianized Jews expelled from the synagogue might well be in some perplexity when the collector of the Temple tax appeared demanding to know if they were Jews or not. After its destruction the question still remained; for the Roman treasury absorbed the tax much in the way that the modern State annexes the tithes when a Church is disestablished. The interest for Mt. lies not in the incident itself but in the unique position given to Peter as Vicar of Christ in relation to external authority. Nothing is in fact said about anything happening, and no miracle is recorded as having taken place. It has all the marks of a community paradigm. (See Appendix, p. 265.)

17^{24}. *The tribute money*, Gk. δίδραχμα. The *drachm* is a quarter of a shekel = about 1s. 4½d. sterling; a tax made on all Jews over 19 for the maintenance of the temple and based on Exod. 23^{15}, 'Thou shalt not appear before Me empty'. Since the *double drachms* were seldom coined, two Jews often combined to pay a *stater*, the coin in verse 27, twice a double drachm.

17^{25}. *tribute*, Gk. κῆνσον, Lat. *census*, the capitation tax alluded to in Mt. 22^{17}. *toll*, Gk. τέλη, local duties collected by publicans.

their sons or from strangers, i.e. of members of the Royal Family or others not so related?

17^{26}. *Therefore are the sons free*, i.e. Jesus Himself and His disciples, the Christians, who are His brethren, are not to be taxed for His own Father's house.

B. DISCOURSE ON THE UNITY OF THE CHURCH, AS DEPENDENT ON THE BEHAVIOUR OF CHRIST'S FOLLOWERS TO ONE ANOTHER.

The basis is a section in Mk. (9^{33-50}) which begins with a quarrel among the Apostles for pre-eminence on the way. This leads to a discussion on toleration, scandals, and peacemaking. Here we naturally expect to find grouped together several teachings of Jesus such as the Apostolic Church found applicable in the course of its great struggle to keep the 'unity of the Spirit in the bond of peace'. It falls into four divisions. (1) Concerning scandal (18$^{1-7}$). (2) The peril of divisions and those who cause them (18$^{8-14}$). (3) The problem of Christian discipline (18$^{15-20}$). (4) Peter's responsibility in the matter (18$^{21-35}$). The whole discourse breathes the same deep longing for unity as in the discourses of Jesus after the Last Supper (Jn. 15–17).

(1) We may note that the quarrel among the disciples which gave Mk. the opportunity of inserting important words of our Lord on religious toleration is significantly omitted by Mt., probably

because it appeared to him in the circumstances in which he lived to go too far. Mt. has a great horror of lawlessness and of the persons who permit it or do things apart from the authorized ministry of the Church. Instead, therefore, of enlarging as he might have done on this theme he goes straight on to (2) the question of offences. At the same time we note that Mt. has given us two further sayings peculiar to his Gospel: (1) that without the child-spirit the disciples, so far from being the greatest in the Kingdom, will not enter it at all (18³). (2) He will be greatest who has the least idea that he is great (18⁴).

18⁵. *receive one such little child* i.e. receive into the fullest Christian fellowship even one who still regards himself as bound by the whole Jewish Law, who has not yet reached the full stature of Christian freedom. Mt. here has in mind the same problem in Christian ethics as occupied S. Paul in Rom. 12–15 and 1 Cor. 8. Insensibly the interest passes from real children to those whom S. Paul calls the weak, i.e. the scrupulous brother of tender conscience who may be induced to act against his conscience by the example of influential and important people whose consciences are robust and able to accept ethical innovations which they are inclined to urge on their less 'advanced' brothers. This is what Mt. means by scandal or causing offence. S. Paul's severe strictures in Rom. 14 and 15 on those who induce others to act against their conscience are, as always, in accordance with the teaching of our Lord. S. Clement of Rome, in his Epistle to the Corinthians, explains the words in this passage in the same way.

18⁶. *great millstone*, Gk. μύλος ὀνικός = a large millstone driven by an ass as distinct from a hand-mill which was usually worked by women (Mt. 24⁴¹).

18⁷. *it must needs be that the occasions come*—Why? The answer is the parable of the Tares (Mt. 13²⁴) which is also concerned with those who work lawlessness. When S. Paul says there *must* be heresies among you (1 Cor. 11¹⁹), he is, as usual, echoing words of Christ.

18¹⁰. *their angels.* A reference to the Jewish doctrine of the angelic administration of the Divine justice to which the little ones appeal. In later Jewish belief each nation has a patron angel. Israel has Michael (Dan. 10¹³), and a development of this idea is seen in the Angels of the Seven Churches (Rev. 1²⁰) who are their Churches' representatives in the Heavenly Court. Similarly Job has an angelic intercessor 'one of a thousand' to whom he appeals to ransom him from his desperate situation (Job 33²³). The angels of the little ones are to be explained in the same way. McNeile sees in the words a reference to the Persian doctrine of the *fravashi* or double souls who, like Peter's angel in Acts 12¹⁵, represent and sometimes even impersonate the bodily presence of their owner.

18¹²⁻¹⁴. *The Parable of the Lost Sheep.* This image sums up the attitude of the Matthean Gospel in which, in spite of all its striking protests against scandals, divisions, and antinomianism, the penalty of excommunication is combined with a gentleness not excelled even in Lk. There is little rigorism in the Gospel.

18¹⁵⁻³⁵. *The problem of Ecclesiastical Discipline.*

1. This discourse is presumably addressed to the Apostles as leaders of the Christian community. Opinion is equally divided among critics as to which of the two 'ecclesiastical texts', Mt. 16¹⁸⁻¹⁹ or 18¹⁵⁻²⁰, is the more original. Dr. Kirk is inclined to think the latter, not only because the commission of the Twelve to bind and to loose is supported by the parallel passage in Jn. 20²³, but also because it was more workable, for whatever Peter may have done at Jerusalem, he cannot have had the exclusive exercise of discipline in the Church at large. Both versions of the Apostolic commission in this passage are strongly Judaistic in phrasing so that there is nothing to choose between them on that ground.

2. This section is, like Mt. 16¹⁸⁻¹⁹, composite. It is based on a saying which stood in Q, as may be seen from the parallel Lk. 17³ᶠᶠ·, where the words refer to wrongs done by one person to another. But Mt. uses the sayings to illustrate the established rule of the Church with regard to sin in general. After the enactment of the procedure for the treatment of sins of Church members by Church officers, instead of proceeding with the instruction in Lk. 17³ to forgive to seven times, Mt. interpolates from an unknown source the saying about corporate prayer, verse 19. This saying appears to be connected with the service of public penance in the Church, known as *exomologesis*, which meant not public *confession*, which never existed normally in the Church, but public *absolution* in which the corporate intercession of the congregation on behalf of the offender was an important feature. Only then does Mt. turn to the injunction about repeated forgiveness, but it is now, as Dr. Kirk remarks, with a significance vastly greater. For it is laid down that the Church, though she is to treat the impenitent sinner as a heathen and a publican, must allow him constant opportunities of reconciliation should he desire it. The motive throughout in Mt. is pastoral and concerned with the *unity* of the Church rather than with its *purity*. 'Thou has gained thy brother.'

3. The primitive Church as a whole did not follow the line laid down in Mt. For the first few centuries of its history the exercise of excommunication was carried out with a severity which eventually defeated its own end. For the most part it took over from Judaism the machinery of discipline. The severest case of discipline in the N.T. is that mentioned in 1 Cor. 5, in which Paul pronounces the terrible sentence of 'delivery over to Satan', a type of excommunication more serious even than the *herem* or *ban* of the Jewish system, and nothing short of the 'destruction of the flesh', i.e. death by anathema or curse, similar to the penalty inflicted on Ananias and Sapphira in Acts 5. Heb. 6⁶, 1 Jn. 5¹⁶, when read in the light of Mt. 12³¹ show that already in the Christian Church the rigorist view prevailed, which allowed no penance or even hope of forgiveness for certain classes of sins.

18¹⁵. *shew him his fault*, Gk. ἔλεγξον, a much stronger expression than R.V. It means the result of a judicial process, 'convict him'.

18¹⁶. Indicates the Jewish character of the procedure. The Mosaic regulations as to witnesses must be complied with (Deut. 19¹⁵).

18¹⁷. *the Gentile and the publican*, this can hardly in view of His attitude to the publican be regarded as a saying of Jesus.

18¹⁸. *bind—loose*. Here, without any doubt, the reference is to excommunication and reconciliation, always carried out in the primitive Church by the Bishop only and not for some centuries delegated to the priesthood.

18¹⁹. 'The Lord is present in the midst of the ecclesia as the true minister of its ordinances', as in 1 Cor. 5⁴. Originally, no doubt, the saying had a wider significance. There are striking Rabbinic parallels to this saying, e.g. 'when two are sitting and the words of the Torah are between them the *Shekinah*, i.e. divine Presence, is among them'.[1] In this connexion the same exalted claims are made for Church authority as in Acts 15²⁸, where the decision of the Council of Jerusalem is regarded as an utterance of the Holy Spirit.

18²¹⁻³⁵. *The Parable of the Unmerciful Servant*. Mt. again introduces Peter as the mediator for obtaining a decision on the question before the Church.

18²⁴. A talent = 6,000 Denarii or £240; 100 Denarii or pence = £4, or $\frac{1}{600,000}$ of his own remitted debt.

---

[1] *Pirke Aboth*, iii. 3. 9.

FIFTH BOOK OF MATTHEW

19¹–26¹. THE MESSIANIC JUDGEMENT

In the fifth and final book, the Gospel mounts steadily to a most tremendous climax. Every opportunity afforded by the material is utilized for heightening the colour of the apocalyptic judgement and emphasizing its nearness. Already in 16²⁷, against the merely general warning of Mk. 9¹, Mt. had given the specific assurance 'that the Son of man is about to come in the glory of His Father with His angels'. 'I give you my word there are some of them that stand here that shall not taste of death till they see the Son of man coming in His Kingdom.' 'Mk.'s aim is to repress apocalyptic excitement after the manner of S. Paul in 2 Thess. 2². Mt. seeks to rekindle its sinking fires' (Bacon). The parables of the Vineyard, the penitent younger Son, the usurping Husbandmen, and the Slighted Invitation form a group well adapted to the situation to which Mt. is leading up in this section. Mt. relies, as usual, for his introductory material almost entirely on Mk. which at this point appears to be an unchronological collection of anecdotes and sayings. (For discussion of Jewish eschatology and apocalyptic see Additional Note G.)

A PRELIMINARY NARRATIVE

19¹. *The Pilgrimage to Jerusalem* (Mk. 9³⁰–10⁵³, Lk. 9⁵¹ ᶠᶠ.). Burkitt has suggested that while Jesus went through Samaria, as Luke relates, Peter and some of the disciples went via Peraea, the route frequently taken by Jewish pilgrims to avoid Samaritan territory, meeting Him at the spot where the pilgrim route crossed the Jordan into Judaea. The '*borders of Judaea beyond Jordan*' is, as Lagrange points out, the plain situated between Jordan and the mountains of the East, a very flourishing region which would belong more to Judaea than the plateaux above it. If room is to be found for a Judaean mission, as recorded in S. John's Gospel, this would appear to be the place and time for it.

19³⁻⁹. *Second teaching on Marriage and Divorce* (Mk. 10¹⁻¹², Lk. 16¹⁸). (On this and the following section see Additional Note F.)

19⁴. Gen. 1²⁷, to which our Lord appeals as against the Rabbinic interpretation of Deut. 24¹.

19⁵. *shall cleave to his wife*, added either by Jesus or Mt. from Gen. 2²⁴. In favour of the former is the use of the quotation in this form by Paul in Eph. 5³¹, 1 Cor. 6¹⁶.

one flesh. Our Lord's own expression, meaning that the principle involved in the creation of man was a complete and indissoluble union.

19⁶. These words were introduced into the actual Marriage Service of the English Prayer Book as defining its doctrine of marriage at a time when the Reformation had introduced laxer ideas of the marriage tie. Formerly they stood only in the Gospel of the Nuptial Mass.

19⁸. *suffered,* Gk. ἐπέτρεψεν, our Lord by the change of word tacitly criticizes the word 'command'. Moses never *commanded* divorce, he only *permitted* it. Moses regulated and thereby conceded the practice of divorce in view of an insistent demand for a low standard of marriage.

19¹⁰⁻³⁰. *The Three Evangelical Counsels of Celibacy, voluntary Poverty, and Obedience.*

19¹⁰⁻¹². *Celibacy.* The meaning of this obscure passage is that celibacy, like the vocation to the married life, is a gift of God to be accepted and used for His purposes. Christians like S. Francis of Assisi have renounced marriage as they have riches, not because they are bad in themselves, but in order to be like Jesus in the world and to be able to give themselves more entirely to its conversion.

19¹³⁻¹⁵. If marriage is hallowed, so are the children: and if marriage is permitted so is the family which is the result of it. The position of this *paradigm* is clearly to show that one of the chief reasons against divorce is that the family is thereby inevitably broken up. It is on the unity of the family that the practice of infant baptism is based and is here meant to be defended. While the greatness of the sacrifice of those who give up all, including children, for the kingdom of heaven's sake is not minimized, it is clearly indicated that marriage and children are blessings not to be despised, as they have been in the interests of a dogmatic rigorism in some periods of Christianity.

NOTE F. DIVORCE AND REMARRIAGE IN THE CHRISTIAN CHURCH

The teaching of Mt. on this subject is found in three distinct passages which, with their parallels in Mark and Luke, must be carefully studied. (*a*) Mt. 5³², 'every one that putteth away his wife saving for the cause of fornication maketh her an adulteress: and whosoever shall marry her when she is put away committeth adultery'. (*b*) Mt. 19⁹, 'Whosoever shall put away his wife, except for fornication, and shall marry another, committeth adultery; and he that marrieth her when she is put away committeth adultery'. (*c*) The strange logion about celibacy in Mt. 19¹².

(a) The first of these texts occurs in the Sermon on the Mount in connexion with the Seventh Commandment. Assuming that the ordinary text is correct,[1] we have here a short statement to the effect that divorce compels the woman to marry again (or starve), but that such a marriage, although permitted under the Deuteronomic law (24[2]) is adulterous and forbidden in the Christian Church. After the words 'putteth away his wife' an exception is added 'saving for the cause of fornication'. Whatever view is taken of the genuineness of this clause, it does not alter the plain meaning of the saying, that even an innocent wife, if divorced, cannot remarry without being guilty of adultery. For in the case of the wife's guilt the saving clause assumes that she is already an adulteress and cannot therefore be made one by any action of her husband. It says nothing about the right of a man to remarry after he has divorced his wife.

(b) The second passage occurs in quite a different context and is in the form of an *apophthegm* or *paradigm*[2] designed to embody an important saying. The test question is asked by the Pharisees, 'Is it lawful for a man to put away his wife for every cause?' Verse 4 is the reply, with the usual appeal to Scripture. In verse 7 the counter-question is put, 'Why then did Moses command to give a bill of divorcement, and to put her away?'; in verse 8 the rejoinder ending in the pronouncement about divorce. Now in this passage it is clear that Mt. has conflated Mk. 10[11], which he follows in this passage, with the Q logion of Lk. 16[18]. Apart from slight differences in Mt. and Mk., Jesus' reply is substantially the same. The divorce legislation of Deuteronomy is, in the view of Jesus, merely a Mosaic ordinance introduced because of the hardness of men's hearts. But the original and divine command is found in Gen. 2[24], and summed up in the emphatic words of Jesus, 'What therefore God hath joined together let not man put asunder'. There follows the prohibition of divorce with remarriage; to which Mk. (*but not Mt.*) adds as a private statement to the disciples, i.e. the Church, 'And if she herself shall put away her husband and marry another she committeth adultery'. Professor Burkitt thinks that the added clause of Mark (10[12]), represents a denunciation of Herodias in the story of the death of John the Baptist, or as Dr. Kirk thinks, it was an intelligent addition addressed by Mark himself to the Roman Church to show that the prohibition of divorce affected both sexes equally, as indeed was the case in Roman law. Again, in the

[1] The D text omits the second clause, which was probably added from the same source as Mt. used in 19[9].   [2] See Appendix, p. 265.

Matthean version of the logion there is the same difficulty, as in 5[32], with regard to the qualifying clause, 'except that it is for fornication.' In any case the answer that Jesus gives in Mt., and presumably in Mt.'s source, is, 'not for every cause but only for adultery'. If this be the case then Mt. in this passage represents Jesus as intervening in a well-known controversy between the two great Pharisaic schools of Hillel on the one hand, who allowed divorce on the slightest grounds (e.g. bad temper or even ill-favoured looks in the wife), and that of Shammai on the other, who allowed it only for adultery, representing the lax and rigorist interpretations respectively of the 'unseemly thing' referred to in Deut. 24[1]. In this controversy He is therefore represented as coming down rather heavily on the side of Shammai. That this is intended by Mt. is shown by the fact that he has added to Mk. the words in verse 3 'for every cause'; which proves that the answer given in Mt. 19[9] is intended to be an answer to that *question only*, and not to any other. In other words, the most that this passage implies is that a tradition of Jesus was current, in the early Church, as saying in effect, 'if I consent to divorce at all (though it is not to be assumed that I do) I could never countenance it beyond the narrow limits laid down by the School of Shammai'. We cannot deny the possibility that this represents a genuine saying of Jesus in the context of such a controversy; but it must at the same time be recognized that this saying does not *explicitly* sanction remarriage after divorce, though it seems to do so implicitly, having regard to the fact that divorce without right of re-marriage was unknown in Judaism. Actually, as Lagrange interprets the saying, the most that it allows is that such cases are *reserved* for special consideration.

Now assuming that such a passage as Mt. 19[9], however apocryphal on the ground of form-criticism its setting may be, represents a true tradition, the further question arises, what does the excepting clause, '*save for fornication*' mean? Four suggestions have been made. (1) A single act of adultery dissolves the marriage bond. But as the Greek for adultery is here *porneia* and not the usual word *moicheia*, especially in the case of a woman, it is impossible to assume this. It certainly seems to be a piece of extreme rigorism to say that a single act of adultery, committed perhaps on the spur of the moment or under stress, dissolves the marriage bond. (2) For this reason it has been suggested that the word *porneia* = prolonged or promiscuous adultery. Again it is difficult to imagine that our Lord so far entered into the minutiae of legal casuistry as to legislate for the cases, obviously rare in the Christian Church, of a practice which even to a Roman such as Juvenal was of a particularly odious and disgusting character. (3) Hence the two explanations that it means pre-nuptial unchastity as in Mt. 1^{18} and (4) relationship within the prohibited degrees of marriage.[1] In the case of these last two the question under discussion would not be divorce and remarriage at all, but the question of nullity of marriage, of a 'diriment' impediment which, according to Jewish law, made the marriage null and void *ab initio*. It may be said at once that the logion in 5^{32} supports this view, for it makes the clause intelligible in that context, where, as we have already seen, if interpreted as meaning *adultery* it adds nothing and is pointless. If this be the correct view then we have among our Lord's words a statement that remarriage after a decree of nullity is lawful for a Christian, while remarriage after divorce (as both S. Paul and two other Gospels unanimously teach)[2] is not. This is the position which the teaching of western Christendom as a whole has consistently supported, and is that of the Canon Law in the Roman Catholic Church. It is also further implied that if this is the true interpretation, the Matthean editor in 19^{9} has misunderstood its meaning; for in this case, as we have seen, he represents our Lord as taking sides in a controversy between two Pharisaic schools of thought. But it is not likely that our Lord ever occupied Himself either with the details of Pharisaic casuistry or with those of the Canon Law. In other words, whether the excepting clause means adultery or nullity, its existence as an *independent* saying of our Lord, *apart from the context in Mt. 19^{9}*, cannot be demonstrated; and until it is demonstrated it cannot be used as claiming the authority of Christ for the remarriage of divorced persons in the Christian Church.

The authorization of re-marriage in the Greek Church was the result of political circumstances and does not in any way represent the general position of the primitive Church.

(3) It remains, however, to consider the curious epilogue to Mt. 19^{9} which is not without its bearing on the question at issue. The words, 'all men cannot receive this saying but (only) they to whom it is given', as we have seen, introduce the principle of the two standards known to Christian moral theology as the 'counsels' and the 'precepts'. (See Additional Note B.) Hence it may have

---

[1] For *porneia* as used in this and other senses, see articles in *Theology* (1927), xv, pp. 89–163.
[2] As in I Cor. 7^{10-17}, Lk. 16^{18}, Mk. $10^{11, 12}$.

been added by the Evangelist to mitigate the rigour of the saying about divorce, i.e. to regard it as a 'counsel' and not as a precept for all. It forms no part of the Marcan tradition, which, as we have seen, ends differently from that of Mt. It did not stand in the source from which Mt. derived the saying (*a*), for in that case he would have made the fullest use of it in that place. And if, as seem probable, Mt. 5³² is an adaptation by Mt. of a saying in Q, it was not in that source either related to the question of divorce. Probably, therefore, the original reference of the saying was not to divorce at all; and in that case, as Dr. Kirk points out, there is no sufficient warrant for suggesting that our Lord intended his prohibition of divorce to be taken merely as a 'counsel', though Mt. may seem to suggest it.

It is idle, therefore, to inquire what were our Lord's actual words on the subject of divorce. As in so many other cases, all that we can say is that the weight of the evidence is in favour of the view that all that is said in the Gospels probably goes back to the single saying in Q (Lk. 16¹⁸). All other sayings are expansions of or additions to that saying, and so S. Paul, who, as we have reason to believe, is the most accurate interpreter of our Lord's teaching, seems without doubt to have understood it. He has no doubt also that, within the limits laid down, the Christian Church has power to make and vary the disciplinary rules of its members in this as in all other matters (1 Cor. 7⁶, ¹², ²⁵).

19¹⁶⁻²². *Second Evangelical Counsel. Voluntary Poverty* (Mk. 10¹⁷ ff., Lk. 18¹⁸ ff.).

The Rich Inquirer. This is one of the passages in which Mt. undertakes to re-write Mk. On the main point all the Evangelists, followed by S. Paul, give what was undoubtedly our Lord's teaching—that there is a vocation to some to renounce not only riches but all property and follow Him. But Mt. introduces the idea, afterwards a prominent feature in Christian ethics, of the *Counsels and Precepts* (see Note B).

19¹⁹. *thy neighbour as thyself.* An addition christianizing the decalogue, after the teaching of Jesus Himself.

19²¹. *If thou wouldst be perfect.* 'For Mk.'s Pauline doctrine that eternal life is not the reward of obedience and good works but of self-surrender without reserve after the example of Jesus, Mt. substitutes a semi-legalist doctrine which only differs from that of the Scribes and Pharisees by a righteousness which exceeds theirs in inwardness and emphasis on good works' (Bacon). Origen, in his Commentary on Mt., quotes from Ev. Heb. a still further development of the original saying.[1]

19^{27-30}. *Third Evangelical Counsel. Obedience.* Mk. 10^{28}, Lk. 18^{28}.

Peter and the two sons of Zebedee had been conspicuous examples of obedience to our Lord's call to close discipleship.

19^{28}. *the regeneration*, Gk. παλιγγενεσία. The expectation of a second or new birth for the nation rested on such passages as Isa. 65^{17}, 66^{22}, and was a commonplace of Apocalyptic writing.

judging the twelve tribes of Israel, i.e. the New Israel, the Christian Ecclesia. It is interesting to note that the promise which in Lk. is placed at the Last Supper (Lk. 22^{30}) is connected with Peter there also; and with the special commission to him to strengthen his brethren.

20^{1-16}. *The Parable of the Labourers in the Vineyard or the Dissatisfied Wage-earners.*

The real moral of this parable is probably not that which Mt. takes such pains to impress on his readers by inserting it between two identical sayings, that the Kingdom shall be taken away from the Jews and given to a nation bringing forth the fruits thereof. It is really a parable of the Kingdom of God in the sense of divine grace as the only basis of admission to eternal life. That grace is a free unconditional gift and not the reward of merit is one of the most difficult and yet the most certain elements in the teaching of Christ, as we can gather from its development by S. Paul and his great disciple S. Augustine.

20^{17-19}. *Third prediction of the Passion* (Mk. 10^{32-34}, Lk. 18^{31-33}).

The words here mark some kind of crisis, which is well brought out in Mk. who describes Jesus at this part as walking alone in advance of the disciples and 'they were amazed'. A final decision, involving an intense inward struggle, as in the garden, must be made, to go to Jerusalem to die. Here the form of execution is specified for the first time. He was going to Jerusalem to offer Himself officially as Messiah—foreseeing the consequences to Himself.

20^{20}. *mother of the sons of Zebedee.* Salome, possibly a sister of the Virgin, in which case the family relationship may have been thought to justify the claim for precedence, cf. Mt. 27^{56}, Jn. 19^{25}.

20^{23}. These words have led to the belief, for which there is some slight evidence, that John as well as James suffered martyrdom (Acts 12^2). The tradition of the Church from the time of Irenaeus

[1] See Appendix, p. 268.

represents John as residing at Ephesus and dying a natural death there at an advanced age in the reign of Trajan.

20²⁸. *a ransom for many*, Gk. λύτρον. It is probable that Jesus had in mind the vocation of the Suffering Servant of Jehovah who in Isa. 53¹² is said to give over his soul to death and to bear the sins of *many*. In LXX the word = an equivalent, e.g. the sacrifice offered in place of the first-born who belonged to God (Num. 3¹³). If the word had not been used by Jesus Himself as a description of His work it would be difficult to understand the repeated use of the word and its synonyms in the N.T.

20²⁹⁻³⁴. *The last miracle* (Mk. 10⁴⁶⁻⁵², Lk. 18³⁵⁻⁴³).

The last stage in the momentous journey now begins. The silence hitherto preserved in public by our Lord and enjoined on the Apostles by the strictest injunction is at this point definitely abandoned and the way prepared for the triumphal entry. The title 'Son of David' here given to Him shows what was already in the mind of the crowd, especially if there be inserted in the interval the miracle of the raising of Lazarus (Jn. 11). There is also the address 'Lord', Gk. κύριε, otherwise used by the synoptic evangelists as a rule only after the Resurrection.

21¹⁻¹¹. *The Triumphal Entry* (Mk. 11¹⁻¹⁰, Lk. 19²⁹⁻³⁸).

The Fourth Gospel (Jn. 12¹⁻⁹) dates the arrival at Bethany six days before the Passover, i.e. Saturday, Nisan 8th, and the entry the following day, Nisan 9th. There can be little doubt from the position of the O.T. quotation in the forefront of the incident that the Evangelist means it to be understood that these words were in our Lord's mind when He planned the incident, and were intended either by Him or by His disciples afterwards as a repudiation of the calumny of which there are probably echoes in the 'Slavonic' Josephus that the crowd on the Mount of Olives assumed at this point the character and dimensions of an armed movement. It is strange that the incident does not appear to have been brought up against Jesus at any of the trials. But we know so little about the charges brought by the witnesses and of what passed immediately before the triumphal entry, that we cannot say what the evidence was. Our Lord, on the other hand, was prepared with His evidence that His movement was from the first to the last a movement of non-violence, in accordance with prophecy (21⁵). Nevertheless, the Messianic idea spread through the city and the authorities evidently so understood the occasion. Otherwise it is difficult to account for the questions about the Capitation Tax and the Son of

David. The Messianic claim was by Jesus Himself made the ground for His delivery to Pilate for sentence (Mt. 27¹¹).

21¹. *Bethphage* = place ot young figs, according to Origen a village of Priests.

21². *village that is over against you*, i.e. Bethany, where Jesus was known to have friends. The words 'the Lord hath need of him' are, like the 'man bearing a pitcher of water' (Mk. 14¹³), a part of a secret and prearranged code of signals. Everything that our Lord does in the last week happens strictly according to plan. Nothing is left to chance—all is foreseen. At the same time nothing that He asked for was refused Him.

21³. *send them*, Gk. ἀποστελεῖ, i.e. Jesus will send them back when he has done with them.

21⁵. A conflation of Isa. 62¹¹, Zech. 9⁹. An 'N' quotation independent of the LXX.

21⁷. As at the accession of Jehu (2 Kings 9¹³) and at the triumph of Judas Maccabaeus (1 Macc. 13⁵¹).

21⁹. *Hosanna*, as in Ps. 118²⁵. The last of the Hallel Psalms sung every year at the Passover. It means in Hebrew 'Save, we pray thee'. It is a simple acclamation addressed to God, as in Mk. 11, which Mt., however, transfers to the 'Son of David', probably in accordance with its liturgical use in the Christian Eucharist, already the practice in the Didache (c. 11).

21¹²⁻¹³. *The Cleansing of the Temple* (Mk. 11¹⁵⁻¹⁸, Lk. 19⁴⁵⁻⁴⁷, Jn. 2¹⁴⁻¹⁶) is reduced in Mt. to a mere incident recorded in the briefest words. In reality it was the immediate cause of the trial and death of Jesus, because He thereby challenged the supremacy and vested interests of the governing body of the Temple, i.e. the Sadducees. There is, however, considerable uncertainty as to when it occurred. Mk. places it on the following day (11¹¹). Lk. has no note of time. The Fourth Gospel, however, puts it at the very beginning of the ministry and connects it with the saying about the destruction of the temple afterwards distorted by witnesses at the trial (Jn. 2¹⁷). But the tradition is strong that our Lord did on this occasion 'suddenly come to his temple' and claim the control of it in His Father's name. That does not, however, prove that our Lord did not at an earlier date make a direct challenge to the authorities, who did not accept it: and for that reason diverted His public mission to Galilee.

The true significance of the incident has been lost sight of by Mt., in whose time the temple was no longer standing. Mk.'s form of the quotation, 'My house shall be called a house of prayer for *all the nations*', shows that there was a great deal more in it than appears in Mt., where it is a mere protest against desecration or dishonesty, for which there is some evidence in Rabbinic stories of extortionate prices. In. Mk. this incident assumes the form of a great dramatic and symbolic act by which old Hebrew prophets were accustomed at times to challenge the policy of the ruling class. In this case the challenge of Jesus is not so much against the desecration of a sacred building as against the whole policy of its official custodians, the Sadducees, whose attitude towards the one purpose for which, according to Israel's prophets, the Temple stood, to be the 'house of prayer for all the nations', was fitly symbolized by the fact that they had cynically made the very court of the Gentiles into a cattle-market. Nor was that all. Their attitude towards the Temple, which they regarded as a private preserve of their own, was itself symbolic of the selfish nationalism of their whole outlook. Their slogan was 'Jerusalem for the Jews'. So far from recognizing any high vocation of Israel to be the Servant of Jehovah to gather the nations to Him, they had by their bitter anti-foreign policy reduced Judaism to a state of siege, which finally involved the whole nation in political destruction. It was indeed their actual alliance with the 'Robbers' of the Jordan valley who carried on a guerrilla warfare against the Government which gave point on more than one occasion to our Lord's denunciations (26^{55}). Like their Robber-friends they were defending their vested interests alike in the Temple and nation, with all the recklessness of robbers defending in a den their ill-gotten gains against all comers. It was undoubtedly this challenge to the official custodians of the sacred shrine of Judaism which sealed our Lord's fate in Jerusalem.

2I^{12}. *the temple*, Gk. τὸ ἱερόν, here the outer Court of the Gentiles called in the Talmud the 'Mountain of the House', in remembrance of Isa. 2^2 and Micah 4^1, where traffic was authorized at all times in what was afterwards known as the 'shop of the Sons of Annas'.

Moneychangers, Gk. κολλυβιστῶν from κόλλυβος, a small coin. Even in those days large profits were made on the exchange, in this case of Greek and other coins, for the 'sacred shekel', at this period the tetradrachma of Tyre, which was the only legal tender in the Temple.

doves. Required by poor people for sacrifices of purification (Lev. 1^{14}, &c., Lk. 2^{24}).

2I^{13}. The quotation is from Isa. 56^7, with an allusion to Jer. 7^{11}.

2I^{16}. Ps. 8^2. LXX. Heb. has 'strength'.

21$^{18-22}$. *The cursing of the fig tree* (Mk. 11$^{12-14, \; 20-24}$).

Like the previous action a piece of prophetic symbolism indicating dramatically that the Jewish nation, for all the luxuriance of its foliage, was still a barren and disappointing tree. This had already been put in the form of a parable in Lk. 13$^{6-9}$, and it is possible that the whole incident here recorded is a dramatized form of that saying, to which Mt. has added other but very appropriate sayings about faith, following Mark 11$^{20-26}$. Cf. Lk. 17$^{5, \; 6}$.

21$^{23-27}$. *The Official Challenge to the Messiah*. Mk. 11$^{27-33}$, Lk. 20$^{1-8}$.

This is by far the most important incident in Mt.'s fifth book, leading as it does directly to the first great denunciation of the Pharisees, and the pronouncement of the final doom. It is the Challenge from the Sanhedrin, with Jesus' reply showing His authority to be from heaven and their control a usurpation.

21^{23}. *these things*, i.e. the temple cleansing and the healings described in 12 and 14.

21^{25}. In the interview with Nicodemus (Jn. 3$^{1-13}$) Jesus gave the same sort of answer to a similar inquiry. Unless a man had accepted the mission and baptism of John, there was little prospect of his understanding or accepting the divine mission of Jesus (Jn. 3$^{1-13}$).

21$^{28-46}$. *The Appeal of the Messiah from the Hierarchy to the People* (Mk. 12$^{1-12}$). *The parable of the Two Sons and of the Usurping Husbandmen* (Lk. 20$^{9-18}$).

The two vineyard parables with which the misplaced parable of the *Dissatisfied Wage-earners* formed a trilogy, all teach the doctrine that the leaders of the Nation being unworthy, those whom they despise will take their place.

21^{42}. In Ps. 118^{22}, the verses preceding the Hosanna cry. This psalm may well have been a triumphal ode for the rebuilding of the walls of Jerusalem in the time of Nehemiah. Then Israel, despised and well-nigh destroyed by the world powers, had been restored. If the quotation was added by Mt. from a collection of proof-texts, the 'stone' is not the nation but its representative, the Messiah (Acts 4^{11}). It was often combined with the 'stone of stumbling' (Isa. 8^{14}), and with the 'Sure foundation stone' (Isa. 28^{16}), as in Eph. 2^{20}, Rom. 9^{33}, and 1 Pet. 2^{6}, where all three thoughts are combined. The statement in verse 44 is in all probability a gloss, and is omitted by D and several versions.

21$^{43, \; 44}$. Probably a reminiscence of the stone in Dan. 2$^{34-45}$ which 'was cut out of the mountain without hands and brake in pieces the iron and clay feet of the image' in Nebuchadnezzar's dream. The mention of a stone has probably led the Evangelist to think of this further reference.

scatter him as dust, Gk. λικμήσει = winnow. To take offence at the Messiahship of Jesus would involve spiritual injury, but to be punished for impudent rejection of Him would involve something far more terrible.

22¹⁻¹⁴. *The Theme continued. The parable of the Slighted Invitation* (Lk. 14¹⁶⁻²⁴).

We may adopt Bacon's view that Mt. in this case has amplified a parable already in Q; but has understood its meaning better than Lk. who makes use of it to enforce our Lord's teaching that we ought to invite those who are unable to repay our hospitality. Mt. reinforces the original application, which was the situation of the Jewish people ripe for judgement, by the addition of a 'targum' at the end, the so-called parable of the wedding-garment. In the addition, however, J. Weiss sees the comment of the Christian Scribe on the new mission to the Gentiles in the Church and a warning that the results are not necessarily accepted by God. The test is the wedding-garment of righteousness according to the Law as in Rev. 19⁸. There is a well-known Rabbinic parable, attributed to Johanan ben Zakkai who may have been a contemporary of Mt., from which the addition was perhaps derived by Mt. himself.[1]

22⁶. These details, which are not in the Lucan story, show that the Matthean version was written after the destruction of Jerusalem (*v.* Introduction, p. 14). They are a reference to the persecution of Christian Apostles and Evangelists.

22⁹. *partings of the highways*, Gk. διεξόδους, frequent in LXX, the central places where the high roads diverge where the people might be expected to hang about.

22¹¹. The idea that there was a custom to supply such garments free of charge at weddings is a pious fiction resting on no other evidence than the parable itself.

22¹². *speechless*, Gk. ἐφιμώθη, was muzzled or gagged; the word used by our Lord in stilling the storm (Mk. 4³⁹).

22¹⁵⁻²². *The Capitation Tax. The defeat of the Pharisees and Herodians* (Mk. 12¹³⁻¹⁷, Lk. 20¹⁹⁻²⁶).

This incident is a perfect example of the controversial apophthegm or pronouncement story ending with a memorable rejoinder to which there is no apparent answer. (See Appendix, p. 266.) As such it was used by Christians for apologetic purposes to prove

[1] *Studies in Pharisaism and the Gospels*, i. 90 ff.

that Jesus was no revolutionary or rebel. But why was there no answer to the statement 'render unto Caesar—unto God'? Would it not have been easy to charge Jesus with evasion or with enunciating a platitude? It is difficult to believe that our Lord deliberately avoided expressing an opinion on a question which meant as much in the daily life of His countrymen as that of British rule does to an Indian. The point lies in the historical circumstances in which the question was asked and answered. Jesus' answer was double-edged—one side aimed at the Pharisees and the other at the Herodians, and both with deadly force. The Pharisees are commanded to render to Caesar the things of Caesar, because it was the *Pharisees* who had demanded direct Roman rule, vexed by the misgovernment of Archelaus (Mt. 2[22]), and secured his deposition in A.D. 6 to the disgust of the Sadducees and their friends the 'Robbers' or gunmen of the Jordan valley. It is a mistake to suppose that the Pharisees or the Jews as a whole were opposed to Roman rule. In fact the people well understood and applauded our Lord's quick rejoinder, that having obtained Caesar they must be prepared to pay for him. It was not His affair but theirs. The Herodians, as the permanent officials of the Herodian government, were notorious, like their master, for their readiness to compromise with the Romans. It was not for nothing that Augustus had granted the tetrarchy to Antipas. It was on condition not to proselytize, and to allow temples to the Genius of Rome and images of the Emperor to be erected in Palestine, as they were openly in the city of Tiberias. In other words the Herodians were prepared to obtain political advantages at the price of loyalty to the Jewish religion. This also the people were well aware of, and there was no answer when our Lord sharply bade them put God before Caesar, and religion before politics.

22[17]. *tribute*, Gk. κῆνσον, as in 17[25]. A capitation tax; one of the two direct taxes levied in the two Imperial provinces of Syria and Judaea; the former a tax on land-values, and the latter a poll-tax, the same for all males over 14 and Jews over 12 up to the age of 65. For the convenience of these taxes a special silver denarius (penny) was struck, with the figure of Caesar and an inscription TIBERIOU KAISAROS.

22[23-33]. *The Defeat of the Sadducees* (Mk. 12[18-27], Lk. 20[27-30]).

22[24]. In Deut. 25[5], the passage paraphrased specifies circumstances in which it is a duty to contract the so-called Levirate marriage, of which the best example is the story of Ruth. It is probable that the practice was obsolete in the time of Jesus.

22²⁸. *The Resurrection.* A belief in the Resurrection, says Dr. Charles, was a fundamental doctrine of Jewish Schools from the second century B.C. But the Jewish scholar C. G. Montefiore quotes evidence that the official doctrine of the later Rabbis about the Resurrection was something far more spiritual than a doctrine of a mere continuation elsewhere of the present life: and our Lord in His answer endorses this view and gives His reasons—namely that the Pharisees did not hold any such crude views as they are here represented as holding. Moreover, although there may be few clear references to a Resurrection in the O.T. and none at all in the Pentateuch, as the Sadducees rightly said, nevertheless, as our Lord proceeds to show by His reference to Exod. 3⁶, the essence of the doctrine of the Resurrection is bound up with almost every word of Scripture. For the Bible is from beginning to end nothing else than the revelation to man of the power and kingdom of God and the Resurrection, so incredible in itself, is the one signal manifestation of that power and kingdom. This is the real meaning of S. Paul's great argument in 1 Cor. 15. It is no doctrine of a natural immortality of the soul like that of Plato, but of a new creative act of the living God calling man, soul and body, from death to life in the spirit. Not to understand this is, as Jesus says, to be in fundamental error as to the nature of God as creative life and power.

22³⁴⁻⁴⁰. *The new Commandment* (Mk. 12²⁸⁻³⁴, Lk. 10²⁵⁻²⁸).

An interesting example of the various forms in which the Q tradition is found in the Synoptic Gospels. Lk. on the whole supports Mk. as against Mt. in this case, but places the saying in a wholly different context. Our Lord's answer to the proof question is the text of Deut. 6⁵, which, together with 11¹³⁻²¹ and Num. 15³⁷⁻⁴¹, was called the Shema (Heb. for 'hear', from its opening words), and was recited in the time of our Lord by devout Jews and gave classical expression to the central article of Israel's Creed, the moral unity of God.

The second commandment is taken from Lev. 19¹⁸. The double injunction was perhaps already known as a summary of doctrines, and is found in the Testament of the XII Patriarchs, an Apocalyptic work of the first century B.C.

22⁴¹⁻⁴⁶. *A Rabbinic Argument* (Mk. 12³⁵⁻³⁷, Lk. 20⁴¹⁻⁴⁴).

Our Lord had answered all His questioners; a single instance is enough to show that they could not answer Him: if David addressed the Messiah as Lord, then must not the Messiah be more than merely his son? It is not a denial of the Davidic descent of the Messiah but an argument that on the strength of the Scriptures themselves the Davidic or nationalist view was inadequate as an expression of the Hope of Israel.

22⁴⁴. *Ps. 110.* Our Lord assumes that the Psalm referred to a Messiah, though that does not appear to have been the current meaning. In the early days of Christianity Jewish teachers applied it to Hezekiah. Box, on the other hand, thinks that this is one of those cases in which the Messianic reference was the current one at the time, displaced for apologetic purposes by the Jews and restored by a Rabbi in the third century A.D. It is frequently quoted in the N.T. as a Christian proof-text and enshrined in the Christian Creed in the words 'He sitteth at the right hand of God'.

22⁴⁴. *The Lord,* Heb. *Jehovah.*

my Lord, Heb. *Adoni,* an honorific title applicable to the Messiah though sometimes used as a substitute for the divine Name from motives of reverence.

23. *The Great Denunciation* (Mk. 12³⁸⁻⁴⁰, Lk. 11³⁷⁻⁵⁴, 20⁴⁵⁻⁴⁷).

A very difficult chapter, not all of which may be directly attributable to our Lord. That there was such a denunciation in Q is shown by the triple tradition supporting it. But the virulence of the denunciation, almost repellent in this chapter, is absent from the other versions. Throughout the chapter the distinction between Scribes and Pharisees has become obscured, indicating the synagogue of Mt.'s time, and not the party system of Palestinian Judaism, which was now a thing of the past. The structure of the chapter, which is largely based on Q, is that of seven woes. In Lk there are only six, in a different order and divided into two groups, one against the Pharisees and the other against the Lawyers or Scribes.

23². *sit on Moses' seat.* Only the Scribes, strictly speaking, were the successors of Moses. As such they claimed to make *ex cathedra* pronouncements on the law, not all of which, as we have already seen, Jesus was prepared to concede (15² ff.).

23⁴. *heavy burdens,* i.e. they appear to be deeply concerned with the religious education of the people, but in fact they do nothing to help them towards the attainment of their object.

23⁵. *phylacteries,* φυλακτήρια in classical Gk. = fortifications or outposts. The Hebrew word to which it appears to correspond means protecting charms or amulets. Here they are 'tephillim' (prayers), small leather cases containing four strips of parchment inscribed with the words of Exod. $13^{1-10, 11-16}$, Deut. 6^{4-9}, 11^{13-21}. Such are still worn at the present day on the forehead and left arm by Jews at the daily morning prayer.

23^9. *Father*, Abba, strictly speaking appropriate to God alone—but used among the later Jews as a title of honour for great men or Rabbis of the past.[1]

23^{10}. is probably a Greek-Christian variant to the Aramaic form in verse 8.

master, Gk. καθηγητής, a master. Plutarch uses it of Aristotle. It is used in modern Greek for 'professor'.

23^{13-33}. *The Seven Woes.*

23^{13-22}. The first three woes directed against the teaching of the Scribes.

23^{15}. It is difficult to see what meaning these words had if spoken in the time of Jesus. They look much more like an allusion to bitter hostility to the Christian-Gentile Missions—the Kingdom of Heaven meaning the Church. Josephus[2] speaks of the length to which strict Jews would go in his day to re-convert adherents of more liberal forms of Judaism. Loisy sees in the words a bitter allusion to the missionary activity of S. Paul. This, however, is incompatible with the liberal outlook of Mt.

proselyte. In the Hellenistic Roman period the Jews of the Dispersion, with a great sense of their own superiority, as S. Paul saw, (Rom. 2^{19}), carried on an energetic missionary campaign among the heathen, to which the poet Horace bears witness:

'ac veluti te
Judaei cogemus in hanc concedere turbam'
(Sat. 1. 4. 142.)

The results were by no means negligible; for every Synagogue became a centre of a group of adherents known as Godfearers, Gk. σεβόμενοι, who were bound to the keeping of the Sabbath and to the food-laws. It was among these, as we learn from the Acts, that Christianity found its greatest opportunity. Actual proselytes were those who submitted to circumcision, baptism, and sacrifice.

23^{16-22}. A piece of casuistry inserted by Mt. similar to that in vv. 15^{4-6}. They ask an inquirer who wishes to free himself from a binding engagement sworn on the temple or altar, as we should say, a Bible oath, Did you also think at the time of the *gold* of the temple or the *sacrifice* on the altar? If not, your oath was not completed and you are free.

---

[1] Dalman, *Words of Jesus*, p. 339.   [2] *Ant.* xx. 2. 4.

23²³⁻²⁸. *Three woes dealing with legalism in the daily life of the Pharisees.*

23²³. *Tithes.* In Lev. 27³⁰ all the seed of the land and the fruit of it was ordered to be tithed; and in Deut. 14²² 'the increase of thy seed' is further defined as corn, wine, and oil. The Scribal tradition extended this to any sort of herb.

faith, Gk. πίστις = faithfulness, as in Gal. 5²²; fidelity not belief.

23²⁵. The fifth woe appears in a somewhat different form in Lk. 1³⁹, though the meaning is the same. External religion is valueless or rather evil if important interior matters are disregarded, e.g. the way things are come by.

within they are full from extortion and excess, i.e. the vessels are defiled because their abundant contents are the result of sweating and profiteering.

excess, Gk. ἀκρασία, a famous word in Greek ethics, defined by Aristotle as an excessive desire for pleasure (*E. N.* vii. 4. 1).

23²⁷. The sixth woe is another form of the same indictment against external prosperity concealing inward wickedness. It was the custom to chalk graves with white marks on 15th of Adar before the Passover so that worshippers might avoid the defiling contact with them. Doubtless such chalking was combined with a general trimming and spring cleaning of cemeteries, which at the time when the words were uttered may be supposed to have been looking outwardly their best.

23²⁹. *Seventh Woe.* The meaning of the charge is again not quite clear. It is easy enough to see it in the light of what afterwards happened, i.e. in spite of their recent adornment of the tombs, as Herod had adorned the Tomb of David at Hebron, they were after all true sons of their fathers. Like them, they were the betrayers and murderers of the Just One (Acts 7⁵²). If the words go back to our Lord Himself, it is the self-righteousness with which they adorned the tombs which is condemned, and which proclaimed them the true sons of their fathers. The explanation often given, 'if your fathers had not made martyrs you could not honour them, so that you proclaim yourselves the sons at any rate of murderers', is, as Montefiore says, ironical, but also rather absurd.

23³². *Fill ye up.* Another reading, 'And you are about to fill up the measure of your fathers', confirms the view that the whole passage is a 'vaticinium ex eventu', cf. 1 Thess. 2¹⁶.

23³⁴⁻³⁹. Jesus seems to turn at this point to the whole nation or to the city of Jerusalem and laments in an apostrophe of extraordinary beauty and pathos. Harnack and others think that it is a quotation from a lost apocalyptic writing. Otherwise it is difficult to explain the words, 'Ye shall not see me till ye shall say "Blessed is he that cometh in the name of the Lord"', when these very words had already been sung at the triumphal entry. This view is confirmed by Lk.'s version which begins: 'Wherefore the Wisdom of God said', i.e. the inspired writing (Lk. 11⁴⁹). If 'Wisdom' stood in Q, Mt. interprets it as referring to Christ Himself as the incarnate Word or Wisdom of God.

23³⁵. *on the earth*, rather 'on the land', i.e. of Palestine—the sacred soil to which bloodshed was a defilement.

23³⁶. *The son of Barachiah*. These words are absent from Lk. and may be an interpolation in Mt. The meaning of Q is quite clear, i.e. all the innocent blood shed in the course of O.T. history from Abel the first martyr to Zechariah the *son of Jehoiada* the High Priest whose death is recorded in the latest book of the Bible (2 Chron. 24²) may be visited on this generation. The murder of Zechariah was a constant theme of discussion in later Rabbinic literature, especially the Midrash. Nebuchadnezzar's capture of Jerusalem was explained as a retribution for it (G. H. Box).

The Son of Barachiah has been thought to refer to the incident in the final Jewish wars recorded by Josephus,[1] the lynching of a Zacharias, son of Baruch, one of the most eminent citizens, and a great lover of justice and liberty. Accused by the Zealots of betraying the city to Vespasian, he stood up and laughed at the accusations, and in a few words confuted the charges. After which, like Stephen, he turned on his accusers and went over all their transgressions of the Law and made lamentation on the confusion to which they had brought public affairs. The seventy judges brought in a verdict of 'not guilty', which made the Zealots so angry that two of them fell upon him in the middle of the Temple and slew him. This case caused, as Josephus says, an intense sensation because of its deliberate travesty of justice. Thus Mt., or the source from which he is quoting, intended to include the latest act of bloodshed in the final siege of Jerusalem, committed as he thought on the very threshold of the great Judgement.

23³⁷. Lk. 13³⁴. Harnack attributes this to the same extra-Biblical source as the previous verse. The words *how often* do not in this case refer to our Lord's visits to the Holy City, which in any case were few and far between, but to the many occasions in the national history in which God had given Jerusalem the opportunity of submitting trustfully to Him.

23³⁸. *Left unto you*—omit *desolate*. God who has hitherto dwelt in the Temple (v. 21) would leave the nation; and so also will Jesus who now stands among them as His messenger to announce the last offer of peace. 'After this I will not see you till I return as the heavenly Messiah in judgement. You will be left alone in your City and Temple.' Of the actual fulfilment of the terrible prophecy

---

[1] *Jewish Wars*, iv. 5. 4; cf. Loeb, *Josephus*, iii. 98–99.

in the fearful desolation of Jerusalem in the siege, Josephus, in the *Jewish Wars* (Bk. II), gives the detailed account. There is no more terrible reading in the whole of history.

24–25. THE DISCOURSE ON THE MESSIANIC JUDGEMENT (Mk. 13, Lk. 17^{20-37}, 21^{5-36}).

In the final discourse beginning with a reference to the destruction of the Temple (24^2) and ending with the tremendous picture of the Great Assize of the Son of man, Mt. has made use of a Marcan discourse, but he has entirely altered the balance of it. Mk. himself built up an apocalyptic discourse delivered to an esoteric body of four disciples based upon an undoubtedly authentic warning of our Lord foretelling the imminent overthrow of the Temple. There is a fourfold tradition for a saying of this kind (Lk. 21^{5-7}, Mt. 24^{1-2}, Mk. 13^1, and Jn. 2^{18-22}). This Mk. combined with a logion from Q on Watchfulness (Mk. 13^{28-37}, Lk. $12^{35\,ff.}$), and, as Colani[1] was the first to point out, an early Christian Apocalypse or prophecy of the year A.D. 40 or thereabouts, which was also used by S. Paul in 1 Thess. 4^{15}, to which he has added extracts from the books of Micah and Daniel, vv. 8, 12, 24–26. Mt. in adopting this combination of sayings, shows his approval of its main lesson, by the words which he emphasizes, 'Behold, I have told you beforehand' (v. 25); looking back, that is, on the events of the great Romano-Jewish War, Mt. sees in them the fulfilment of Jesus' warnings to repentance; but he extends the prediction to a wider horizon and a considerably later date than even Mk. does. For the word '*immediately*' in verse 29 is not, as Bacon has pointed out,[2] intended to imply that the *parousia* is to take place immediately after the capture of Jerusalem, but after 'tribulation' and 'sufferings' not only of a local character in Palestine as in Mk., but worldwide and involving the whole Church. In other words, since Mk. wrote, the Church has experienced the persecutions not only of Nero but of Domitian, and it is at the end of them—an indefinite term—that Mt. places the *parousia* (vv. 29–31). As has already been remarked, Mt. marks the swing of the pendulum, after the death of St. Paul, towards the Jewish Branch of the Church and its apocalyptic fervour.

24¹. *the buildings of the temple.* This Temple was begun by Herod the Great in the 18th year of his reign, 20 B.C., and not finished till A.D. 64, twenty-four years before it was destroyed by fire. It was a monument of engineering skill. Its stones are stated to have measured $25 \times 8 \times 12$

[1] See Rawlinson, *St. Mark*, pp. 180 ff.   [2] *Studies in Mt.*, p. 68.

cubits and they were 'white and strong'. It had doors with lintels of the same height as the Temple itself; it was these vast gates that were shut on S. Paul when he was nearly lynched on his last visit to Jerusalem (Acts 21). The whole building was surrounded with cloisters or, as they are called in the N.T., 'porches', one of which was Solomon's Porch in which our Lord taught (Jn. 10²³) and the Apostles preached (Acts 3). Another of the cloisters looked down on the precipitous side of the valley of the Kedron from a giddy height from which it was impossible to see the bottom. According to the description in Josephus the outer face of the Temple on its front was covered all over with sheets of gold of great weight, 'which at sunrise reflected a fiery splendour'—but to strangers the temple appeared from a distance like a mountain covered with snow, for the parts of it which were not gilded were exceedingly white. On the top it had spikes with sharp points to prevent any pollution by birds sitting on it.[1]

24³. *privately*, as a secret revelation to a chosen few—a standing feature of Jewish Apocalypses.

coming, Gk. παρουσία, the technical term in N.T. for the Advent of Christ in glory.

end of the world, Gk. συντέλεια τοῦ αἰῶνος, completion of the era. Cf. 13³⁹.

24⁶. *must needs come to pass*—divinely decreed, according to the strict view of Jewish Monotheism that God is the creator of all that happens whether good or evil, cf. Isa. 45⁷.

24⁸. *beginning of travail*. The universal wars and convulsions that are to precede the end of the age are again a commonplace of Apocalyptic; and were called in Rabbinic writings the 'birth-pangs of the Messiah'.

24⁹⁻¹². Mt. has already used some of the Q material in 10¹⁷⁻²¹, and accordingly curtails it here, but adds the reference to *lawlessness* and *decay of faith* which was the sign of his own times.

24¹⁵⁻²². *The Little Apocalypse* of Mk. 13¹⁴⁻²⁰.

Mt. at this point returns to the Marcan form of the discourse and inserts a passage which could have had no other reference than to the destruction of Jerusalem. Streeter and Sir J. Hawkins were the first to suggest that this was an ancient oracle of the Palestine community warning Christians to flee from Jerusalem while there was yet time. Eusebius relates that in obedience to such an oracle the Christians fled to Pella in the mountains of the Jordan valley.[2] The words in Mk. 13¹⁴, *Let him that readeth understand*, look as if they referred to some such written document, but Mt. has turned them into a reference to Dan. 11³¹. It is to this little apocalypse that Paul probably refers in 1 Thess. 4¹⁵ as a word of the Lord, i.e. a prophetic message of the Risen Lord to the Church.

[1] Josephus, *Jewish Wars*, v. 5. 6.   [2] Euseb. *Hist. Eccl.*, iii. v. 3.

24[15]. *The abomination of desolation.* The LXX translation of the Hebrew of Dan. 11[31], 12[11], 'an abominable thing that layeth waste'; with reference to a heathen altar with an image of the Olympian Zeus erected in the Temple by King Antiochus Epiphanes at the time of the Maccabean revolt (2 Macc. 6[1-13]).[1] Mk., following Paul, understood by the expression the appearance of Anti-Christ, but Mt. refers to the Holy Place and it must be a reference either to the desecration of the Temple by the Zealots just before Titus besieged the city or to the erection of the statue of Titus on the site of the ruined Temple. Josephus (*Jewish Wars*, iv. 3. 6–8) thus writes of the Zealots: 'They used the Temple of God as a stronghold for themselves and as a place whither they might resort in order to avoid the troubles they feared from the people. So the sanctuary became a refuge and a shop of tyranny.'[1]

24[22]. *shortened*, Gk. ἐκολοβώθησαν, amputated, meaning that the reign of anti-Christ is 'cut short' by a fixed period, as in Dan. 9[24-27].

(3) *False Prophets and the great Deception*, vv. 23–25.

All such are to be disbelieved, for when the true Messiah appears there will be no need to seek for Him in hiding, doubtful whether He is really there; for His *parousia* will be a mighty world-event visible to all eyes, like the lightning which is visible over a vast area.

24[26]. *the wilderness*, as in 11[7], the ancient scene of theophanies.

24[28]. *wheresoever the carcase is*, a proverbial saying. There is no reference to the Roman eagles. It merely expresses the inevitableness of the event; for if the world is ripe for judgement, the judge will come with unfailing certainty.

(4) *The world-wide Revelation of the Son of man and the End*, vv. 29–51.

Mt. adds to the Marcan account one more terrifying sign—that of the Son of man Himself. Mt. and his readers knew what this was, for it was the subject of a public prophecy which S. Paul knew all about (2 Thess. 2[3ff]). We do not know what is meant, but Mt. must be thinking of something terrible, e.g. an announcement of judgement at which all men will break out into loud lamentation. There appears to be a close connexion between this passage and Rev. 1[7]. The double allusion in both passages to Zech. 12[10-11] and Dan. 7[13] points to dependence of one upon the other or of both

---

[1] Prof. C. H. Dodd states that the phrase in Daniel is clearly an opprobrious parody of the Hebrew equivalent of Ζεῦς οὐράνιος.

on a common source. The author of the Apocalypse adds, 'they also that pierced Him' (cf. Jn. 19^{37}), indicating that the sign is to recall the death of Christ, hence the lamentation prophesied in Zech. 12^{10}. This is probably the origin of the Patristic interpretation, the sign of the cross in the heavens, as in the story of the Labarum, to which the conversion of Constantine was attributed.

24^{29}. Convulsions of the heavenly bodies normally moving so unerringly in obedience to divine law are an outstanding feature of Apocalyptic.

24^{30}. *power*, i.e. the hosts of angels.

24^{36}. *that day and hour*. There is considerable evidence for the omission of the words 'neither the son' in Mt., but there is no doubt that he wrote 'the Father only'. Whole christologies have been built upon these words as they have been upon Phil. 2^7, especially with regard to the doctrine of the Kenosis or self-emptying of the Son of God. But they are far more likely to be an expression of the unconditioned transcendence of God's Kingdom, its absoluteness and independence of any human power, agency, or co-operation.

24^{37}–25^{46}. *Epilogue to the eschatological discourse.* A Q passage (Lk. 17^{26}) and three parables.

(1) 24^{45-51}. *The parable of the Good and Bad Servant.*

24^{51}. *cut him asunder*, Gk. διχοτομήσει, a form of execution mentioned by Herodotus (2. 1. 39), cf. the story of Susannah vv. 53–59.

(2) 25^{1-13}. *The parable of the Ten Bridesmaids.*

The feminine form of the preceding parable. The imagery of the parable is not quite clear and some have thought that it is a parabolic form of the saying in Lk. 12^{35}. For one thing there is no mention at all of a bride, unless with some MSS. 'and the bride' is added at the end of 25^1. A trace of Palestinian or Syrian marriage customs lies beneath the detail of the parable. To this day there is in some districts a custom for marriages to be celebrated at the house both of bridegroom and bride. At midnight the whole company assembled in the bridegroom's house sets forth to the house of the bride in order to celebrate the festival first there. It is this part in the proceedings that appears in the parable.[1]

(3) 25^{14-30}. *The parable of the Entrusted Funds* (Lk. 19^{12-27}, Mk. 13^{34-37}).

The immediate purpose of the parable was to expose the Jews

---

[1] For this and many other interesting survivals of customs alluded to in the Gospels see *The Syrian Christ* by Abraham Rihbany, an Orthodox Christian from the Lebanon district.

who entrusted with the treasure of the divine revelation had concealed it from the world and now forfeit it. But its moral is that human activity ought to be employed in the interests of God so as to serve Him in some way, since He recompenses it and punishes him who, without doing anything wrong, simply refuses to work for Him.

25²⁴. **hard**, Gk. σκληρός, used in Jn. 6⁶⁰ of a hard or repellent saying. Here it sums up the master's character as that of a hard money-making Jew (McNeile). The slave even accuses his master of illicit gains; he has reaped another man's field, and secured returns even where he had not put out money to interest.

25²⁹. The master accused of avarice, justifies himself not by words but by an act of generosity, and the Evangelist means to say that this liberality, like the chastisement of the idle servant, was justified by the proverb already mentioned in 13¹², Mk. 4²⁵, Lk. 8¹⁸. But as in the parable of the Dissatisfied Wage-earners, the master does not think it necessary to account for his preference.

25³¹⁻⁴⁶. *The Conclusion of the great discourse on Judgement. The Judgement of the Son of man.*

In the magnificent climax not only to the Fifth book but to the entire series of the sayings of the Lord, many have seen the work of the Evangelist rather than the actual words of Jesus. Based as it may well have been on the apocalyptic doctrine of the Son of Man as Judge, there is no doubt that it preserves actual teaching of Jesus. The picture itself is not so much a parable as a piece of what the Jews called 'haggada' or pious narrative like the story of the Temptation. Almost every word in it is strikingly Jewish and 'it is marked to an extraordinary degree by the characteristic features of Hebrew poetical composition' (Box). It is, however, addressed primarily to the 'nations', the Gentiles, who though ignorant of the Law of God have it written in their hearts. Cf. Rom. 2², 12¹⁶.

NOTE G. ESCHATOLOGY AND APOCALYPTIC

Eschatology, or the doctrine of the last things, is the term used to describe the hopes and fears for the future whether of his race or of the world which were at all times a marked feature of the Jew's religion. 'Apocalyptic' is the name given to a certain type of eschatological writing which depicted the future in a series of visions, like those in the Book of the Revelation, and was for the most part pseudonymous, i.e. anonymous writings named after saints, heroes, and prophets of the O.T., such as Daniel, Enoch, or

Baruch. Next to the Law itself, the national hope was by far the most important element in later Judaism before Christ. It has been described by Bousset as its 'second centre'. When the Jew of this period in faith and hope directed his thoughts towards the future, he thought first and foremost not so much of a Messiah as of the sovereignty of his nation—dreamed of its glory and found in these hopes the centre of his creed. As we have already seen,[1] the hope of Israel was summed up in the idea of the Kingdom or Sovereignty of God and its universal acknowledgement, for which the vindication of the chosen people before the nations wast he indispensable condition. Hence the idea of the sovereignty of God in course of time became identified with that of the chosen people; 'for that kingdom shall not be given to another people' (Dan. 2[44]). In the O.T. the belief appears under the form of the Day of Jehovah, when it was expected that God would destroy the nations hostile to Israel, but which the prophets warned them would be more likely to be a day of judgement for Israel itself (Amos 5[18]). This faith in a 'good time coming' for the nation, already strong in the O.T. (cf. Isa. 4, 35, &c.), received a new and powerful stimulus in the successful fight for independence under the Maccabees (165–100 B.C.) when many of the Jews believed themselves to be living in the Messianic age; though a more spiritual hope was kept alive in the nation by the Chassidim, the spiritual ancestors of the Pharisees. Inaugurated by the Book of Daniel this is the beginning in Jewish literature of the age of Apocalyptic. Later, when the brilliant Maccabean epoch came to an end in the century before Christ, there emerged anew the hope of a Messiah of the family of David. This is the theme of the Psalms of Solomon, a Pharisaic document dating from 25 B.C., and we have an echo of it in the prologues of the First and Third Gospels. In the Pharisaism of the Herodian era the hope of the future faded a good deal into the background and interest centred, as we can see from the Gospels, in the cultivation of the Law and the refinements of Rabbinic piety. Very few eschatological utterances are to be found among the teachers of the Pharisaism of the first century A.D., such as Hillel, Gamaliel, and Jochanan ben Zacchai. The greater part of our Lord's teaching has been handed down in Rabbinic moulds, whereas it was probably far more eschatological than the records alone would suggest. Certainly among the people there existed throughout the Roman period a strong Messianic expectation. As time went

---

[1] See Note on the Kingdom of Heaven, p. 188.

on the feeling grew more and more intense until we reach the era of false messiahs and prophets in the time of the Emperor Caligula, A.D. 40, when the rising torrent of fantastic Messianic fanaticism drove the Jews into their final breach with Rome. Even in the very last hours of the siege of Jerusalem, when the Temple was the only barrier left against the inrush of the Roman armies, belief, as Josephus relates, was unshaken in the intervention of God in sorest need.[1] The sack of the city gave a fresh impetus to Apocalyptic writing, of which the best-known examples at the time were the Sibylline Books, Baruch and IV Ezra, and the Apocalypse which has a good deal of Jewish material in its composition. The Messianic hope lasted on into the reign of Hadrian, and ended in the rising of Bar-Kokba (A.D. 130), a title which means 'the Son of the Star' (Num. 24[17]). It survived in the form of millenarianism in the Christian Church and in modern times it has re-emerged in the strange speculations of the British Israel Movement, and in the non-religious form of Bolshevism, itself largely Jewish in origin.

In the period of later Judaism it is possible to distinguish two main streams, which of course often crossed and combined with each other. (1) The more strictly Messianic hope; a faith in Jehovah and the Nation which was the inheritance from the prophets. A certain group of clearly distinguishable ideas is associated with this nationalist hope—the Kingdom of Heaven, the vindication of Israel by victory over the heathen, the deliverance of Palestine from a foreign yoke, and final destruction of the heathen world powers; rebuilding of Jerusalem and the Temple; the reign of a Messiah of David's line in a happy and prosperous Palestine; the gathering of the dispersed of Israel and the subjection under them of the remnants of the heathen. All these features are easily recognizable both in the O.T. and N.T. (cf. Isa. 40–61, Acts 1[6]). The character of the hope is thoroughly 'this-worldly'. It reveals more than anything else the 'particularism' of the religion of Israel in the post-exilic period.

(2) Within this intensely nationalist and often fanatical Messianism dominating the religious feeling of the masses, there emerged a second group of eschatological ideas, in which the interest is no longer national but universal, and the horizon is enormously widened. Men began to be concerned not so much with the future of the nation, perhaps because that had become hopeless, but with the end of the world. The place of nationalist expectation is taken

---

[1] *Jewish Wars*, vi. 2. 1; 5. 2.

by cosmological speculation. The worldly character of the ancient hopes disappears, and a transcendental and other-worldly tendency becomes more and more apparent; and there is a new interest in the spiritual and ethical welfare both here and hereafter of the individual. Just as the Messianic hope centred in the idea of God's sovereignty, so the prevailing thought in Apocalyptic is the New Age—the life of the world to come. It was this thought especially which lifted the Messianic hope on to a higher and supernatural plane; for not only a new world but a new world *order* is by the grace of God to supersede the old. In the same way the conflict of Israel with the world powers becomes a contest between God and the powers of evil, 'the world rulers of this darkness' as they are called in the Epistle to the Ephesians (6¹²). In place of the victory of Israel over their enemies there is the triumph of God and His angels over the Devil and the Demonic powers; instead of the restoration of the Jewish people and their city, the judgement and destruction of the whole world and a new creation by God. In Daniel, the earlier part of Enoch (1–36), the Book of Jubilees, and some of the Sibylline Books, the figure of the Messiah does not appear at all. The writer's interest is concentrated on the 'age to come' and the events which are to precede it. In the remaining Apocalypses, in place of the Son of David or the ideal King, there appears a heavenly, mysterious, and pre-existent Being, who is called the *Son of Man*. This is the origin of that expression in the Gospels. As Dalman has shown, the idea of a pre-existent Being is foreign to Jewish ideas and it is not easy to say from what source it came into the Apocalypses of later Judaism. In the Book of Daniel the Son of Man is clearly only a personification of the nation of Israel in contrast with the heathen nations who are symbolized by beasts (Dan. 7⁹). It looks as if the Apocalypses subsequent to Daniel had combined into one figure two different conceptions—that of a Messiah in the ordinary meaning of the word and the widespread idea of the original Man, the Man from Heaven, the prototype of humanity which appears in many different forms in the oriental mysticism which afterwards became known as Gnosticism. It was this figure which our Lord adopted in order to express the mystery of His Person and the universality of His claim. (For the best discussion of this phrase see T. W. Manson, *The Teaching of Jesus*, pp. 211–36, and 258 ff.)

EPILOGUE

26–28. The story of the Passion and of the Resurrection.

The reason for the elaborate character of the Passion stories in all four Gospels was probably that they were from the first used liturgically in the celebration of the Eucharist. Mk.'s narrative represents the earliest official form, and for this reason it is followed by Mt. with all the reverence due to a church document. Such additions as appear ($27^{3-10, 19, 24-25}$) are secondary and not very trustworthy. Lk. deserts Mk. in his account of the Passion and Resurrection, and follows an independent source for which he evinces a most decided preference.

26^{1-5}. *The Plot to kill Jesus* (Mk. 14^{1-2}, Lk. 22^{1-2}).

26^2. *after two days.* Jewish reckoning of time was inclusive, so that if Friday was the day of the crucifixion, then this would be Wednesday. The Passover began on the evening of Nisan 14 (Lev. 23^5), while the Feast of *Unleavened Bread* (Mk. 14^{12}) began on Nisan 15 with the Paschal Meal at 6 p.m. on that day. But even Josephus uses the expression 'feast of Unleavened Bread' for both, so that there is excuse for Mk.'s statement which Mt. has been so careful to correct. The Paschal lambs were offered in the Temple in the afternoon of Nisan 14; but were actually eaten after sundown when Nisan 15 had, according to Jewish reckoning, already begun. Mt. regards the Crucifixion as bound to take place for symbolical reasons on the Feast of the Passover; that is the meaning of the words which immediately follow 'and the Son of Man is delivered up to be crucified' (v. 2).

passover. The word is Tyndale's brilliant coining of an English word to translate the Hebrew Pesach, and the Aramaic and Greek Pascha; containing an echo both of the original word and of its significance.

26^3. *court,* Gk. αὐλή, not 'palace' as A.V. but 'quadrangle', where our Lord was taken after the arrest in Gethsemane.

Caiaphas. Joseph Caiaphas was High Priest A.D. 18–36, said by Josephus to have been son-in-law of Hanna, High Priest A.D. 6–15. He had been appointed by Gratian the Procurator who preceded Pontius Pilate and made and unmade several High Priests in succession. Mt. leaves no doubt whatever that it was the Priestly party, the Sadducees, who were immediately responsible for the death of Jesus. They hated and feared the Romans and were watchful against any premature attempt to rise against them which might have the effect of forfeiting even the small shred of independence which Rome still allowed them, cf. Jn. $11^{47\,\text{ff.}}$. Such an attempt they probably inferred from the events of Palm Sunday; they prepare a counterplot.

26⁶⁻¹³. *The Anointing in Bethany* (Mk. 14³⁻⁹, Jn. 12¹⁻⁸). The Lucan parallel to the story (Lk. 7³⁶⁻⁵⁰) represents an independent tradition. The woman is identified by S. John with Mary the sister of Martha and Lazarus. Simon the Leper is commonly supposed to have been their father. Bacon thinks that the significance of the woman's act lay in the idea that she was already anointing Him as the Messiah and that our Lord's reply, 'she has done it for my burial', meant in effect 'not a crown but a martyrdom awaits me'. He also suggests that it was this fact which was the substance of the information given by Judas to the High Priests and which provided them with evidence on which to bring a charge against Jesus of blasphemy in claiming the Messiahship. The Church came afterwards to see in what was an act of devotion or of penitence on the part of the woman, a rectification of the omission to anoint the body of the Lord after His death (Mk. 16¹).

26¹³. *This gospel.* We do not know what word or words the Greek word *gospel* is here intended to represent. As it stands, the saying seems to be an obscure reference to the atoning death of Christ implied in the former words.

26¹⁴⁻¹⁶. *The Betrayal* (Mk. 14¹⁰⁻¹¹, Lk. 22³⁻⁶).

The treachery of Judas is placed in striking contrast with the devotion of the woman. Nothing whatever is said about the motive of the traitor, but it was probably political, in spite of John's allegation of a mercenary motive (12⁶). Mt. evidently regards the whole affair as predestined; a fulfilment of prophecy. That is enough for him. He is not interested in motives (see note on 27³⁻¹⁰).

26¹⁵. *weighed unto him.* Gk. ἔστησαν = weighed. The words are taken directly from Zech. 11¹², LXX. 'They weighed for my wages thirty pieces of silver', i.e. shekels, a coin equivalent to a stater, the word which the D Text has in this place (cf. 17²⁷). The whole price, therefore, = £4 16s., the price fixed in Exod. 21³² as compensation for the loss of a slave; perhaps a large enough sum for a hungry and desperate man.

26¹⁷⁻²⁹. *The Farewell Supper* (Mk. 14¹⁷⁻³¹, Lk. 22⁷⁻³⁸).

The action of our Lord implies the same careful planning of the course of events and the same steady control of the situation which characterized His actions from the first moment of the arrival in Judaea. Nothing is left to chance—there is nothing that in the least suggests waiting upon events or submitting to circumstances. Even the traitor himself is made to serve the purpose for which the

Son of man is come. Hence He proceeds to communicate with His friends by a secret code of signals because He does not wish His last meal to be interrupted by the traitor, who is waiting for his opportunity (v. 16), and perhaps arranging for the house to be surrounded. Many think that the house was that of the mother of John Mark, which was afterwards used as a centre for Christian gatherings. Dr. Sanday[1] thinks that the evidence favours the view that the traditional site of the Cenaculum, the earliest Christian Church in Jerusalem, is authentic; having been built on the site of the house of John Mark (Acts 1[13], 12[12]).

NOTE H. THE LAST SUPPER AND THE CRUCIFIXION IN RELATION TO THE PASSOVER

In view of the clear statement of the Fourth Gospel that the death of our Lord took place on the Preparation day before the Passover, i.e. on Nisan 14, and that the Sabbath on which the bodies could not be allowed to remain on the Cross was a high day (Jn. 19[31]), i.e. both the Sabbath and also the first day of Unleavened Bread, Nisan 15; it is extremely difficult to find the reason why the Synoptic writers should state unanimously (a) that our Lord died on the Feast Day itself, when one at least of them has said that the High Priests were agreed that it must not be during the Feast (Mt. 26[5]); (b) that the Last Supper moreover was an actual observance of the Passover, when the Johannine account of it clearly indicates that it was not so. Mk. is the most flagrant offender in respect of this contradiction. According to him, the disciples themselves carried arms; a meeting of, and a trial before, the Sanhedrin took place; Simon of Cyrene came out of the country, presumably from work, and carried the Cross; Joseph of Arimathaea bought linen, and the women spices: and all this on the day which, according to Exod. 12[16], was to be regarded as the equivalent of a Sabbath. The actual trial of Jesus may have been irregular and unjust, but at least the formalities of the law were observed: it was no mere assassination or lynching like that of S. Stephen. Even Herod waited till after the Passover was over to bring Peter out for execution (Acts 12[4]). For this reason it must be regarded as certain that our Lord suffered the day before the Passover, Friday, Nisan 14; on which day in the afternoon the Paschal lambs were slain. It was with this thought in his mind that S. Paul wrote to the Corinthians that

[1] *Sacred Sites of the Gospels*, p. 77.

'even Christ our Passover is sacrificed for us' (I Cor. 5[7]). And the same authority records the tradition, at his time universally received in the Church, that the Last Supper took place on the night in which He was betrayed, i.e. Thursday, Nisan 13 (I Cor. 11[23]).

It must, however, be admitted that S. Matthew's Gospel has been careful to expunge from the record all these contradictory statements of Mk. and the still more damaging statement in Mk. 14[12], 'When they killed the Passover', and has obviously done his best to bring his own narrative into line with what must be called the commonsense view of what is possible.

1. Granted these omissions, Allen holds that 'the rest of the narrative of Mt. is intelligible and in no sense in conflict with the Johannine account'. The room for the Last Supper is prepared as for the Passover, but a day or even two days in advance. Everything is ready except a lamb, which could not be obtained before the proper day and then only by the head of the household in company with as many of its members as could be got together. Our Lord, conscious of the traitor's plot, proposes a counterplot by anticipating the meal. It is of course not a real Passover meal for there is no lamb. But there was Bread which he declared to be the Body which God 'had prepared for him' (Ps. 40[7]) and that was a sufficient substitute. The disciples, of course, at that time did not understand either the need for a lamb or the meaning of the rite thus instituted; though John indicates in his sixth chapter that it was not the first time that he had alluded to a doctrine of Bread.

2. G. H. Box adopts a view not dissimilar from that of Allen, except that he holds with many other authorities that our Lord made no attempt to celebrate a Passover of any kind, but a *Kiddush*, a meal of fellowship celebrated privately by a Jewish family or group of friends, at the conclusion of which a solemn thanksgiving was uttered over a cup of wine by the President. This ceremony took place on the afternoon before the Sabbath, and before great days, such as the 'Preparation' was. This view has the support of Lk.'s independent account of the Supper in which Jesus took a cup and gave thanks, saying, 'With desire I have desired to eat this Passover', i.e. I have desired but my desire was frustrated by the traitor's plot (Lk. 22[15]). This appears to be a perfectly satisfactory solution of the difficulty.

3. It has been suggested by Strack-Billerbeck[1] and others that the real solution is to be found in a dispute between the Pharisees

---

[1] *Kommentar Z.N.T.* ii, pp. 346ff., and Rawlinson, *S. Mark*, p. 262.

and Sadducees about the Calendar, which fixed the beginning of the important month Nisan inaugurating the ecclesiastical year. The result was that the Pharisees who disputed the date were allowed as a concession to celebrate the Passover a day earlier and that they were followed in this case by Jesus and His disciples.

4. It is, however, more probable that the records themselves have been coloured by the variations of contemporary observance in the primitive Church. We know that as late as the end of the second century a controversy arose about the time of keeping Easter and was referred to Rome for solution. It was called the Quartodeciman controversy. The Eastern Church, relying on the Johannine tradition, was accustomed to celebrate Christ's death as the Christian Passover on Nisan 14, irrespective of the day of the week on which it fell in any particular year. In the Roman Church, regarding the Jewish Passover as having been replaced by the Christian Eucharist, which was celebrated on Easter Sunday, the Friday, which we still observe as Good Friday, was kept as the commemoration of the Passion, irrespective of the day of the week on which Nisan 14 happened in any year to fall. Hence it is probable *either* that the Fourth Gospel, true to the position of the Asian Church, adapted the Gospel story for symbolical purposes so as to make the date of our Lord's death coincide with the time at which the Paschal lambs were slain; *or* that Mk. and Lk., followed by Mt., have erroneously described the Last Supper as a Paschal meal in the interests of the view that the Eucharist is the true Christian Passover. For a full account, see Brilioth, *Eucharistic Faith and Practice*, pp. 1–58.

26²³. *in the dish*, Gk. τρύβλιον, a deep bowl. Those who identify the meal with the Passover refer this to the Haroseth, a sauce composed of fruits, spices, and vinegar in which bread was dipped. Mt. understands that the dipping marked out the traitor in an indirect way.

26²⁴. *as it is written.* e.g. Ps. 22, Isa. 53.

26²⁶⁻³⁰. *The Institution of the Eucharist.*

26. *brake it.* The idea of the *fraction* as containing a symbolic reference to the death of Christ is not found in early Christian Eucharistic thought. In 1 Cor. 11²⁴ the word 'broken' is not in the best MSS. and the symbolism of the Fourth Gospel is against the idea (Jn. 19³³⁻³⁶). Christian theology in the West has looked for the symbolism of death, not in the breaking, for our Lord's body was not broken, but either in the communion, the eating and drinking

of the sacramental elements (S. Augustine), or in the separate consecration of bread and wine representing the separation of the Body and Blood in death, as in Jn. $6^{55\,\text{ff.}}$ (S. Thomas Aquinas). Our Lord is clearly using the language (1) of sacrifice, (2) of symbolism, as Christian belief has always recognized, whatever explanation it may have sought at different times of the 'inward part or thing signified' in the Mystery.[1]

26^{27}. *Drink ye all of it*, an alteration by Mt. of what in Mk. is a statement of fact, '*They all drank of it*', perhaps lest it should be supposed that Judas partook.

26^{28}. *blood of the covenant*, Gk. διαθήκη. The words refer to Exod. 24^{4-8}, the inauguration of God's covenant with Israel at Sinai. The point is that it is sacrificial blood. Jesus, by His bloodshedding, of which the Eucharist is a representation, inaugurates a covenant for those whom He had drawn from the old Israel to be the New People of God.[2] 'This is my counterpart of the blood of the Covenant at Sinai.' It has, however, been suggested that there is a further reference in these words to the prophecy of Isa. 42^6 where the Servant of Jehovah is spoken of as being given for a 'covenant of the people' for a light of the Gentiles.

Rawlinson connects the 'Covenant' not only with Exod. 24^7 but with the idea of the propitiatory value of martyrdom, especially in the book of the Maccabees, when Jewish martyrs are said to have 'offered up both body and life for the Law of their Fathers, entreating God that He would speedily be propitiated for their Nation'.[3] Jesus in the same way made at the Supper 'an act of self-dedication' by which He covenanted that the life He was willingly surrendering in the cause of the Kingdom should be a sacrifice to God on Israel's behalf. Jesus, therefore, thought of His blood as being Covenant blood (Zech. 9^{11}). S. Paul (1 Cor. 11^{25}) received the words as 'the *new* Covenant'; with reference to the new Covenant of the 'heart' predicted in Jer. 31^{31}. We cannot definitely say what was in our Lord's mind; we only know how the primitive Church interpreted the words of which they found echoes and anticipations in the whole of Scripture.

shed for many, Gk. περὶ πολλῶν. Cf. Isa. 53^{11-12}.

remission of sins. An addition of Mt. to the words as recorded both

---

[1] On the meaning of the 'Body of Christ' see the suggestive article by Dr. A. E. J. Rawlinson in the volume *Mysterium Christi*, pp. 226 ff.

[2] Cf. note on 'Ecclesia' in Mt. 16^{18}. The meaning given there to this expression is supported and illustrated by the Eucharistic action.

[3] 2 Macc. 7^{36-39}.

in Paul and Mk. The words appear to be taken from Mk.'s account of John's Baptism where Mt. omits them (Mk. 1⁴). In placing the words here Mt. continues the thought of the Eucharist still further, by allusion to the sin- or peace-offering of which the central thought is reconciliation.

26²⁹. *I will not drink henceforth of this fruit of the vine.* The Eucharist is not only a memorial of the death of Christ but also a pledge of future glory. The eschatological idea is as inseparable from the Eucharist as the sacrificial. Thus S. Paul teaches that the Eucharist is to be celebrated 'till He come' (1 Cor. 11²⁶); and the ancient Christian liturgy embodied in the Didache has the same thought: 'We give thanks for the holy vine of David Thy servant which Thou didst make known to us through Jesus Thy servant. May grace come and this world pass away.' The Messiah is the true vine in which His people will participate. Cf. Jn. 15¹.

Professor N. P. Williams remarks that 'to an Evangelist of the date of Mt. these words must have been an equivalent to a command to continue the Eucharist. "This fruit of the vine" can hardly have meant anything else to him but the Eucharist, the *sacrum convivium*, which is the centre of the Church's life, "the Kingdom of My Father"' (*Essays Catholic and Critical*).

26³⁰⁻⁵⁶. *In the Garden of Gethsemane* (Mk. 14³²⁻⁴², Lk. 22³⁹⁻⁴⁶, Jn. 18¹⁻¹¹).

26³¹. Zech. 13⁷ from the Aramaic translation agreeing neither with the Hebrew nor the LXX. The apparent weakness of Jesus in the face of His enemies is hereby explained to Christian believers as part of the predestined purpose of God for the Christ.

26³⁴. *cock crow*=i.e. the third Roman watch, 12 to 3 a.m., before dawn.

26³⁶. *Gethsemane* = olive press. Lagrange remarks that since the fourth century a church had been built on the place of the prayer in the Garden. It was discovered in 1920. (Vincent Abel, *Jerusalem*, vol. ii, p. 1007.)

26³⁷. *sorrowful*, Gk. ἀδημονεῖν, to be bewildered or feel fear, implying a restless distracted feeling of impending horror which one shrinks from but cannot escape.

26⁴². The second prayer as given by Mt. shows an advance upon the first, as though our Lord had steeled Himself to realize that the 'cup' would not pass from Him.

26⁴⁶. *let us go*, Gk. ἄγωμεν, expression of purpose, 'go out to meet them', 'Do something definite'. Our Lord's human self-respect made Him shrink from the arrest taking place with His own disciples sprawling on the ground around Him.

26⁵⁰. *Friend, do that for which thou art come*, Gk. ἐφ' ὃ πάρει. The words are not found elsewhere, nor is it clear what they mean, some such words as 'do' or 'say' may have dropped out.[1]

26[52]. The teaching of Jesus on this occasion has always been upheld by Christians in the face of persecution. It has not been regarded as forbidding them to bear arms 'at the commandment of the magistrate'. But no brave man struggles on the scaffold.

26[55]. *a robber*, Gk. λῃστής. Ironically addressed to the emissaries of the Sadducees, whose friends the Robbers were, see 21[13].

26[57-68]. *The Trial of the Messiah before His people* (Mk. 14[53-72], Lk. 22[54-71], Jn. 18[12-14]),

26[57]. *scribes and the elders*, i.e. the whole Sanhedrin. The law contained in the Mishnah required only twenty-three members as a quorum in criminal cases, but such cases must be tried and punished in the daytime. But G. H. Box thinks it doubtful whether these rules would have been observed by the Sadducee Priesthood of the time.

26[59]. *false witness*. Instead of Mk.'s 'witness'. An example of the growth of anti-Semitic feeling in Mt.'s Gospel, which reflects the bitter relations between Jews and Christians in his day.

26[61]. *destroy the temple of God*. Some authentic utterance of Jesus lies behind the charge. In its original form the saying was probably eschatological as the reference in Jn. 2[19] to the Resurrection shows; and referred to the new age in which the worldly sanctuary would be replaced by a new temple, not made with hands. As this belief belonged to the group of ideas associated with the Messianic hope, the charge implied a claim to the Messiahship which was regarded as blasphemous in the circumstances. Stephen was afterwards condemned for repeating this prophecy, Acts 6[14].

in three days. A complete interval as in Hos. 6[2], where after three days seems to mean 'after death has been completed', cf. 15[32], but the original saying probably meant after the complete and final destruction of the present building.

26[63]. *I adjure thee*, Gk. ἐξορκίζω, i.e. he put Jesus on His oath. It was suggested by Schweitzer that what Judas betrayed was the secret revealed at Caesarea Philippi that Jesus claimed the Messiahship, and that is how the High Priest knew. But, as we have seen, the charge of the witnesses itself involved the claim and in its strongest form to be the Christ, the Son of God.

26[66]. If a formal capital sentence was passed, the rule in the Mishnah, if at that time in force, was broken, for the final proceedings in the case of a verdict of 'guilty' had to take place on the following day

[1] The words are found inscribed on drinking vessels. See Deissmann, *Licht vom Osten*, pp. 100 sqq. (1925).

in order to avoid precipitate action. But it has been suggested that the Sanhedrin was acting as a sort of Grand Jury formulating the charges on which Jesus was to be arraigned before the legal tribunal.

26^{67-68}. A reminiscence of what appears in Lk. as horseplay on the part of those who had arrested our Lord while waiting in the outer court for the trial to begin (Lk. 22^{63-65}). It is hardly likely that the Sanhedrin itself would have been so forgetful of judicial propriety as to indulge in such offensive conduct. Mk. (14^{65}) adds the interesting detail that they covered his face after the pronouncement of sentence, as was the custom with condemned criminals (Esther 7^8), and this is the probable explanation of the strange action described in verse 68.

26^{69-75}. *S. Peter's Denial* (Mk. 14^{68-72}, Lk. 22^{55-62}, Jn. $18^{17, \ 25-27}$).
    26^{69}. *the court, v.* on 26^3. It would be below the Council Chamber.

27. *The Final Scene.*

27^{1-2}. *The Second Meeting of the Sanhedrin* (Mk. 15^1, Lk. 22^{65-71}).
    This is one of the few cases in which Mt. differs from Mk. in his Passion story. It may have been an attempt on the part of the Council to adhere in some fashion to the rule already mentioned of the Tractate of the Mishnah. Apparently confirmation of a sentence of death by the Procurator was required at this period. Pontius Pilate was appointed Procurator Fiscal, i.e. under the direct control of the Emperor, of the province of Judaea by Tiberius in the year A.D. 26 and remained for ten years, when he was sent back to Rome by Vitellius, at that time in command in Syria, in consequence of cruelty in crushing a Samaritan rising. According to Josephus, whose account may be exaggerated, his record was bad. But he attempted to keep order in a country seething with discontent. (Josephus, *Ant.* xviii. 3; *Jewish Wars*, ii. 9. 2 ff.; and Schürer, *History of the Jewish People*, Div. I, vol. ii, pp. 44 ff.)

27^{3-10}. *The End of the Traitor.*

    The fact that Judas at once knew that Jesus was condemned led E. A. Abbott to suggest that he was 'that other disciple' referred to in Jn. 18^{15}, but not named from horror, who followed from the Garden with Peter and brought him in. If so, it was not the first time that Judas had been the evil genius of Peter. (Cf. Jn. 6^{70}, Mt. 16^{23}.)
    Mt.'s account of the suicide of the Traitor is related in sharpest

condemnation of the Jewish hierarchy. Gruesome legends have always gathered round the end of traitors; and this story which Mt. relates from his N source is only one of at least three different accounts of the death of Judas. Both this story and that in Acts 1^{19} appear to be aetiological in character, and are related to explain the origin of a place in Jerusalem known as Akeldama = field of blood, which may itself be a corruption of its Aramaic name = Field of Sleeping, i.e. Cemetery. In any case late Christian tradition in Jerusalem from an early date explained the name of this place of ill fame either (1) as the field in which Judas met his bloody end (Acts 1^{19}) or (2) as the field purchased with blood-money as in Mt., while the name 'Potter's Field' in Mt. may be an attempt to bring the story into close agreement with the prophecy cited in verse 7.

27^5. *sanctuary*, Gk. ναόν, not the Holy of Holies but the buildings surrounding it, which may have been a rendezvous for Judas when he wished to see the chief priests on private business.

27^6. *Treasury*, Gk. κορβανᾶν, peculiar to Mt.; a Graecized form of the Hebrew *Korban*. (Cf. Mk. 7^{11}.)

27^7. In this passage Mt. again quotes texts without knowing exactly where they come from. The passage is in the main from Zech. 11^{12-13}, not from Jeremiah at all. The only connexion with Jeremiah is that the prophet was commanded to go to visit a potter and that he purchased a field at Anathoth on the very eve of the Exile as a sign to his people of the certainty of the return (Jer. 18^2, 32^6). The quotation, which as in all N passages, is from the Aramaic version and not the LXX, depends for its point on the similarity between the Heb. *Ôsā*, treasury, and *yosēr*, potter. (G. H. Box.)

27^{11-26}. *The Trial of the Messiah before the heathen* (Mk. 15^{2-15}, Lk. 23^{1-25}, Jn. 18^{12-40}).

27^{16}. *Barabbas*. There is an interesting variant reading known to Origen, the MS. Θ and several of the Syriac versions, which inserts the name *Jesus* before *Barabbas*. There can be no doubt that it is the original reading because it is one of the variants which could not have been interpolated from outside. Burkitt suggests that Mt. derived the name from some tradition known to him. But McNeile thinks that Mk.'s unusual phrase, 'there was one who was called Barabbas' (Gk. ἦν δὲ ὁ λεγόμενος Βαραββᾶς) (15^7), may also point to an original sentence 'there was a Jesus who was called Barabbas'. Certainly in Mt. it is impossible to account for the phrase in verse 17, 'Jesus who is called Christ', unless it was to distinguish Him from another Jesus who was called Barabbas. Deissmann traces the gradual process by which every instance of the name of *Jesus* belonging to another than the Saviour has been carefully eliminated from the New Testament. Deissmann adds the acute observation that the elimination of the name in Mt. 27^{16} is one of the most decisive proofs of the historical truth of Jesus and of the story of His death. Otherwise later Christians would not have been at pains to tamper with records many years after the events to which they refer.[1] (See note on 1^{21}.)

27^{19}. An N passage. Tradition gives the name of Procla or Claudia Procula to Pilate's wife in the Apocryphal Gospel of Nicodemus. There is nothing improbable in the anecdote. Tacitus records a decision of the Senate that Governors in the provinces might have their wives with them (*An.* iii. 33). Strack-Billerbeck mentions similar cases of interference by wives in the administration of justice. The historian Appian relates a story that Calpurnia, wife of Julius Caesar, had a similar terrifying dream before his death, on the strength of which she implored him not to proceed to the Forum.

27^{21}. As McNeile remarks, each of the Synoptics leads up to the fatal sentence in his own way. Lk. emphasizes Pilate's lack of courage. Mk. catches the political situation (15^{15}). Mt. inserts from his N source the incident of the washing of the hands, and uses it with tremendous effect to exonerate the Roman authority and to pile up the guilt upon the apostate nation. It reflects the intense anti-Semitism of the Christians of his day.

27^{25}. *all the people*, Gk. πᾶς ὁ λαός, not the crowd but the Holy People, the nation and its rulers in their corporate capacity, solemnly assembled for the Feast.

27^{27}. *The Second Act in the Passion.*

27^{31}. *The Mocking by the Soldiers* (Mk. 15^{16-20}, Jn. 19^{2-3}).

Professor C. H. Turner suggests that Pilate's sentence named a definite hour for the execution, leaving an interval which the soldiers filled up with this 'ragging'.

27^{27}. *the palace*, Gk. *Praetorium*, originally the general's head-quarters in a camp, now the official residence of a Governor: in this case, as most modern archaeologists think, the former palace of Herod the Great on the Western Hill. There was a main street leading from the Temple area and the Council Chamber of the Sanhedrin to this palace.[2]

the whole band, Gk. σπεῖρα, Lat. *manipulus*, a company or detachment

---

[1] *Mysterium Christi*, p. 19.
[2] Acts. xxiii. 35, cf. Josephus, *Jewish Wars*, ii. 15. 5.

of a cohort, 500 or 600 men, under a company commander called a centurion.

27²⁸. *scarlet robe*, Gk. χλαμύς, Lat. *sagum*, a soldier's scarlet cloak.

27²⁹. *crown*, Gk. στέφανον, not a royal diadem but a garland such as would be won either in a battle or in the games (1 Cor. 9²⁵).

27³²⁻⁴⁴. The Via Dolorosa and the Crucifixion (Mk. 15²¹⁻³⁷, Lk. 23²⁶⁻⁴⁶, Jn. 19¹⁷⁻³⁰).

27³². *Cyrene*, a town between Alexandria and Carthage, capital of the ancient Pentapolis, now Tripoli, had one of the largest settlements of Jews. Mk. knew the man's sons either at Jerusalem or Rome (Mk. 15²¹, Rom. 16¹³).

compelled, Gk. ἠγγάρευσαν = impressed, see on 5⁴¹.

27³³. *Golgotha*, probably a skull-shaped mound, hence the Lat. *Calvarium*, the traditional site of which is not far 'without the city wall' by the gate near the Praetorium.

27³⁴. Cf. Ps. 69²¹ and Lam. 3¹⁹.

Jesus wished 'to taste death' voluntarily and for this required the full unnumbed exercise of will and consciousness to the last (Heb. 2⁹).

27³⁵. Ps. 22¹⁸.

27³⁶. *watched him*, as was usual, to prevent possibility of rescue of the crucified by friends. The D text of Mk. 15²⁵ has 'guarded him'.

27³⁸. *robbers*, see on 21¹³. Their execution is evidence of Pilate's determination to stamp out terrorism in Judaea, probably in this case connected with the rising of Barabbas. Tradition gives names to them, Dysmas and Gestas.

27³⁹. Ps. 22⁷.

27⁴⁴. As C. H. Turner remarks, the impression emerges that the story is told from a distance. Luke and John have detailed knowledge; Lk. especially about the conduct of the Crucified and its diverse effect on the various 'assistants' at the Passion (Lk. 23⁴⁴).

27⁴⁵. Mt.'s first note of time. The Crucifixion, according to the evidence of the Fourth Gospel, took place at 12 noon (Jn. 19¹⁴). Mk.'s 'It was the third hour', if not a later addition, was omitted by Mt. and Lk.

The darkness, though quite explicable as a natural phenomenon, is not so regarded by the Evangelist who is influenced in his description of the portents at the death of the Messiah and by O.T. predictions of coming catastrophe in which failure of light is always one of the most common features (cf. Amos 8⁹, Isa. 60²).

The longer text of Lk. gives a natural reason, 'the sun being eclipsed'. But this is impossible at a time of full moon.

27[46]. Ps. 22[1]. There is no reason whatever to imagine, with some critics, that Jesus died with words of despair on his lips. The words quoted are only the first words of a Psalm which ends on a note of triumph.

Eli, Eli. The words as they stand are Hebrew, whereas in Mk. and according to some important MSS. in Mt., they are in Aramaic. In their Aramaic form, it is difficult to see how they could possibly have suggested the name 'Elijah' to the bystanders. In no case could any Jew possibly have confused the name of God (Heb. *El*) with any other name. For this reason the words in verse 47 have been supposed to refer to the heathen guards. But what would they have been likely to know about Elijah? Turner's comment upon the parallel passage in Mk. 15[34] notes that the Old Latin MS. k has in verse 35 not *Heleian* but *Helion*, Gk. ἥλιον, the sun; and thinks that it may originally have referred to the darkness; especially if at this moment the sun appeared. But as they stand the words are only intelligible as deliberate mockery on the part of the bystanders. (See *New Commentary ad loc.*)

27[50-55]. *The Death of the Messiah and the portents attending it* (Mk. 15[38-41], Lk. 23[44-49], Jn. 19[30-37]).

27[50]. *yielded up his spirit*, Gk. ἀφῆκε τὸ πνεῦμα, i.e. as a voluntary act. Lk. adds the final word from the Cross adapted from Ps. 31[5], 'Father, into thy hands I commend my spirit': Jn. has the single word τετέλεσται, 'It is finished'.

The portents accompanying the death of the Messiah are taken from Mk.'s account, but one is added, the opening of the tombs and the preliminary Resurrection, from the N source.

27[51]. *veil of the temple*, Gk. καταπέτασμα τοῦ ναοῦ. More than one veil is mentioned both by Josephus[1] and in Rabbinic writings. It may have been either that between the outer court and the Holy Place, or that between the Holy Place and the Holy of Holies. It was the latter which the author of the Epistle to the Hebrews had in mind when he used this passage for the purpose of his symbolism (Heb. 10[20]). A story is told in the Talmud, that forty years before

---

[1] *Jewish Wars*, v. 4 and 5. The rending of the veil is one of the references to the Gospel story which occur in the Slavonic Josephus, a very dubious document which cannot be traced back beyond the Middle Ages. It may contain some genuine readings but, according to Professor Dodd, numerous interpolations of which this is almost certainly one.

the destruction of Jerusalem one night the doors of the Temple, shut on the previous evening, sprang open of their own accord. Both these events point to the earthquake which in Christian tradition was bound up with the moment of Christ's death.

27^{52}. This is one of the passages quoted by S. Ignatius (Magn. 17). The writer evidently regards the emergence of the Saints from the rock tombs thrown open by the earthquake as a kind of first-fruits of the Resurrection, while the words 'after the Resurrection' are inserted to guard the doctrine that Christ was Himself the 'first-fruits of them that sleep' (1 Cor. 15^{20}, Col. 1^{18}). It looks rather as if Mt. was here combining tradition about the 'harrowing of hell' by Jesus (as in 1 Pet. 3^{19}, 4^6) with a Jerusalem story of visions of 'saints' seen after the death of Jesus. For saints see on Mt. 17^4, and the popular belief there quoted. As Lagrange remarks, the description is vague and does not contain historical detail as does that of the Resurrection of Jesus of which the witnesses are named.

27^{53}. *after his resurrection*, Gk. ἔγερσιν, only in this place in the N.T.

27^{54}. *centurion*. Known to Christian tradition in the Gospel of Peter as Petronius.

the Son of God—rather 'a Son of God': in the mouth of a pagan the phrase would mean a superhuman person or hero (Rawlinson, *S. Mark*, 1. 1, *N.T. Doctrine of Christ*, pp. 90 ff.).

27^{56}. *Mary the mother of James and Joses*. See note on Mt. 13^{55} where James and Joseph are called brothers of the Lord. If they are the same as those referred to here, then the woman, their mother, is perhaps the same as she who is mentioned in Jn. 19^{25} as the sister of the Virgin, and the wife of Cleophas or Alphaeus. See Turner's note on Mk. 15^{40-41}, *New Commentary*.

27^{57-61}. *The Burial of the Body of Jesus* (Mk. 15^{42-47}, Lk. 23^{50-56}, Jn. 19^{38-42}).

In no case would the Jews have suffered the Body to remain on the Cross on the Sabbath; they would have claimed it themselves had not the unexpected death of Jesus given Joseph his opportunity. The careful burial of executed criminals was prescribed by Deut. 21^{23}, but they were not to be buried in the tomb of their fathers. This act of Joseph manifests, therefore, a unique devotion. Burials were not allowed within the Holy City, they had to be fifty ells from the Tower of Antonia. Rock tombs were especially popular for families, and holes in the rock were often artificially deepened and widened to the requisite size.

27^57. Just before 6 p.m. at which time the Sabbath begins.

Arimathaea, identified with the city of El Kanah in Ephraim; but Eusebius places it near Diospolis or Lydda. Cf. 1 Macc. 11^34.

rich man. An allusion to Isa. 53^9. Mk. has 'honourable', Gk. εὐσχήμων, which had come to mean 'rich'.

27^61. *the other Mary*; in Mk. 15^40 the mother of James, named, so Turner says, as being Mark's special informant. Mt. implies that the women are witnesses of what is described in the next few verses.

27^62-66. *The Events of Easter Eve.*

From the source N, and evidently intended by Mt. to dispose once and for all of the canard of the Jews that the Body of Jesus was stolen. According to Bacon 'this addition, unknown to the Palestinian community, represents the story of a great controversy between the Christian Church and the Synagogue; which arose as a result of Mk.'s account of the empty Tomb'. Mt., who has kept hitherto very close to the Marcan account of the Passion, advances at this point a step farther; he takes cognizance of objections raised by the Jews to Mk.'s account. The answer to that had been that the disciples stole the body by night in order to support the false belief which they champion. To this charge the Christian apologist replies by a new assertion. Removal of the Body was impossible because the Jews were forewarned and had taken elaborate precautions. To which the rejoinder was, 'in that case the guards would have seen and reported the alleged miraculous occurrence of the Resurrection'. To which again the counter-rejoinder replied, 'they were bribed not to', and as Mt. adds, 'the report of the transaction is current among the Jews to this day' (Mt. 28^15). This passage is noteworthy for the number of words in it not found elsewhere in the Gospel, e.g. *deceiver*, Gk. πλάνος; *guard*, Gk. κουστωδίαν, a Latinism which Mark might have used.

27^62. *the Preparation*, i.e. Friday, which was called the evening before the Sabbath.

27^64. *the third day.* The whole story assumes that predictions about the Resurrection on the third day were common property. This in itself is most unlikely; unless the Jews so interpreted the words about the destruction of the Temple in 26^61. But it is wholly improbable in any case that the High Priest would have taken action involving association with the pagan Governor and the soldiers on the very Feast day itself.

28. *The Resurrection and Appearances of the Risen One.*

This chapter is a triumphant assertion of the doctrine of Christ's

Resurrection. As Dr. Goudge remarks, 'perhaps there is no book in the literature of the world which possesses so splendid a conclusion'.[1] Mt. no longer has Mark to follow, because the ending of Mk.'s Gospel, if ever written, was lost before Mt. received it, otherwise he would have reproduced it.[2] In place of it he has composed for his readers a picture, almost in the style of a great Italian painter, of what he conceived to have taken place at the Tomb. For this purpose he combines two traditions of the Resurrection, namely (1) that of Mk. and Jn., both of which centre in the story of the empty Tomb; and (2) that which placed the scene of the appearances in Galilee (John 21 and the apocryphal Gospel of Peter, cf. Mt. 26^{32}, Mk. 16^{7}). A supernatural being of terrifying aspect here takes the place of the young man in white whom the women saw *inside* the Tomb. The appearance of Jesus Himself to the women (vv. 9–10) seems from its details to be a variant form of the appearance to Mary Magdalene in the Garden (Jn. 20$^{11-18}$).

28^{1}. *late on the sabbath day*, Gk. ὀψὲ δὲ σαββάτων. Mt. here uses a technical phrase because he wants to indicate a precise time, namely what was known as the 'outgoing of the sabbath'—not *late on the sabbath day*, but the *dawn of Sunday*.

28^{10}. *my brethren* refers either to the early Christian disciples in Palestine who were known as the 'Brethren' or to our Lord's actual relations. An appearance to James, the Lord's brother, is mentioned by S. Paul in 1 Cor. 15^{7}.

28$^{11-15}$. *The Jewish Council.* See note on 27$^{62-66}$.

28^{15}. *The Jews*, Gk. Ἰουδαίοις, as in 27^{37}, no longer the Holy People but the enemies of the Christian Church, as always in the Fourth Gospel.

28$^{16-18}$. *The Appearance of the Risen One to His Ecclesia.*

At this point Mt. breaks off the account of the Jerusalem appearance and turns to an independent source, as is implied in the mention of *the* mountain, which was evidently well known but is not further specified. Unknown facts underlie the story, but the historical character of the expression is vouched for by the testimony of S. Paul in 1 Cor. 15^{6} which refers to persons at that time alive who were prepared to testify to the experiences in question.

---

[1] *New Commentary, ad loc.*
[2] On the lost ending of Mark, see Rawlinson, *S. Mark*, p. 267, and Bp. Blunt in this series, *ad loc.*

28¹⁷. *some doubted,* inserted probably to harmonize the story with that of S. Thomas in Jn. 20²⁴ᶠᶠ.

worshipped him, Gk. προσεκύνησαν, a term of divine adoration not used elsewhere in the Synoptic Gospels except in Mt. 14³³ which, as we have seen, may itself embody a Resurrection appearance.

28¹⁸⁻²⁰. *The Apostolic Commission.*

The final words corresponding to the Commission to the Apostles in Jn. 20²¹ are intended to be the reinstatement of the Disciples into their Apostolic office forfeited by their failure at the Passion.

28¹⁸. *All authority hath been given unto me.* A direct reference to Dan. 7¹⁴: 'And there were given unto him power . . . and all the nations of the earth according to their races and languages worshipping him.' (LXX.) Cf. also the ascription in Eph. 1¹⁹⁻²³.

28¹⁹. *into the name of,* Gk. εἰς τὸ ὄνομα. In inscriptions, which are common, soldiers were said to swear themselves 'into the name' or possession of the most High Zeus. So also in financial matters a sum of money is said to be paid 'into the name', i.e. account or possession of some one. Accordingly in the present passage the baptized may be said to be translated into the possession of the Father, Jesus Christ, and His Spirit at that moment operative in the fullness of the Divine activity in the Christian community (*v.* note on 7²²).

28²⁰. 'With the concluding words of the Gospel not only are the first disciples comforted with the assurance of the speedy return of the Lord but the whole Church with His abiding presence in the Spirit which guarantees its continued life' (S. Chrysostom).

NOTE I. THE APPEARANCES AND SAYINGS OF THE RISEN CHRIST

1. The story of the Resurrection appearances of Jesus as it has been handed down in the Christian Church is only a reminiscence of a much richer tradition of which the traces are to be found in the oldest portions of the N.T. That record forms, however, a nucleus from which the historian can still recognize the fact that certain experiences of the Risen Christ were related at an early date by eyewitnesses, many of whom were still alive in the year when 1 Cor. 15 was written (A.D. 54). These appearances took place in different places, in Galilee, Jerusalem and its neighbourhood, near Damascus, and in different circles, and after a certain time wholly ceased. It is out of these experiences, rather than from

the fact of the empty Tomb, that the belief in the Resurrection arose.

What, then, was the nature of the appearances? In the first place it is important to understand that the Resurrection of Jesus Christ is never in the N.T. regarded as a case of mere survival after death. There is nothing in the N.T. analogous to the Greek doctrine of the natural immortality of the soul, the idea to which the death of Socrates gave so great an impetus among western peoples, that a loved and honoured master was still alive. The disciples' experiences as described by them were something quite different. Nor were they anything in the nature of a mystical vision. S. Paul distinguishes quite clearly between his own great experience, belated though it was, on the way to Damascus and the 'visions and revelations of the Lord' which he received in the seventh heaven (2 Cor. 12[1]). Such visions are always those of individual persons and liable to recur, but the Easter experiences happened simultaneously to a number of persons, and within a measurable interval suddenly came to an end. As we have already seen (see note on Mt. 22[30]), the Resurrection is always regarded in the N.T. as an eschatological event, closely connected with the Kingdom of God, and that of Jesus is never spoken of apart from the Resurrection of the dead as a whole. To judge from the interpretation of S. Paul, the Resurrection appearances were to the disciples an experience in some overwhelmingly convincing form of an act of the Living God, which they felt to have been the fulfilment of all the prophetic and apocalyptic revelations of the past. The event had happened according to the scriptures; it was the dawn of the age to come and of the new life in the Spirit of which Christ Himself was the 'first-fruits, afterwards they that are Christ's at His coming' (1 Cor. 15[23]). They had experienced what another writer in the Epistle to the Hebrews called the 'powers of the world to come' (Heb. 6[5]). It is for this reason, because it was an entirely new and creative act of God raising up Jesus from the dead, that no description of the Resurrection or of the Risen One could be given in the N.T., for no one can behold the mighty works of God except in their effects (Jn. 3[8]). 'The miracle of Easter', as a recent writer remarks,[1] 'is not the fact of the Easter visions nor the empty grave, but the act of the living God 'who raised up Jesus from the dead', summoning man, soul and body, from death to life in the Spirit. In the Easter fact the final end of history enters in some way into history.' When

---

[1] *Mysterium Christi*, p. 95. Sasse notes that the Jews, like the Persians, regarded the Resurrection as strictly analogous to the Creation.

the primitive Church went out into the world with the message 'the Lord is Risen', it was not only the Easter events that it preached, but the *act of God* which lies behind them and which, as S. Paul says, is still operative in the Christian Church (Rom. 8¹¹, Eph. 1¹⁹⁻²⁰). It was to this 'act' that S. Paul, with true understanding of it, referred in his speech at Athens recorded in Acts 17³¹: 'God hath given assurance unto all men (of the judgement to come) in that he raised him up from the dead.'

(2) Much has been written against the concluding words of the Gospel as authentic sayings of Jesus. There is no variant of any one of them in any MS. but it is not necessary to claim them as *ipsissima verba* of Jesus any more than similar utterances in the Fourth Gospel. The fact is, the early Church failed to distinguish between the sayings of the Lord while on earth and sayings of the Risen One and of His Spirit in the Christian Ecclesia. In any case post-Resurrection sayings of Jesus must by their very nature be incapable of phonographic reproduction. They belong to a mysterious order, the world of the Spirit, the experience of which can be only very imperfectly interpreted in the words of earthly language. The sayings have raised three serious problems:

(a) The command to evangelize all the nations was apparently unknown in the primitive community in Palestine which, according to the Acts (8¹⁴, 10, 11, 13¹³, 22⁸⁻²²), looked with suspicion on the Gentile and even the Samaritan Mission. Even Peter had to be convinced by a special vision from heaven and that in spite of the statement in Acts 1⁸. The words, as we have them, reflect the liberal attitude which we know from other sources to have been characteristic of the Nazarene Church of northern Syria from which we have had reason to believe S. Matthew's Gospel originally sprung. The close connexion with Antioch and S. Paul's missionary efforts, as well as a strong local missionary tradition, are enough to account for the belief that work like that of S. Paul was commanded by the Spirit of Jesus; Acts 13¹⁻³ supplies the very occasion when such a command is given through the mouth of a Christian prophet.

(b) The command to baptize is not found elsewhere in the N.T. Mt. refers to baptism as a well-established Sacrament of the Church, complete with matter and form, and together with the observance of the new law, 'as generally necessary to salvation'. The Trinitarian formula, though not the usual baptismal invocation in the Palestinian and Pauline communities (Acts 2³⁸, 8¹⁶, 10⁴⁸, Gal. 3²⁷), was already established early in the second century A.D. in Syria, as can be seen from its use in the Didache, and in Asia and prob-

ably Rome from its occurrence in the Apology of Justin Martyr
(A.D. 150). It clearly implies that by that time the solemn
service of Baptism was thought to require the fuller richness and
more efficacious and creative Name of the Threefold One.

(c) There is no doubt that we find the threefold Name in use
very early in the primitive Church—not of course in ordinary
language, but in exalted utterances, i.e. in passages which in
form and origin have already something liturgical about them,
and appear to be rudimentary forms of the Christian Creeds.
Such may be found in 1 Cor. 12[4-6], 2 Cor. 13[14], 2 Thess. 2[13-14],
Eph. 4[4-6], in which S. Paul does not seem to be making up the
threefold Name for the first time at the moment of writing, but
to be using a recognized formula which was already filled with
a definite content. Similar, though not exactly the same, forms
are to be found in other parts of the N.T., e.g. the glory of the
Son of man, of the Father, and of the Holy Angels (Mt. 16[27]), the
solemn invocation in 1 Tim. 5[21], God, Jesus Christ, and the elect
angels; and the greeting in Rev. 1[4], from the Almighty, from
the Seven Spirits (in the second place), and from Jesus Christ.
The varying forms of expression for the Third *Person* (to use an
ancient though very inadequate term), as also the uncertainty
in the order of the Sacred Names (cf. 1 Pet. 1[2]), prove that the
Trinitarian belief had not yet in the primitive Church received a
fixed dogmatic form. Even as late as the middle of the second
century we find Justin Martyr in his Apology using such an
expression as 'Father, Son, and the whole host of heaven' (1[6]).
It is remarkable that in not one of the seven authentic Epistles
of S. Paul is the greeting given as we should expect in the
threefold Name, unless the 'grace and peace' are intended to
represent the Spirit (Rom. 1[7]). This makes it all the more certain
that the Trinitarian formula was no creation of S. Paul, but
appeared when the Holy Spirit was as *personally* experienced
as were the Father and the Son. There is reason to believe that
this took place in the Hellenistic communities rather than in
those of Palestine.

(d) The words as they stand in Mt. are doubtless intended to be a
dogmatic or credal statement, the earliest that we possess, of
the Christian Church. The meaning of dogma is often misunderstood. It is not in its true meaning a speculative definition to
which an intellectual assent is absolutely demanded, although
it has often been imposed in this sense; nor is it a statement
of individual opinion; but always an expression of a common

faith in the strength of which a common life is lived by a community of people; in the case of Christianity, a faith in God, Father, Son, and Holy Spirit. In other words, the formula is the

The Emblem of the First Evangelist; from a painting on the tester of the tomb of the Black Prince in Canterbury Cathedral.

expression of the central principle of Christianity, as the manifestation of the Divine Goodness in the flesh (called the Incarnation) in Jesus as the Son of God first, and then through His Spirit, in the members of His mystical Body, the Church, into which they are admitted by Baptism. All the rest of what is known as Christian Dogma springs from this one source, apart from which Christianity in its historical meaning cannot be held. But dogma finds its true setting only in the common worship of the Body of whose belief it is the expression. This is the truth that is contained in the words of the ancient Christian statement of faith called the Athanasian Creed, 'The Unity in Trinity, and the Trinity in Unity is to be worshipped'.

APPENDIX

THE TRADITION OF THE WORDS OF JESUS

1. The intention of Matthew, as Papias rightly judged, was to make an orderly compilation of the Lord's oracles. The question may be asked what evidence is there that we possess the genuine sayings of Jesus? It can hardly be doubted that in a great deal that passed in the primitive Church for actual sayings of Jesus, i.e. the discourses in the Fourth Gospel, we have not the *ipsissima verba* of Jesus but the teaching of Jesus as it has passed through the medium of the mind of the Evangelist or the Community to which he belonged. No one would think of denying that the discourses in the Fourth Gospel represent perhaps even more than the Synoptic Gospels, the *Spirit* of Jesus.[1] But this very expression the 'Spirit of Jesus' raises a problem which has recently become very prominent in the study of the New Testament. It is thought that the primitive Church did not always distinguish between the words of the Lord in His earthly life and those after His resurrection and exaltation, i.e. those which are elsewhere in the New Testament called the words of the 'Spirit'. Speaking of Q, Professor Bartlet says 'we must be ready to recognize among the Logia, along with the voice of the Church's Lord, echoes awakened in the Church's experience. The material of our First Gospel reflects the practical needs of the first days.' The so-called Second Epistle of Peter even seems to regard the word of 'prophecy' as of greater authority than the written word. 'We have', he says, 'also (in addition to the records of Peter and other eyewitnesses of the Incarnation) a more sure word of prophecy whereunto ye do well to take heed as unto a light that shineth in a dark place.' But he adds the necessary condition of authorization, 'knowing this first that no prophecy of Scripture is of any private interpretation' (1^{19}). In the same way the author of the Apocalypse again and again attributes to Jesus Himself the words spoken by the Seer, adding more definitely towards the end 'The testimony of Jesus is the spirit of prophecy' (Rev. 19^{10}).

[1] At the same time there is a growing opinion among scholars that the discourses in the Fourth Gospel embody a considerable number of genuine sayings of Jesus transmitted in the *form* of miracle stories.

While therefore it is obvious that the vast majority of the sayings collected in the Synoptic Gospels are the actual words of Jesus translated into Greek, there is no need to question the considered judgement of the conservative scholar Schlatter, who has analysed the sayings of Jesus in Matthew with a minuteness which no one else has attempted:

We have no Sayings of Jesus which have not come down to us other than under the supervision of the original Christian Community which believed them to be the Sayings of a divine Person. Behind that framework we cannot get. The evidence fails us.

2. The Words of Jesus have come down to us in two forms: (1) embodied in short anecdotes; (2) in collections of Logia. Much attention has been given by recent scholars to the *forms* in which the Gospel material has been moulded. It has been discovered that the division into teaching and narrative is very largely misleading. There is very little pure narrative, but for the most part narrative embodying teaching. If we examine the Synoptic Gospels with care, we can see that they are composed of a large number of disconnected anecdotes, miracle stories, sayings, and poems put together so as to form what appears to be a connected whole. While we can distinguish the main outlines of the public life of Jesus, it is clear that the arrangement in the Gospels is topical rather than chronological. The incidents are grouped according to a certain plan, but it would be impossible to say to what period the separate events belong. This had been largely forgotten, because the first Christians were not interested in the particulars of Jesus' life. Now it has been observed that these separate fragments fall into the same pre-literary groups, or *forms* (such as anecdotes, proverbs, legends, ballads, &c.) which are commonly assumed in folk-lore and other community traditions, which have not been consciously created by individuals, but developed by the force of constant oral repetition. The study of these groups is known as *form-history*; and the material of which the Synoptic Gospels are composed obviously offers a valuable field to the work of the 'form-critic', because we have here what was obviously the original oral tradition of a community, innocent of conscious literary art. Without going into detail, it may be safely asserted that the analysis applied by this method to the

'*pre-Synoptic*' materials of the Gospel has yielded the following results:

1. A very large number of the Gospel stories are employed as a framework to preserve a short logion or saying of Jesus. This does not of course mean that the stories themselves had no foundation in fact (form-criticism has no concern with the question of historicity), but only that the chief reason why they were remembered and written down was because of the saying which they preserved.

To these brief anecdotes, enshrining a saying of Jesus, Dibelius gives the name of '*paradigm*', i.e. an anecdote or illustration for a sermon or lesson, because he holds that the anecdote was employed as material for the earliest Christian preaching. Bultmann, however, and K. L. Schmidt have established the name *Apophthegm*, a term well known to Greek literature for the form in which the sayings of great men like Socrates have been preserved.[1] Dr. Vincent Taylor prefers to use the less technical name of *pronouncement stories* because they invariably lead up to a weighty pronouncement of Jesus with reference to the moral, spiritual, controversial, or liturgical needs of the Community.

Apophthegms fall roughly into two divisions: (a) Those in which a short logion or saying is found embodied in a somewhat artificial or conventional framework. These are found chiefly in the form of 'controversy' questions, such as we know to have been common in our Lord's day between the Rabbis (cf. Mk. 12¹³⁻³⁷). The controversial type of apophthegm always starts from an action or circumstance either of Christ or His disciples, on which an enemy fastens, e.g. the plucking of the ears of corn, and makes his complaint in the form of an accusation or of a question, as the Evangelist often puts it, 'tempting' him (Mt. 19³; 22³⁵). The defence usually consists of a counter question (Lk. 10²⁶) or a proverb or sometimes both together, or it may even take the form of an appeal to Scripture, as in Mk. 2²⁵. With regard to these apophthegms we note two important features: (1) with few exceptions

---

[1] Of the pioneers in the methods of form-criticism of the Gospels, Dibelius emphasizes the homiletic, Bultmann the apologetic and legislative, and K. L. Schmidt the liturgical needs of the primitive community in the formation of the Gospel tradition. The last, as we have seen, possibly accounts for the detailed features of the Passion narrative in the four Gospels.

they were concerned with questions which were of vital concern to the primitive communities of Christians: e.g. marriage, infant baptism, the Sabbath, the relation of Christians to the civil power, &c. In other words, they have been preserved because they served some need of the community. (2) Another feature which has been observed in the controversial apophthegms, is that in many cases it is the *disciples* who are attacked rather than Jesus Himself. In this case it is thought that we can see the Christian community being attacked and defending itself by appeal to its Master in similar circumstances. (Cf. Mt. 15^2; 17^{24}.) This is in striking contrast to what we find in the Apocryphal Gospels and the papyri, in which Jesus Himself is invariably placed in the forefront, showing that the interest has shifted from the saying to the story itself. In the same way many apophthegms centre in what may be called 'disciple questions', equally common in the Rabbinic schools, and concerned with domestic discussions in the Community itself, e.g. about the *Parousia* (Mt. $24^{3\mathrm{ff.}}$).

(b) *Biographical apophthegms*, i.e. short stories designed to place an *obiter dictum* of Jesus in an interesting context which may or may not have been that in which it was originally uttered, or to show Jesus in a particular light. Examples of these are seen in the calling of the disciples in Mt. (Mt. $4^{18\mathrm{ff.}}$), of the Publican Levi (Mt. 9^9), the calling of the children (19^{13}). In all of these the word of Jesus which they contain stand at the end and rounds off the story, e.g. 'I will make you fishers of men', 'of such is the kingdom of heaven'. Similarly the decisive word of Jesus is provoked by a request or a question (Mt. 8^{18-22}; Lk. 10^{40}, 13^{14-16}; Mk. 3^{31-35}; 14^3; Mt. 9^{10}), by a relationship (Mk. 6^{1-6}); more rarely spoken by Jesus on His own initiative (Mk. 1^{17}). Some of these stories may well be ideal situations in the sense that they bring to expression, some of the features of which are ideal, a truth about Jesus or the community which extends beyond the immediate situation, so as to possess a symbolical or ideal character. The miracle stories of the Johannine Gospel obviously partake of this nature. Nothing is more interesting than to trace the evolution of a biographical apophthegm, e.g. that of the Rich Young Ruler, from its simple and original form in Mk. 10^{17-22} through its Lucan and Matthaean form to its final shape in Ev. Heb. (see note on Mt. 19^{16})[1]. It is to these very interesting biographical apophthegms that Dibelius's term 'paradigm' is especially appropriate; they must have been much used in Catechetical instructions and preaching, and they are to this day easily learned and remembered in the 'Gospels' for the Sunday—they were indeed composed for no other purpose. In course of time the apophthegms of both sorts were strung together into catechetical or mnemonic form, of which we have a good example in the loosely connected string of incidents in Mk. 10$^{1-31}$ containing a whole series of sayings useful to the community upon a variety of topics, and preserved for that reason.

(2) The Second Form in which the Sayings of Jesus have come down to us is that of *Logia* which have no accompanying story. They may be divided into three kinds: (1) isolated pronouncements of a proverbial or parabolic character; (2) prophetic and apocalyptic utterances; and (3) what Bultmann calls 'law-words' or rules for the community, e.g. Mt. 16^{19}. These correspond roughly to the threefold division of Jer. 18^{18}; from the wise man we expect counsel, from the prophet the word of the Lord, and from the priest the oracle or guidance. To which we may add; (4) the parable which, as we have seen, is rather to be reckoned, after the manner of Jewish 'haggada', with narrative rather than sayings; and lastly (5), the interesting collection of what we may call 'I' sayings, in which the Fourth Gospel, the Apocryphal Gospels, and late collections of *Logia* in the Papyri especially abound, e.g. Mt. 9^{13}; Jn. 10$^{1-18}$.

It is not possible to discuss in detail here these various classes of sayings. While the greater part of these sayings in the Synoptic Gospels bear the hall-mark of genuineness, the 'I' sayings are most likely to belong to the period of later reflection on the teaching of Jesus. It is, however, interesting to note that the evolution of sayings which we see going on in the Apocryphal Gospels and the so-called Agrapha is the continuation of a process which had already begun in the canonical gospels.

[1] See M. R. James, *Apocryphal N.T.*, p. 6, for the version of the incident of the Rich Young Ruler (Mt. 19$^{16-22}$) as recorded by the Ev. Heb., which adds 'but the rich man began to scratch his head and it did not please him, and the Lord said to him, "How sayest thou that I have obeyed the law and the prophets, when it is written in the law thou shalt love thy neighbour as thy self? And how many of thy brethren, the sons of Abraham,

From an analysis of all these 'forms' we gather that tradition early assembled the words of the Lord, enlarged and extended them, in some cases beyond their original meaning. It likewise included other material, prophetic, apocalyptic, and Rabbinic, which it carefully prepared for adoption into the treasury of Christian instruction. Perhaps the most ancient material is to be found in the short parables and in the words of conflict which bring the moral attitude of Jesus most clearly to expression as against Jewish formalism, e.g. Mt. 9^{11-13}. The next stage was the collection of all kinds of sayings into catechisms such as the Sermon on the Mount or the discourses on the Mount of Olives. We may note especially in this connexion how beautifully Mt. has amplified and rounded off the little catechism of Mk. 9^{33-50} in the discourse of the fourth book (Mt. 18). From this point it was only a step to the assembly of the catechisms into the large collections first of Q and then of the Gospels themselves.

To sum up, while much in the conclusions of Form-criticism remains hypothetical, it is probably true that most of the stories and sayings of Jesus reached our Evangelists as the copyright of some important person or centre, such as Peter or Jerusalem, and were stamped with their authority. That is why the wording of them appears to be so stereotyped and is treated with such reverence by those who incorporated them in the Gospels, in spite of the opportunity which all the Evangelists must have had to obtain first-hand accounts from other sources. The Gospels are therefore in every sense of the word 'community documents', the working materials of a great missionary movement designed to serve its own purposes and not merely to gratify the natural desire, which arose in a later generation, for biographical details about Jesus. The detailed precision of the stories of the Passion in all four Gospels may, as we have seen, be due to the fact that they were used for recitation in the weekly eucharist wherein the

are clothed with filthy garments and dying of hunger and thy house is full of many good things and nothing whatever goeth forth from it to them?'' Compare with this saying the story in Mt. and Mk., and the development can plainly be seen. We may also compare the statement in another context (Mt. 20^{27}) which is added by certain 'Western' texts: 'But do you seek to increase from that which is little and to become less from that which is greater.' Possibly from the Gospel of the Nazarenes. (Cf. Jas. 1^9.)

Lord's death was commemorated. Other stories crystallized the decisions of the community upon some point of dispute, whether internal or external to the Church, based upon a treasured saying of the Lord or one of His characteristic actions. In any case the Gospels of Matthew and John do seem to echo in a greater degree perhaps than the others, the problems, needs and aspirations of the later apostolic age. That is perhaps as far as we can safely go. But so far from detracting from the historicity of the Gospels, the close connexion which Form-criticism has shown to exist between their sources and the parent community is a valuable guarantee of their substantial accuracy. The 'sayings' especially have come down to us with the 'Imprimatur' of communities of Christians contemporary with our Lord and His apostles.

Thus it may be truly said that while the Gospels do not claim to provide us with a 'talking picture' of Jesus, nevertheless, as Dr. Vincent Taylor remarks, 'We see Jesus better, for we behold Him not only in the final form, which the tradition assumes in the Gospels, but also in the lives, thoughts and desires of men throughout the formative period.' (For further exposition of Form-criticism in relation to the Gospels and kindred subjects, see R. H. Lightfoot, *Bampton Lectures 1935*, and Hoskyns and Davey, *Riddle of the New Testament*.)

INDEX

Index

PRINTED IN GREAT BRITAIN
AT THE UNIVERSITY PRESS, OXFORD
BY VIVIAN RIDLER
PRINTER TO THE UNIVERSITY